DELIVERING REHABILITATION

Do offenders have the right to be rehabilitated and should the state be responsible for their rehabilitation? Should the public expect punitive and coercive approaches to offender rehabilitation? Why should the state be interested in the reform of individuals and how can helping offenders be justified when there are other disadvantaged groups in society who are unable to access the services they desperately need? Finally, why does the state appear to target and criminalise certain groups and individuals and not others?

These are just some of the questions asked in this new text, which offers an analysis of the delivery of rehabilitative services to offenders over the past two decades. It focuses particularly on the ideological and political imperatives of a neoliberal state that intends to segment the work of the Probation Service and hand over the majority of its work to the private sector. Issues covered include:

- governance, politics and performance of probation,
- occupational culture and professional identity,
- markets, profit and delivery,
- partnership, localism and civil society,
- citizenship, exclusion and the state.

This book is aimed at academics, practitioners, managers and leaders within the field of corrections and wider social policy. It will also appeal to undergraduates and postgraduates specialising in criminal justice, criminology, politics and social policy.

Lol Burke is a Senior Lecturer in Criminal Justice at Liverpool John Moores University.

Steve Collett worked for three North West probation areas over four decades, retiring from Cheshire Probation in December 2010 after ten years as its chief officer.

'This is a timely and well-judged book that offers an acute analysis of probation's recent past, combining many perceptive and original insights with a searing critique of the political ineptitude and cynicism that have destabilised – and perhaps wrecked – the probation service. Its account of the way in which social problems are constructed and managed in our times makes the book of value not only to students of criminal justice, but to anyone with an interest in modern social policy.'

Rob Canton, Professor in Community and Criminal Justice, De Montfort University, UK

'They say "timing is everything", and what an incredible time this is for a book on the politics and governance of probation in the UK. Yet, *Delivering Rehabilitation* also addresses timeless and crucial questions about the right to rehabilitation in a democratic society. If there is any justice left, this transformative book will have a longer lasting and more profound impact on probation than the latest Government shake-up.'

Shadd Maruna, Dean, School of Criminal Justice, Rutgers University – Newark, USA

DELIVERING REHABILITATION

The politics, governance and control of probation

Lol Burke and Steve Collett

LONDON AND NEW YORK

First published 2015
by Routledge
2 Park Square, Milton Park, Abingdon, Oxon OX14 4RN

And by Routledge
711 Third Avenue, New York, NY 10017

Routledge is an imprint of the Taylor & Francis Group, an informa business

British Library Cataloguing in Publication Data
A catalogue record for this book is available from the British Library

Library of Congress Cataloging-in-Publication Data
Burke, Lol.
Delivering rehabilitation : the politics, governance and control of probation / Lol Burke, Steve Collett.
1. Probation—Great Britain. 2. Criminals—Rehabilitation—Great Britain. 3. Rehabilitation—Great Britain. I. Collett, Steve. II. Title.
HV9345.A5B87 2014
364.6'30941—dc23 2014014636

ISBN13: 978-0-415-54036-0 (hbk)
ISBN13: 978-0-415-54038-4 (pbk)
ISBN13: 978-0-203-10734-8 (ebk)

Typeset in 10/12 Bembo
by codeMantra

In memory of Joan Feenan and Ray and Christa Collett

And for Sandra, Daniel and Megan Burke

CONTENTS

ACKNOWLEDGEMENTS

We have wanted to write this book for a while and when the opportunity came along, the timing could not have been better. We have been working on and developing the themes and ideas presented here during a highly turbulent period in the history of the Probation Service and so have never been short of argument and debate with regard to developments affecting the future of the Probation Service, as well as the form and delivery of the rehabilitative endeavour.

We are also fortunate in being involved academically and through practice and management in an area of public policy that demands and receives incredible commitment from a broad range of individuals – academics, practitioners, leaders, critical friends, colleagues within the criminal justice system and, on occasion, some of our political representatives. It would be invidious and impractical, therefore, to mention individuals by name given the debt of gratitude we owe to so many people. However, readers who know the world of probation will understand why we would want to acknowledge two individuals – the late David Mathieson who died in 2013 and David Scott. Mathieson, a career probation officer and chief probation officer of Merseyside Probation Service until his retirement in 1999 never let us forget the importance of humanitarian values to the work and effectiveness of the Service. David Scott, likewise a career probation officer who led London Probation Service during a highly volatile and politicised period, maintained his honesty, decency and integrity while some around him lost theirs.

Our partners, Sandra Burke and Sue Egersdorff have maintained their support and encouragement to ensure that we finished what we started. Heidi Lee, editorial assistant, provided timely but unobtrusive advice at various stages which greatly assisted the completion of the book.

Part of Chapter Seven draws significantly on Steve Collett's 2012 McWilliams Lecture – *Riots, Revolution and Rehabilitation: The Future of Probation* – which was published by John Wiley & Sons Ltd. in the *Howard Journal*, (2013) 52(2): 163–189.

ABBREVIATIONS

ACOP	Association of Chief Officers of Probation
ASBO	Anti-Social Behaviour Order
AUR	Automatic Unconditional Release
BCU	Basic Command Unit
CAFCASS	Children and Family Court Advisory and Support Service
CCTV	Closed-Circuit Television
CDRP	Crime and Disorder Reduction Partnership
CJ Act	Criminal Justice Act
CRC	Community Rehabilitation Company
CSP	Community Safety Partnership
DOM	Director of Offender Management
DIP	Drug Interventions Programme
HMCS	Her Majesty's Court Services
HMIP	Her Majesty's Inspectorate of Probation
HMP	Her Majesty's Prison
HMPS	Her Majesty's Prison Service
IOM	Integrated Offender Management
LCJB	Local Criminal Justice Board
LDU	Local Delivery Unit
LGA	Local Government Association
LSE	London School of Economics
LSP	Local Strategic Partnership
NAPO	National Association of Probation Officers
NOMS	National Offender Management Service
NPD	National Probation Directorate
NPM	New Public Management

NPN	No Page Number
NPS	National Probation Service
PA	Probation Association
PbR	Payment by Results
PCA	Probation Chiefs Association
PFI	Public Finance initiative
PPO	Prolific & Priority Offender
PSE	Poverty and Social Exclusion UK
RCVP	Riots, Communities and Victims Panel
MAPPA	Multi Agency Public Protection Arrangements
MARAC	Multi Agency Risk Assessment Conference
OCJR	Office of Criminal Justice Reform
ODPM	Office of Deputy Prime Minister
ROM	Regional Offender Manager
SEU	Social Exclusion Unit
SFO	Serious Further Offence
YJB	Youth Justice Board
YOT	Youth Offending Team

ABOUT THE AUTHORS

Lol Burke is a Senior Lecturer in Criminal Justice at Liverpool John Moores University. He has worked as a Probation Officer and Senior Probation Officer and was involved in the delivery of probation training prior to his current appointment. Lol has written extensively on probation policy, practice and training issues and is co-author of *Redemption, Rehabilitation and Risk Management: A History of Probation* (2011) with Prof. George Mair. Lol is currently editor of the *Probation Journal* and a member of the editorial board of the European Journal of Probation. He is also a member of the Howard League for Penal Reform's Research Advisory Group, the European Society of Criminology Working Group on Community Sanctions and CREDOS (an international collaboration of researchers for the effective development of offender supervision).

Steve Collett worked for three North West probation areas over nearly three decades, retiring from the Cheshire Probation Trust in December 2010 after ten years as its chief officer. He also taught social work and social policy in further/higher education in the early 1980s before returning to Probation to take up a joint appointment with Merseyside Probation & Liverpool University (1987–1991). Steve has been an Honorary Fellow within the Department of Sociology, Social Policy & Criminology since then and following his retirement in 2011, he was made an Honorary Reader in criminology within the School of Law at Manchester University. In 2012, he was made an Honorary Fellow of Liverpool John Moores University. Steve has been a member of the *Probation Journal* Editorial Board for over 20 years and was a founding vice chair of the Probation Chiefs Association.

1
INTRODUCTION

> 8 November, Leeds. Walking along Wellington Street towards City Square I pass the offices of the probation service, now plastered with protest leaflets and posters from Napo against the selling off of the service, protests that in my view are wholly justified. The notion that probation, which is intended to help and support those who have fallen foul of the law, should make a profit for shareholders seems beyond satire. As indeed is the proposal to take the East Coast line out of what is virtually public ownership and reprivatise it for the likes of the expatriate Branson. I never used to bother about capitalism. It was just a word. Not now.
>
> *(Alan Bennett 2013)*

Covering the ground

Beginning a book is a difficult and precarious task, but there are times when serendipity delivers exactly what you were looking for. In our case, it is this extract from Alan Bennett's diary of 2013 that we landed on by good fortune. Not only does he hint at the current situation the Probation Service finds itself, but places our predicament within a wider context. His humanitarian concerns are, in essence, what this book is about. A great many other questions arise: Do offenders have the right or expectation to call on the resources of the state for their rehabilitation from a life of crime? Should the public expect punitive and coercive approaches to offender rehabilitation? Other than incapacitating offenders in prison for the protection of the individual and the wider public, why should the state be concerned with prisoner reform; beyond that, how, can helping offenders be justified when there are disadvantaged groups who are unable to access the services they desperately need? Finally, why does the state appear to target and criminalise certain groups and individuals and not others?

The range of questions, issues and potential approaches that need be included in *Delivering Rehabilitation* is clearly daunting. Indeed, the interested practitioner, policy-maker or scholar has only to browse through the pages of relatively recent edited readers – for example, *Handbook of Probation* (Gelsthorpe and Morgan 2007), *Moments in Probation: Celebrating the Century of Probation* (Senior 2008), or *Offenders or Citizens* (Priestley and Vanstone 2010) to appreciate the dilemma authors may have in refining their focus. There are also so many excellent books that engage the interested reader in both historical analysis and contemporary debate about offender supervision, rehabilitation and the role of probation. Indeed, the title of Whitehead and Statham's 2006 book, *The History of Probation – Politics, Power and Cultural Change 1876–2005* might suggest that much of the *Governance, Control and Management* referred to in our title has already been covered and all that is required is an update. Alternatively, our inclusion of *Delivering Rehabilitation* might also suggest that we are traversing similar ground to that covered so superbly by Rob Canton in *Probation – Working with Offenders* (2011).

The truth is that whilst we draw heavily on the work of many probation and criminal justice academics, commentators and practitioners, we have also attempted to fashion a more general, theoretical, and politically informed analysis, one that is critical of post-modernity and the hegemonic nature of neoliberalism as it has developed into a global force, ostensibly accepted by both the left and right of the political spectrum. Therefore, publications such as Emma Bell's *Criminal Justice and Neoliberalism* (2011) and *Organising Neoliberalism: Markets, Privatisation and Justice* (2012) edited by Philip Whitehead and Paul Crawshaw, have also been informative. Without, hopefully, doing an injustice to the necessary detailed analysis of probation over the past two decades we have also drawn on the work of authors Loic Waquant, Danny Dorling, Richard Wilkinson, Kate Picket, Michael Sandel, Christopher Lasch and Guy Standing. These authors have influenced the general thrust of our arguments. We are also interested in the role of specific events and personalities in shaping probation's future. In essence, we have attempted to capture a critical, ever-evolving period in the history of probation, whilst keeping in mind the practical realities of working with individuals who offend.

What do we mean by Probation?

In the quote from Bennett's diary, he specifically mentions *probation service* but also refers to *probation*. It is not clear whether he is using the latter term as shorthand for Probation Service or as a reference to the concept of probation – of putting someone on test to behave better in the future – or indeed as a reference to supervision under the guise of a probation order. Throughout this book, we use *probation* in a similarly ambiguous way and unless we intend it to have a specific meaning, we leave it to the reader to interpret whether we are referring to specific organisational and bureaucratic features, a concept and a set of values for conducting offender supervision or indeed as a (now defunct) sentence of the court.

We use probation in this generalised way as an umbrella for the rehabilitative endeavour because our understanding of the practical and professional world of probation and the Probation Service is one of a complex value-laden and politicised environment within which committed work with individuals is undertaken on the personal and bureaucratic level to deliver rehabilitation. Furthermore, whether we use terms like offender management, risk management and assessment, control, surveillance or compliance, we nevertheless believe that what has motivated generations of probation staff has been to give individuals who are policed, arrested, prosecuted and sentenced, the opportunity to lead crime-free, productive lives that have meaning for themselves, their families, and the wider community.

Our arguments will acknowledge that whilst punishment has been the enduring core in the state's response to the treatment of offenders and past approaches to rehabilitation sometimes conveyed more about the aspirations of burgeoning social work and medical professions than the real needs of poor working class people, the state nevertheless maintained a relatively even-handed approach to rehabilitation. However, on the back of rising post-war crime rates, the crime debate became increasingly politicised and despite long-term trends in falling crime and ever decreasing levels of victimisation over the past fifteen years, the penal arms race has been used to the wider political advantage of both Tory, Labour, and now Coalition administrations. This battle for the right to use crime control for party political fortunes now, however, pales into insignificance compared to the insidious impact of neoliberal thinking on the construction of crime, problem populations and the delivery mechanisms for penal big business.

Structuring the debate

The opening chapter – *Contextualising Rehabilitation* – sets out the general terrain and context for understanding the concept of rehabilitation and begins signposting events that have had a significant impact upon the development and delivery of rehabilitative services over the past two decades. In Chapter Three – *Governing Rehabilitation: Politics and performance* – we show how a heady mix of ideology, mezzo politics, personalities and events have shaped probation and ultimately led to the future it faces under the Coalition's *Transforming Rehabilitation* project. The higher profile given to law and order in recent years has meant battling crime has increasingly been viewed as a mechanism for securing electoral support. Prime Minister Blair's oft-repeated *tough on crime, tough on the causes of crime* effectively introduced ambiguity into both public and professional understanding of criminal justice policy approaches to rehabilitation. Contemporary probation practice has therefore had to operate within a heightened and volatile political environment that has often been dominated by anti-liberal rhetoric fuelled by negative media representations. This chapter analyses the ambiguities, continuities and discontinuities of government policy and its impact on the Probation Service. The changing political landscape and drive for public sector modernisation under the precepts of *New Public Management* (NPM) has also fundamentally altered the relationship between probation and central government. We will question why, given its relative size and influence, the Probation Service has been a particular concern for central government. Rather than being a participant in the decision-making process, the Service has found itself subsumed into a prison service dominated by a command-and-control environment and culture. This has had profound implications on the character and governance of probation and its relationship with local communities. Ultimately it raises questions, we argue, about the significance of losing traditional probation values for local communities and for wider society.

In combination, our first two chapters aim to set out the concepts and the contexts for the rehabilitative endeavor. The remaining chapters take on a more thematic approach to an understanding of *delivering rehabilitation*. Chapter Four – *Providing Rehabilitation: Occupational culture and professional identity* – reflects on why so much consideration has been given to a service that has effectively been in perpetual reorganisation since becoming a national service in 2001. We pay particular attention to the operational and professional culture within probation and how its public and political image has changed over the past two decades. We also consider how workers reconcile the care and control aspects of their job and their personal and professional values within the changing requirements of contemporary policy and practice. These requirements include developing new ways of working and different types of relationships with other agencies within and beyond the criminal justice system. Finally, we consider the potential impact of the Coalition government's *Transforming Rehabilitation* project upon the occupational culture, training and working practices of probation staff.

Part of the rationale for the creation of the National Offender Management Service (NOMS) was to deliver a system of *contestability* that hoped to introduce the concept of *market tension* into the monopoly of community-based corrections. The avowed goal was to improve the quality and effectiveness of public provision. However, the debate has developed into a politically-motivated initiative to privatise aspects of probation as part of a wider desire to expose the criminal justice system to competition and private capital. In Chapter Five – *Competing Rehabilitation: Markets, profit and delivery* – we discuss these developments in light of recent policy initiatives such as *Payments by Results* (PbR) and the uses of social impact bonds. This will lead to a discussion of the future role of the state and the private sector in the delivery of the core tasks of offender management and whether or not the arrangements envisaged will lead to greater effectiveness or dangerous fragmentation.

Chapter Six – *Widening Rehabilitation: Partnership, localism and civil society* – considers a key feature of contemporary criminal justice planning in the concerted attempt to control crime through partnerships of statutory, private and voluntary organisations. Similarly, the idea of *joined up* government to tackle wider social problems through multi-agency partnerships represents a significant break with the idea of centralised power. The discussion in this chapter encompasses the role of the state in the pursuing reductions in levels of crime and re-offending through non-criminal justice agencies as well as crime agencies and Local Criminal Justice Boards (LCJBs). The chapter will further examine the Prolific and Other Priority Offender (PPO) initiative and explore the workings of Multi-Agency Public Protection Arrangements (MAPPAs) established by the Criminal Justice and Court Services Act 2000. Both will be analysed in terms of effectiveness and questions of appropriate levels of intrusion and intervention into offenders' lives.

The recent experience of criminal justice agencies has been one of an overpowering sense of management, control and direction from their respective central government departments (Home Office/Ministry of Justice). This feature of the Blair years helps to account for and shape much of what has been covered in the preceding chapters. However, the end of the Labour administration heralded a move to localism and the Coalition government has seized on the political and ideological opportunities afforded by a return to the *local*. Localism has significant potential to tackle local problems but it also exposes the tensions of operating a sentencing framework for England and Wales within the context of local action and community engagement. This chapter will conclude by critically examining what the much heralded but little understood notion of *Big Society* might mean for managing and rehabilitating individual offenders.

Chapter Seven – *Blaming Rehabilitation: Citizenship, exclusion and the state* – takes the discussion into a more discursive ideological environment by considering the rehabilitative endeavor in the context of forty years of neoliberal economic and cultural hegemony. Our aim is to analyse how social problems are defined and institutional responses determined. Specifically, we are interested in how *responsibilisation* has moved beyond the individual to agencies of the state, including probation. A case study of the 2011 riots is used to highlight the way assumptions about the poor are reinforced in negative stereotypes that justify reactionary responses to their plight. We also consider how notions of equality of opportunity and social mobility within a notional modern meritocratic society are deployed to further isolate undeserving groups whilst justifying massive and increasing inequalities in income and wealth.

The title of our conclusion – *Reimagining Rehabilitation* – suggests, despite our reservations concerning the direction in which probation is being moved structurally and philosophically, that there is optimism at the margins. The debate about the balance between the responsibilities of the individual to behave in a law-abiding manner and those of the state to ensure the preconditions for the good life have been central to debates within probation and wider social policy for generations. Notwithstanding the current domination of neoliberal thinking, we consider that this debate has not atrophied to the extent that community and citizen engagement in the rehabilitative endeavor is beyond the imagination. It will require, however, new ways of working with offenders.

The last decade has seen significant innovation in the multi-agency approach to targeting offenders, and the correctional services have enhanced their ability to differentiate between different kinds of offending and levels of risk. Probation, in particular, has had to respond to working with dangerous and high risk offenders in ways that have impacted on its organisation and operational culture. Yet there is emerging evidence that the relationship between worker and offender remains critical to successful outcomes. In a number of important ways probation has changed for the better over the recent past. Still, reimagining rehabilitation is as much about renewing and reinvigorating features of the rehabilitative endeavor that have been lost as it is inventing new technocratic approaches to supervision that have accountability to shareholders rather than the local community.

References

Bell, E. (2011) *Criminal Justice and Neoliberalism*, Palgrave Macmillan: London.

Bennett, A (2014) *Diary: What I did in 2013, London Review of Books*, 36(1) 9 January. http://www.lrb.co.uk/v36/n01/alan-bennett/diary (Accessed 13 January 2014).

Canton, R. (2011) *Probation: Working with Offenders*, Abingdon, Oxon: Routledge.

Gelsthorpe, L. and Morgan, R. (eds) (2007) *Handbook of Probation*, Cullompton: Willan.

Priestley, P. and Vanstone, M. (2010) *Offenders or Citizen: Readings in Rehabilitation*, Cullompton: Willan.

Senior, P. (ed) (2008) *Moments in Probation – Celebrating the Century of Probation*, Crayford: Shaw & Sons.

Whitehead, P. and Crashaw, P. (2012) *Organising Neoliberalism: Markets, Privatisation and Justice*, London: Anthem Press.

Whitehead, P. and Statham, R. (2006) *The history of Probation – Politics, Power and Cultural Change 1876–2005*, Crayford: Shaw & Sons.

2

CONTEXTUALISING REHABILITATION

> What I really need is the chance to become an acceptable, responsible, productive member of my community. A voice that can be heard. A voice that can speak for its own self. The guilt, the shame, the remorse, it's made me feel worthless. Surely my solution lies behind re-evaluated self-esteem and re-directed purpose. I'll grow when I'm ready! Just help me plant the seed, 'cos' hope is the drug that every offender needs. A new identity indentation. A source of inspiration! So show me examples of the people that succeeded, so I too can believe that I'm valued and needed.
>
> *(Duncan 2013: 13)*

For me there were two significant relationships that in different ways gave me hope, determination and the courage to change. First, when I was aged 22, I met an older guy in prison who was nearing the end of a life sentence. He was previously involved in organised crime and had credibility in my eyes. During our time together he spoke about earlier beliefs, values and experiences that all conspired to result in his life sentence. More importantly, perhaps, he also spoke about the stark realities of crime and his 'wasted life' and he basically gave me a framework to examine the futility and destruction of my own offending behaviour and the effects this was having on my life and the people who cared about me. Given his past experiences, no-one else would have held so much sway over me in the same manner. Indeed, this was my first experience of a positive male role model; a convicted murderer. The second relationship came in to play when I was released from the same prison sentence and involved the social worker I had had since childhood. On reflection, her value for me wasn't necessarily in her profession, but her

> personality. She was a lovely, caring individual who believed firmly in the concept of change and rehabilitation, and she never lost sight of me during all those years of bedlam.
>
> *(Weaver 2013: 7)*

Innate evil and mindless selfishness

We begin this chapter with quotes from two individuals who have experienced the rehabilitative endeavour of our correctional services. Although those who offend, sometimes seriously and persistently, can find ways of expressing their own journeys, it is often within the confines of academic literature, agency publicity or occasionally through the processes of the criminal justice system itself. It is much more likely that the general public will receive information about offenders from the media. On 22 February 2010, 27-year-old Jon Venables reported to his probation supervising officer that he thought his identity had been compromised. This began a series of investigations that quickly led to Venables being arrested and subsequently charged with offences relating to the downloading of pornographic images of children. On 24 February, he was recalled to prison in breach of the terms of his post-release life licence and he remained in custody until he appeared before the Central Criminal Courts on 23 July. He was sentenced to two years imprisonment for those child pornography-related offences. The case was subject to considerable scrutiny and media hysteria because as a 10-year-old boy, he had been convicted along with his co-accused, Robert Thompson, also aged 10, of the murder of 2-year-old James Bulger, abducted from a shopping centre in Merseyside by the older boys in 1993. Jon Venables and Robert Thompson were, therefore, just above the age of criminal responsibility when they killed James Bulger. They were eventually tried, convicted and sentenced in an adult Crown Court to be detained for life at Her Majesty's pleasure.

The child's body was found on a railway track, but it was the CCTV footage of the two boys holding the hand of James Bulger as they led him away from the shopping centre, along with news coverage of the subsequent baying crowds outside South Sefton Magistrates' Court that were to become iconic images and defining moments in the history of modern British criminal justice. Robert Thompson and Jon Venables became the youngest children in England and Wales to be convicted of murder in the twentieth century. The case was controversial from the outset and was complicated by legal argument in the European Court of Human Rights over the suitability of the court proceedings involving such young children in an adult court. There was also intense political debate over the appropriate length of sentence they would have to serve before being released on life licence. Following their release in 2001, both Robert Thompson and Jon Venables were provided with new identities so as to protect them from the depth of public feeling aroused by their crime. The extent to which the threat to both was real and enduring and the subsequent identity planning and security arrangements have been documented in

Sir David Omand's *Serious Further Offence* review of the Venables case, where Omand concluded that "it was the right judgement to create a complete new identity for Jon Venables given the police assessment of the level of threat" (2010: 41).

Rather than presenting the offence as aberrant or resulting from the interplay of a complex range of social, economic, biographical, cultural and psychological factors, the media portrayals of the two boys tended to pathologise them in simplistic and absolute terms. Germaine Greer observed at the time, that it seemed that almost everyone who dealt with the two children (as well as those who hadn't) was able to offer an opinion about their moral character and decided they were *innately evil*, interpreting "their every gesture whether nervous or vacant or frightened or uncomprehending as a manifestation of evil"(cited in Collett 1993: 185). The concomitant vying for professional ascendancy between so called experts was unsightly, but it was also ideological in that classifying both the crime and the perpetrators as evil "may serve to remind us that the only guarantee of safety in this increasingly dangerous society is by placing ourselves behind the thin blue line" (Collett 1993: 185).

On another level, the enduring impact of the murder of James Bulger can be seen in part as the result of a number of political contingencies fuelled by the breakdown in the post-war Butskellite consensus that had "implicitly rested on the non-partisan character of crime and on the merit of gradual shifts towards rehabilitative policies for its control" (Downes and Morgan 1997: 128). In this respect, the murder was presented as symptomatic of a deeper moral malaise within British society; a condition that required remoralisation and condemnation through tough and uncompromising policies. For the revitalised Labour Party under the leadership of Tony Blair, "Out-toughening the Tories on law and order also included the legitimisation of simplistic, doom-laden, tabloid rhetoric that was usefully employed to convince voters that they were on the brink of a moral crisis, one which the Tories had allowed to occur and which New Labour was better equipped to address" (Green, 2008: 198). Similar crisis narratives would be invoked nearly two decades later in David Cameron's response to the riots that occurred in the summer of 2011:

> When we see children as young as 12 and 13 looting and laughing, when we see the disgusting sight of an injured young man with people pretending to help him while they are robbing him, it is clear that there are things that are badly wrong with our society. For me, the root cause of this mindless selfishness is the same thing I have spoken about for years. It is a complete lack of responsibility in parts of our society, people allowed to feel the world owes them something that their rights outweigh their responsibilities and their actions do not have consequences. Well, they do have consequences. We need to have a clearer code of standards and values that we expect people to live by and stronger penalties if they cross the line. Restoring a stronger sense of responsibility across our society in every town, in every street, in every estate is something I am determined to do.
>
> *(Quoted in New Statesman 2011)*

High profile events such as child murder or urban rioting are relatively rare but they have far-reaching consequences. This is not simply because of the extreme nature or impact of such occurrences but because they bring into question issues of public trust and confidence in the legitimacy of those institutions within society charged with protecting the public. They also challenge the role and legitimacy of professional expertise. It was perhaps inevitable, therefore, that Jon Venables' recall to prison for committing a serious further offence (SFO) would once again challenge the very notion of rehabilitation, especially for those convicted of the most serious offences, along with the efficacy of the organisations that were responsible for their supervision in the community. The media coverage surrounding Venables' recall inevitably tended to focus on some of the more salacious elements of the case. There were reports that he had had a sexual relationship with one of the residential care workers during the period of his first incarceration for the murder. Although he was a minor (13 years old) at the time, the press nevertheless hinted at his continued supposedly depraved character, thus one newspaper reported, "*Fury over Bulger killer's tryst with girl guard: 'Why was Jon Venables' sordid encounter in secure unit covered up?, asks James' mother*'" (Daily Mail, Feb 27 2011). In any other context, what happened to Venables would be viewed as institutional child sexual abuse!

Moreover, on 21 April 2011 the BBC televised a documentary entitled *What Went Wrong* which indicated a failure in the supervision and management of Venables in a provocative manner even though the Independent Serious Further Offence Review of the case led by Sir David Omand had concluded assessments made on Venables that he posed only a minor risk to the public were correct on the evidence then available and that he was appropriately managed and supervised by the Probation Service (2010). Incidents such as the recall of Venables highlight the intensely politicised nature of crime control in England and Wales rather than the real options for offender rehabilitation and the moral and philosophical bases for individual redemption within a modern democracy – as Green argues "Political culture and political economy clearly condition the ways in which crime is featured in political debates" (2008: 215). We will consider the politicisation of crime in more detail in Chapter Three but first need to analyse what delivering rehabilitation tells us about the changing nature of the state's response to crime, public protection and reducing re-offending.

So what is offender rehabilitation?

A key starting point in this task will be to discuss exactly what is meant and understood by the term *rehabilitation*. It is used in a variety of ways by those who are employed within the correctional services and it is therefore not surprising that the public are confused by the term. Does, for example, rehabilitation mean reform? These two words are often used interchangeably within official policy documents, even criminal justice statutes. For example, section 142 (1) of the Criminal Justice

Act 2003 outlines five purposes of sentencing of which the third is the *reform and rehabilitation of offenders,* (the others are punishment, crime reduction, protection of the public, and making reparation by the offender to persons affected by their offence). There is no further guidance and indeed the act does not indicate that one purpose should be more important than the other. In effect, the sentencer has the job of deciding how to apply the purposes and what the balance between them should be (see Sentencing Guidelines Council 2004: 3).

Do the public have specific expectations about the role of the state in rehabilitating individual offenders and indeed should the offender have any expectation about their own entitlement to rehabilitation? How can society best support individuals to desist from crime? Is rehabilitation different from desistance? Where and how do the rights and responsibilities of the individual and of the state play themselves out? Should probation recast itself within a framework of community justice and restorative approaches? What is success and how is it measured? Are the goals of rehabilitation absolute in the sense of individuals stopping offending, or do they reflect other relative measures relating to the level of harm and dangerousness of the offending act? Should we even consider the well-being of the offender in contrast to that of the victim? These questions are endless and the implied goals, as Raynor and Robinson suggest,

> … reflect the different values placed on different kinds of outcome, and these values themselves often draw on further assumptions about human nature or human purposes.
>
> *(2009: 5)*

Rehabilitation was originally conceived as a means of legal requalification of individuals through the removal of the stigma of a criminal conviction (Carlen 2012, McNeill 2012). In this sense, the outcome for the individual is the regaining of their full status as a citizen and non-offender. Essentially, rehabilitation referred to the endpoint or outcome of a process that involved settling the putative debt implicit in the commission of an offence. Reform, on the other hand, has been more concerned with affecting a change in the individual in order to aid their reintegration into society with the attendant rights and responsibilities of citizenship. It has tended, historically at least, to assume a moral enterprise, backed up by help and direction (*advise, assist and befriend* in old probation parlance). Nowadays, as our reference to the current sentencing framework suggests, these terms are often used interchangeably along with more modern terms like desistance and reintegration. To complicate matters further, some definitions of rehabilitation ascribe a particular type of approach to reducing re-offending whilst others identify outcomes not just for offenders but for individual victims, communities or wider society (see Ward and Maruna 2007: Chapter 1). Finally, these terms are often not recognised by offenders who talk instead of *going straight* or *getting sorted.*

For us, the notion of rehabilitation includes both process and outcome. The process involves helping individual offenders to *go straight* by working with them to lead crime-free lives and meet their personal, family and community responsibilities. The process may be quick or drawn out over many years and will often involve setbacks. The outcome ultimately involves the restoration of the individual to their rights and obligations as full citizens whereby they no longer consider themselves or are considered an offender. This implies action by the state to both provide the resources to support the process and to acknowledge the outcomes. Our view of rehabilitation draws heavily on a burgeoning literature on desistance which moves thinking from why people commit crime to what might help them stop offending (Farrall and Calverley 2005, Maruna 2001, McNeill 2006, McNeill and Weaver 2010). A review of this literature is beyond the scope of this chapter but we wish to emphasise the following. Firstly, despite the *technicist* trends within the correctional services over the past decade or more, rehabilitation is a moral enterprise in which we should do with individuals and not to them (Burke and Collett 2008 and 2010). Secondly, techniques and structured interventions have their place and sometimes surveillance and control are necessary but often it is the expansion of and connection with personal, social and economic resources that offenders request and need. As individuals operating within a social context, the help identified and offered will be more effective if it is negotiated within a relationship that offers belief in the capacity of the individual to change and a professional commitment that it can be achieved, however difficult the circumstances. In this respect we would support Fergus McNeill's contention

> That offender management services need to think of themselves less as providers of correctional treatment (that belongs to the expert) and more as supporters of desistance processes (that belong to the desister).
>
> *(2006: 46)*

Transition, transformation or adaptability?

Notwithstanding our attempt to loosely define the rehabilitative endeavour, notions of rehabilitation can only be understood within their historical and ideological context. Nowadays, we tend to discuss rehabilitation in terms of community corrections and community-based responses to support offenders and ex-prisoners, but historically, the penitentiary, as a site of confinement, was perhaps the first practical expression of the reformative power of religious contemplation and penance through hard labour (Rotman 1990), leading to what the French philosopher Michel Foucault described as *coercive soul-transformation* (Foucault 1977). Gradually those religious ideals were supplanted by more medical and therapeutic models of rehabilitation characterised by their clinical, individualised and treatment-orientated practices (Robinson 2008). These ideas fitted well with the penal-welfare complex that emerged in the early twentieth century, with its emphasis on collective security and the provision of a safety net for the most disadvantaged through universal social benefits under the umbrella of a burgeoning welfare state. However, from the 1960s, as the power of professionals in clinical setting came under critical scrutiny, their role too was challenged both on the grounds of efficacy and morality. This resulted in the reformulation of rehabilitative practices "not as a sort of quasi-medical treatment for criminality but as the re-education of the poorly socialised" (McNeill 2012: 22).

The challenge to clinical notions of rehabilitation came from across the political spectrum and not necessarily from the usual contemporary suspects, such as the media. Rehabilitation was particularly criticised by left-wing civil libertarians because it was adjudged to interfere too much in the lives of individuals and seemed to operate unquestioningly in the interests of the state, consciously or unconsciously propagating its prevailing ideology. A fictionalised account of rehabilitaion, Ken Kesey's novel, *One Flew Over The Cuckoo's Nest* (1962) reflected this perspective. In the field of psychiatry on both sides of the Atlantic, practitioners were questioning the ideological and medical basis of then current practice (see Szasz 1962, Szasz 1974, Boyers and Orrill 1972). Additionally, the anti-psychiatry movement itself was contested by socialist radicals such as Sedgwick who placed greater emphasis on the social context of illness and the political response to human problems (1982).

Professional knowledge and practice, ideology and socio-economic context were similar themes within the criminal justice arena. The ideological underpinning of the rehabilitative endeavour was criticised for ignoring the social context of crime and by implication presenting criminal behaviour as a *social disease* that could be treated in much the same way as a physical ailment (Bean 1976). However, the critical issues were not simply about social and economic disadvantage, but also about how far delinquent or criminal behaviour was symptomatic of individual pathology. Theoretical perspectives such as labelling theory in turn articulated the view that interventions could make matters worse by reinforcing deviant behaviour. *Due process* lawyers drew attention to the problems of injustice which stemmed from indeterminate sentencing and questioned whether unreliable predictors of future behaviour – based on the unsubstantiated claims of professional wisdom – should continue to influence sentencing. Instead, it was argued that rehabilitation should be provided within the context of a determinate sentence, the length of which should be proportionate to the seriousness of the offence (see Hudson 1997, Hudson 2003: 63). The law and order lobby, on the other hand, argued that rehabilitation was soft on crime and put the needs of the offender before those of the victim (Murray 1990). Rising crime rates during the post-war period and the absence of empirical evidence about impact of rehabilitative measures also appeared to suggest that treatment was failing to reduce criminal activity.

> Within a very short time it became common to regard the core value of the whole penal-welfare framework not just as an impossible ideal, but, much more remarkably, as an unworthy, even dangerous policy objective that was counter-productive in its effects and misguided in its objectives.
>
> *(Garland 2001: 8)*

Pat Carlen has argued that the net result of these divergent challenges was to erase "the citizen-subjects of the welfare state from the penal frame, replacing them with the risk-laden techno-entities of surveillance and security fetishism" (2012: 95). On the surface then, rehabilitation would seem to sit uneasily with the emergence of a risk-based penality (Feeley and Simon 1994) more concerned with providing a cost-effective means of managing *dangerous* individuals than reintegrating them into their communities. From this perspective rehabilitation, whatever we may want it to mean in terms of direct humanitarian work with individuals to help them turn their lives around, is in fact much more ideologically instrumental. Toward the millennium then:

> The task of the new penology is managerial, not transformative, and its discourse is characterised by an emphasis of systematic integrity and on internal evaluation based on formal rationality, rather than on external social objectives such as the elimination of crime or reintegration into the community. Consequently, it is concerned less to diagnose and treat individuals than to identify, classify and manage unruly groups sorted by dangerousness.
>
> *(Brownlee 1998: 79)*

For David Garland the replacement of the broader project of penal-welfarism with more intrusive forms of social control and surveillance can be located in the social, economic and political drivers of late modernity. Rehabilitation, with its emphasis on the collective did not resonate or was unable to respond to the increasing insecurity amongst the middle-classes and their distrust of professional penal expertise.

> The dominant voice of crime policy is no longer the expert or even the practitioner but that of the long-suffering, ill-served people – especially of "the victim" and the fearful, anxious members of the public.
>
> *(Garland 2001: 13)*

Garland's analysis of late modernity is considered in greater detail in Chapter Three but looking back on the immediate period after *The Culture of Control* was published (2001), McNeill *et al.* pick up on widespread concerns that the orthodoxy of management of risk and dangerousness, so clearly dominant in the first decade of the new millennium, has meant that "to the extent that rehabilitation endures at all, it survives only in a hollowed out managerialized form, not as an over-riding purpose but as a subordinate means" (2009: 421).

In some quarters, then, rehabilitation has become somewhat tainted, but the concept has nevertheless displayed qualities of endurance and adaptability. According to Robinson, this is because it has been able to adapt to prevailing, sometimes conflicting meta-narratives (2008). In this respect, rehabilitation, and by implication the Probation Service, has been largely successful in repositioning itself within the dominant contemporary policy and practice discourses of managerialism and risk. These developments are perhaps best encapsulated in the emergence of the *What Works* project (discussed further in Chapter Three) whose instrumentalism rested on claims that certain approaches would reduce reconviction (Canton 2012: 584). The subsequent National Offender Management Model (NOMS 2006) in which the individual's risk profile largely determines their eligibility for, intensity and type of intervention demonstrates both managerialism and risk discourses. In some senses this is not surprising given that "there is bound to be a strong motivation to seek results – such as a significant impact on offending behaviour – not least as a way of securing the future of the probation service" (Millar and Burke 2012: 318).

Rehabilitation as social utility

With the championing of *What Works* by the newly reorganised National Probation Service (NPS) in 2001, the mantra of probation increasingly became *risks, needs, and responsivity* (RNR). In essence the RNR approach was predicated on research evidence that reductions in re-offending could be achieved by closely matching the resources put into an intervention to the level of risk of re-offending posed by the individual. In short, the higher the risk the greater the resources deployed. This match of risk and needs required appropriate interventions to be delivered in a way that was responsive to the learning styles of the individual. The corollary was that a mismatch of resources particularly in relation to low risk offenders was not only wasteful but could actually increase the risk of an individual re-offending (Andrews and Bonta 2006, Underdown 1998, Ward and Maruna 2007).

The attraction of risk assessment tools was, according to Nash, that "they offered an alternative to the 'subjective' clinical interview, a method increasingly discredited in political circles. By utilising scientific method it was suggested that the assessment would be more accurate and less likely to be influenced by professionals' subjective feelings and experience" (2005: 22). Concomitantly, National Standards had also been introduced in 2001 to emphasise the timeliness of processes rather than their quality or effectiveness (Robinson *et al.* 2012) and until recently they required increasingly restricted decision-making by the worker particularly in relation to offender compliance, breach and return to custody. The increasing regimentation of probation practice and its packaging into more measureable actions and outcomes also fitted in with new ways of organising and managing the rehabilitative endeavour. As Corner contends:

> Risk-based targeting of people's needs allows commissioners, but perhaps more importantly procurement officers, to satisfy themselves that they are achieving the greatest good for the greatest number with the least resources.
> *(2012: 5)*

In a contemporary sense, therefore, the appeal of rehabilitation has tended to lie in its ability to protect the wider public and effectively manage risks rather than the needs and interests of those under its supervision. As such, rehabilitation has been promoted mainly in terms of its social utility. Furthermore, for the Probation Service, participation in such forums as Multi-Agency Public Protection Arrangements (MAPPA) and Multi-Agency Risk Assessment Conferences (MARAC) discussed in Chapter Six have enhanced its credentials as a partner alongside other criminal justice partners, particularly the police and prison services, where previously ideological conflict would have made such partnerships problematic, if not unthinkable (Nash 1999, Robinson *et al.* 2012).

Problems arise, however, when the social utility of the rehabilitative endeavour is questioned as fundamentally as it was in the wake of the summer riots of 2011, when the Coalition launched an attack on the correctional services for a failure to deliver higher levels of reduced re-offending. The ideological and political climate facilitated an attack not just on the concept of rehabilitation, but also on the efficacy of the state's delivery mechanisms. Although it wasn't mentioned by name, the response of Justice Secretary Ken Clarke clearly implied that the riots of 2011 were in part a reflection of Probation's failure to deliver (discussed further in Chapter Seven).

No escaping punishment: So that's what the public want?

Despite the move to making the state, in the form of the public sector, responsible for criminality, there nevertheless remains a very strong focus on individual offenders, their families, and the communities to which they are seen to belong. All too often this growing emphasis on individual responsibility has been orientated more toward apportioning blame rather than an understanding of need (Millar and Burke 2012: 321). What clearly follows from blame, though, is the apportionment of punishment, and the enduring existence of the rehabilitative endeavour can be partly explained through its adaption to the requirements for punishing offenders. As Robinson *et al.* points out, in many European jurisdictions the idea of punitive community sanctions is an anathema (2012). Indeed, implicit in the notion of probation is the avoidance of state punishment and for much of its history in this country, it was used *instead* of punishment (Canton 2012: 578). Recent attempts to promote rehabilitation's punitive credentials have been evident in attempts to rebrand community-based sanctions as *punishments in the community* providing a cheap and credible alternative to custody for less serious offenders. This has involved the *creative mixing* of multiple conditions and requirements as part of a single sanction (Bottoms *et al.* 2004). It has also been evident in the development of new *hybrid* sanctions such as the Intensive Supervision and Surveillance Programmes (ISSPs) for young offenders and the Intensive Alternative to Custody (IAC) for adults. These latter disposals have been explicitly packaged as alternatives to custody (ATC). However, in reality they do not include anything that could not have been included within a straight-forward community order, and their success seems to have depended more on the intensive management and support that was made available to the individual through supervision rather than the specific content of the order or threat of imprisonment in breach proceedings (Humberside Probation Trust 2012).

Schedule 16 of the Crime and Courts Act 2013 amends section 177 of the Criminal Justice Act 2003 by now making it a requirement that every community order must include *at least one requirement imposed for the purposes of punishment.* By prioritizing the infliction of punishment, this legislative change threatens to undermine the balance of sentencing outcomes and the underlying principles of proportionality and fairness in sentencing. The rationale for such a move appears to be based on the perennial perception of a lack of confidence in community sentences amongst the general public. This view persists despite existing research finding little evidence that the public want community sentences to be unproductively harsh (Hough and Roberts 1999, Maruna and King 2004). Indeed, adding punishment purely for the sake of general deterrence and increased public confidence has shown to have limited positive effects. Moreover, as Robinson and Ugwudike point out, equating *toughness* with *legitimacy* is extremely problematic (2012). Making community orders overly harsh and punitive in a misguided attempt to match the damaging impact of imprisonment ultimately undermines notions of legitimacy, without which compliance and desistance are jeopardised. As McNeill has noted, whilst "community punishment makes sense as a way of securing positive payback that benefits communities; it can't compete with prisons when it comes to imposing penal harm. When community punishment tries to do that, it also undermines its capacity to secure a positive contribution from reforming citizens" (2012b).

Unintended consequences: Widening the net

It has been argued that this *punitive turn* in the use of community sanctions has been largely driven by good liberal intentions to reduce the use of custody (Robinson *et al.* 2012). However, one of the unintended consequences has been the emergence of mass supervision in the community, alongside rather than diminishing the use of imprisonment (Burke and McNeill 2013: 108). The use of community sentences by the courts in England and Wales increased by 28 per cent between 1999 and 2009 (Ministry of Justice 2010a). A key driver behind this expansion has been the desire to use community sentences as a mechanism for controlling the prison population.

The *Breaking the Cycle* Green Paper estimates that the *vicious cycle* of re-offending by ex-prisoners costs the UK economy between £7–10 billion per year (Ministry of Justice 2010b). The potential role of community sentences in reducing these costs has become a key interest of contemporary penal policy, particularly in relation to using community sentences to displace shorter custodial sentences, which have higher costs per day and are typically associated with high reconviction rates. For example, a recent enquiry has calculated that diversion from custody to residential drug treatment produces a lifetime cost saving of approximately £60,000 per offender (Make Justice Work 2011). Some argue that, as well as being much less expensive than imprisonment, community sentences can produce lower re-offending rates. According to government figures, proven re-offending of those individuals receiving community orders in 2008 was 8.3 per cent lower than for those who had served prison sentences of twelve months or less, even after controlling for differences in terms of offence type, criminal record and other significant characteristics (Ministry of Justice 2012: 10). There are of course risks as well as opportunities here. It is important that the creation of intensive community punishments does not generate a net-widening effect resulting in less serious offenders being given sentences which are wasteful of limited resources and ineffective at reducing re-offending. The late Stan Cohen warned of this in his seminal work, *Visions of Social Control,* as long ago as 1985 and, notwithstanding the political and ideological consideration highlighted by Cohen, it represents a needless and ineffective waste of public resources. The evidence to date for the displacement of short-term custody by community orders remains depressing, and the prison population has continued to rise remorselessly over the recent past. The Ministry of Justice's own figures show that between 1993 and 2008 the prison population rose on average by 4 per cent annually, fuelled by increases in the number of people sent to immediate custody, increase in sentence length including the use of indeterminate sentences and increases in the numbers recalled to custody for breach of licence conditions (Ministry of Justice 2013: 6). Despite a modest fall for the first time between June 2012 and June 2013, the prison population standing at nearly 84,000 is almost twice what it was in 1992 (Ministry of Justice 2013: 8) and this against a trend of falling levels of crime since the mid-1990s.

Don't get mad, get even!

David Downes once suggested that "*the more secure we are the more insecure we feel*" (2010: 396), and attempts to allay public fears and insecurity within a highly politicised environment is itself fraught with risks. As governments become more certain about how they will deal with crime, this paradoxically heightens anxiety and fear of crime amongst the very communities they seek to protect. The impossibility of providing complete security and the inevitability of some failure means that whatever protections are provided, they will never be enough, creating profound organisational and personal consequences (see Chapter Three). The dilemma for the Probation Service is that its

> … traditional mechanisms of protection – for want of a better expression – are to be found in the support of long-term change processes which provide relatively little security and reassurance in the short-term. Thus, although changed ex-offenders who have internalised and committed to the responsibilities of citizenship offer, a better prospect for a safer society in the long term, change programmes and services look somewhat feeble when set against the increasingly threatening offender that communities are taught to fear.
>
> *(McNeill 2009: 22)*

Of course, politicians and the political process itself find it difficult to tolerate longer-term strategies for effective rehabilitation and few if any recent Secretaries of State have shown any desire to build public confidence to support these *longer-term change processes*. Rather they exhibit knee-jerk responses to events; short-termism becomes the order of the day. One consequence is the absence of rhetoric, public policy or legislation directed toward punishment. Indeed, punitiveness has an expressive quality in the sense that it is not just the supposed instrumental benefit of punishment but its powerful emotional expressiveness that serves politicians and the political process well during times of wider pressure. It is difficult, therefore, to envisage how short-termism can ultimately strategically support a desistance-based approach to rehabilitation which by its nature requires long-term political commitment, ironically mirroring the exact same commitments to be expected from criminal justice workers and their clients!

It can also be argued that contemporary rehabilitative practices chime with the expressive nature of punishment in the sense that programmes which encourage individuals to think and behave differently and become more empathetic to their victims resonate more with neo-classical perspectives that emphasise personal responsibility. Punishment and rehabilitation both communicate, as Gwen Robinson notes,

> … censure in response to criminal acts and seek to instil within the offender a moral compass to guide his or her future actions. Thus the 'treated' offender is presented as an individual capable of managing his or her own risks without recourse to externally imposed sanctions or controls.
>
> *(2008: 440)*

This notion of the expressive or symbolic form of punishment is in fact an instrumental means of achieving wider political and administrative goals. *Communicative* theories of punishment, on the other hand, are very different. Building on the communicative theories of the legal philosopher Antony Duff, this approach aims to give wrongdoers an opportunity to redeem themselves and ultimately to be reconciled to the community. As Ward explains:

> A significant feature of communicative theories of punishment is that crime is conceptualized as a community responsibility rather than simply an individual one. While offenders are held accountable to the community their core interests are not neglected. Relatedly, victims are not ethically required to forgive offenders but do owe them a meaningful opportunity to be reintegrated within the community once they have served their sentences. Thus, the community is obligated to actively help offenders in the process of integration by the necessary internal and external resources such as education, work training, accommodation, and access to social networks.
>
> *(2009: 118).*

In other words, rehabilitation is a two-way street and critically, findings from the desistance literature referred to earlier suggest that intervention should not be solely about the prevention of further offending but should equally be concerned with constructively addressing the harms caused by crime by encouraging offenders to make good through restorative processes and community service (in its broadest sense). As McNeill argues:

> Rehabilitation, therefore, is not just about sorting out the individual's readiness for or fitness for reintegration; it is as much about rebuilding the social relationships without which reintegration is impossible. Any would-be supporter of rehabilitation has to do more than try to sort out 'offenders'; s/he needs to mediate relationships between people trying to change and the communities in which change is impeded or impelled; s/he also has to mediate the role and limits of the state itself in the process.
>
> *(2012a: 13)*

One of the advantages of strength-based approaches, such as the *Good Lives* model (Ward and Maruna 2007) is that they provide an antidote to a preoccupation with risk-based offender management strategies. Rather than labelling offenders as criminal *others*, they are presented as having the same needs and basic human nature as the rest of us, actively searching for primary human goods in their environment which emerge from such basic needs as relationships, a sense of belonging, self-worth and the potential for creativity. In this respect, strength-based approaches shift the attention toward supporting the conditions necessary for offenders to achieve these primary human goods rather than solely focusing on their personal deficits. They provide an incentive to change by focusing on the individual's own life goals and ambitions. Commenting on this approach, Robinson argues that "correctional intervention should focus on assisting offenders to identify the functions that offending has served in their lives and to adopt ways of achieving the goods that they desire more pro-socially" (2011: 15).

However, developing the social capital of a vilified group is not easy in insecure, late-modern societies. No amount of individual support will be enough if the legal, economic and social barriers to change are not also tackled. Narrowing the scope of rehabilitation to some residual form of social utility goes against Kantian (1724–1804) conceptions of the individual as a moral being capable of choice, rather than an instrument of other people's purposes. As Malcolm Millar and Lol Burke have argued, committing criminal offences does not constitute a justification for social exclusion or for withdrawing the respect which individuals, as persons, are due.

> Forcing offenders to wear brightly-coloured jackets as a shaming form of 'punishment in the community' (Casey 2008); imposing disproportionate restrictions on individuals based on the *possibility* of further offending; or recall decisions which are of dubious legitimacy (Digard 2010) – these topics all raise moral issues; and particularly in a punitive climate, those who venture to examine them in terms of their questionable humanity in individual cases enter contentious territory.
>
> *(2012: 324)*

The domination of managerial and punitive discourses in contemporary penal policy and practices, as Canton (2012: 577) points out, has relegated the human rights of individual offenders to an issue of secondary importance and apart from some improvements in the prison system, the rights of offenders have been eroded rather than upheld (Robinson 2011: 11). Those who have argued for a system of *state-obligated rehabilitation* (Cullen and Gilbert 1982, Rotman 1990) contend that the state has a moral duty to offer rehabilitative measures in return for the individual's future compliance. However, state-obligated rehabilitation can be articulated within a wider social and economic context. Making a direct link to the work of probation and the rehabilitative endeavour, Peter Raynor expresses it in this way:

> Probation flourishes best in societies which believe that the legitimacy of government rests partly on recognising a substantial share of responsibility for the welfare of its citizens. This social contract requires that in return for expecting us to obey its laws, the State should make available, as far as it can, the resources that help and enable us to pursue satisfactory lives within the law. This is the essence of the theory of State-obligated rehabilitation.
>
> *(2012: 186)*

From this perspective a rehabilitative criminal justice strategy should form part of a social policy agenda that recognises everyone's right to have their basic needs met. The strength of these approaches, as Sam Lewis argues, is that they acknowledge that "both citizen and state have duties and that citizens are more likely to comply with the law if the demand that they do so is experienced as legitimate" (2005: 123). Legitimacy in turn cannot be achieved without professionally competent staff (see Chapter Four).

Whilst the notion of *state-obligated rehabilitation* might sound philosophically and practically aloof, the notion of long-term strategies to support the reintegration of offenders into their families and communities for the benefit of the wider communities as well as for the individual offender is not. Politicians deliver punishment because they tell us that the public want it. However, when people are engaged in the criminal justice process and particularly when they have both direct and indirect contact with offenders, all the evidence is that their desire for punishment is usually mediated and often over-ridden by the desire to see the individual supported on their travels back to citizenship. The public appear to understand the notion of *don't get mad, get even*, even if our politicians do not.

Summary: So that's what offender rehabilitation is

> Justifications for rehabilitation are essentially moral arguments about what society *ought* to do in relation to offenders.
>
> *(Raynor and Robinson 2009: 5)*

Of course, such moral arguments are deeply contested and the delivery of state-mandated punishment and rehabilitation happens against a complex set of expectations and political pressures. Successive administrations have their own ideological purposes and find themselves at the mercy of public opinion, which they hope to shape for their own purposes. Whilst many people experience crime at first hand and form their own opinions based on that experience, we can also see the impact of a powerful news media on public attitudes to both crime and those who commit it. The public are fed ideologically-framed and highly subjective information about both individual offenders and more general aspects of crime. This in turn chimes with wider feelings of insecurity – as Shadd Maruna *et al.* note "public punitiveness is more a symptom of free-floating anxieties and insecurities resulting from social change than a rational response to crime problems" (2004: 277).

Whilst there is much talk of punishment in the community and alternatives to custody based on arguments of effectiveness and cost, the question has to be asked whether the dominance of imprisonment is tolerated as a relatively cheap alternative to longer-term social and economic change. The cost of mass incarceration could, from one perspective be seen as a cheap price to pay for the control of particular problem populations and the maintenance of the current socio-economic order. The language of rehabilitation acts a Trojan horse for the position that punishment holds within the criminal justice system, but it could be further argued that punishment extends beyond the penal system to the ability to access a range of goods and services. This leads us to the thorny question of the role of the state in reproducing and perpetuating deprivation. As Carlen has argued:

> Prime Minister Cameron was wrong when, in a speech last month, he put renewed emphasis upon punishment and rehabilitation in the community. He was wrong for several reasons, but he was fundamentally wrong because the poor, the young, the disabled and the indigent elderly and many others are already being severely punished in communities deprived of the most basic access to housing, jobs, and general welfare. In such a situation it seems obvious to me that all questions of crime and punishment have to be linked to, and most probably subsumed by, questions of social justice and inequality.
> *(2012: 1)*

The moral arguments for the justification of the rehabilitative endeavour, the link to questions of social justice and inequality, the vested interests and the overriding political and ideological determinants of service delivery mechanisms all help to define and shape what we think rehabilitation is. It is a complex set of considerations, but at the end of all this, we remain clear that rehabilitation is about helping individuals to go straight and get sorted.

References

Andrews, D.A. and Bonta, J. (2010) *The Psychology of Criminal Conduct*, (5 ed), Newark: LexisNexis.

Bean, P. (1976) *Rehabilitation and Deviance*, Oxon: Routledge.

Bottoms, A., Rex, S. and Robinson, G. (eds) *Alternatives to Prison: Options for an Insecure Society*, Cullompton: Willan.

Boyers, R. and Orrill, R. (1972) *Laing and Anti-Psychiatry*, Harmondsworth: Penguin.

Brownlee, I. (1998) *Community Punishment: A Critical Introduction*, London: Pearson Education.

Burke, L. and Collett, S. (2008) Doing with or doing to: What now for the probation service? *Criminal Justice Matters*, 72: 9–11.

Burke, L. and Collett, S. (2010) People are not things: What New Labour has done to Probation, *Probation Journal*, 57(3): 232–249.

Burke, L. and McNeill, F. (2013) The Devil in the Detail: Community sentences, probation and the market in Dockley, A. and Loader, I. *The penal landscape: The Howard League guide to criminal justice in England and Wales*, Oxon: Routledge.

Canton, R. (2012) The point of probation: On effectiveness, human rights and the virtues of obliquity, *Criminology and Criminal Justice*, 13(5): 577–593.

Carlen, P. (2012) Against Rehabilitation; For Reparative Justice, 2012 Eve Saville lecture, Centre for Crime and Justice Studies. http://www.crimeandjustice.org.uk/resources/against-rehabilitation-reparative-justice (Accessed 14 March 2014).

Cohen, S. (1985) *Visions of Social Control: Crime, Punishment and Classification*, Polity Press: Cambridge.

Collett, S. (1993) Beyond reason and understanding: The everyday understanding of crime, *Probation Journal*, 40(4): 184–187.

Corner, J. (2014) *What is the nature of the opportunity that Transforming Rehabilitation represents?* Clinks AGM, 29 January 2014.

Cullen, F. and Gilbert, K. (1982) *Reaffirming Rehabilitation*, Cincinnati: Anderson.

Daily Mail (2011) *Fury over Bulger killer's tryst with girl guard: Why was Jon Venables' sordid encounter in secure unit covered up?, asks James' mother*, 27 February.

Downes, D. (2010) Counterblast: What went right? New Labour and Crime control, *The Howard Journal of Criminal Justice*, 49(4) 394–397.

Downes, D. and Morgan, R. (1997) *Dumping the 'Hostages to Fortune'? The Politics of Law and Order in Post-War Britain* in Maguire, M., Morgan, R. and Reiner, R. *The Oxford Handbook of Criminology*, (2nd Edition) Oxford: Oxford University Press.

Duncan, S. (2013) Judgement room: a life story, *Euro Vista*, 3(1): 11–13.

Farrall, S. and Calverley, A. (2005) *Understanding desistance from crime*, Maidenhead: Open University Press.

Feeley, M. and Simon, J. (1994) Actuarial justice: the emerging new criminal law, in Nelken, D. (ed) *The Futures of Criminology*, London: SAGE.

Foucault, M. (1977) *Discipline and Punish* [English translation], London: Allen Lane.

Garland, D. (1985) *Punishment and Welfare: A History of Penal Strategies*, Aldershot: Gower.

Garland, D. (2011) *The Culture of Control*, Oxford: Oxford University Press.

Green, D.A. (2008) Suitable vehicles: Framing blame and justice when children kill a child, *Crime, Media, Culture: An International Journal*, 4(2): 197–220.

Hough, M. and Roberts, J.V. (1999) Sentencing trends in Britain: Public knowledge and public opinion, *Punishment and Society*, 1(1): 11–26.

Hudson, B. (1987) *Justice Through Punishment: A Critique of the 'Justice' Model of Corrections*, London: Macmillan.

Hudson, B. (2003) *Understanding Justice: An Introduction to Ideas, Perspectives and Controversies in Modern Penal Theory* (2nd ed), Buckingham: Open University Press.

Humberside Probation Trust (2012) *Response to Punishment and Reform: Effective Community Sentences* (Consultation Paper CP8/2012), Humberside: Humberside Probation Trust.

Kesey, K. (1962) *One Flew Over The Cuckoo's Nest*, London: Picador.

Lewis, S. (2005) Rehabilitation: Headline or footnote in the new penal policy, *Probation Journal*, 52(2): 119–135.

Make Justice Work (2011) *Community or custody? A National Enquiry*. www.makejusticework.org.uk (Accessed 14 March 2014).

Maruna, S. (2001) *Making good: How ex-convicts reform and rebuild their lives*, Washington DC: American Psychological Association.

Maruna, S. and King, A. (2008) Selling the public on probation: Beyond the bib, *Probation Journal*, 55(4) 337–351.

Maruna, S., Matravers, A. and King, A. (2004) Disowning our shadow; a psychoanalytical approach to understanding punitive public attitudes, *Deviant Behaviour*, 25(3): 277–299.

McNeill, F. (2006) A desistance paradigm for offender management, *Criminology and Criminal Justice*, 6(1): 39–62.

McNeill, F. (2009) What Works and What's Just? *European Journal of Probation*, 1(1): 21–40.

McNeill, F. (2012a) Four forms of 'offender' rehabilitation: Towards an interdisciplinary perspective, *Legal and Criminological Psychology*, 17(1): 18–32.

McNeill, F. (2012b) *Not big, not tough, not clever, June 16*. Discovering Desistance. ESRC Knowledge Exchange. http://blogs.iriss.org.uk/discoveringdesistance/2012/06/16/not-big-not-tough-not-clever/ (Accessed 14 March 2014).

McNeill, F. and Weaver, B. (2010) *Changing lives? Desistance research and offender management*, Glasgow: Scottish Centre for Crime and Justice Research.

McNeill, F., Burns, N., Halliday, S., Hutton, N. and Tata, C. (2009) Risk, responsivity and reconfiguration: Penal adaptation and misadaption, *Punishment & Society*, 11(4): 419–442.

Millar, M. and Burke, L. (2012) Thinking Beyond 'Utility': Some Comments on Probation Practice and Training, *The Howard Journal of Criminal Justice,* 51(3): 317–330.

Ministry of Justice (2010a) *Offender Management Caseload Statistics 2009.* Ministry of Justice Statistics Bulletin, London: The Stationary Office.

Ministry of Justice (2010b) *Breaking the Cycle: Effective Punishment, Rehabilitation and Sentencing of Offenders*, London: The Stationary Office.

Ministry of Justice (2012) *Punishment and Reform: Effective Community Sentences* – Consultation Paper CP08/2012, London: Ministry of Justice.

Ministry of Justice (2013) *Prison Population Projections 2013–2019 England and Wales*, Ministry of Justice Statistical bulletin, 7 November.

Murray, C. (1990) *The Emerging British Underclass*, London: IEA Health and Welfare Unit.

Nash, M. (2005) The probation service, public protection and dangerous offenders in Winstone, J. and Pakes, F. *Community Justice: Issues for probation and criminal justice*, Cullompton: Willan.

New Statesman (2011) Cameron searches for the "root cause" of the riots, *New Statesman*, 10 August.

NOMS (2006) *The NOMS Offender Management Model 1.1*, London: Home Office.

Omand, D. (2010) *The Omand Review: Independent Serious Further Offence Review: The Case of Jon Venables*, London: Sir David Omand GCB.

Raynor (2012) Is Probation still possible? *The Howard Journal of Criminal Justice,* 2(2): 173–189.

Raynor, P. and Robinson, G. (2009) *Rehabilitation, Crime and Justice*, Basingstoke: Palgrove Macmillan.

Robinson, A. (2011) Foundations for Offender Management: Theory, Law and Policy for Contemporary Practice, Bristol: Policy Press.

Robinson, G. (2008) Late-modern rehabilitation: The evolution of a penal strategy, *Punishment & Society*, 10(4): 429–445.

Robinson, G. and Ugwudike, P. (2012) Investing in 'Toughness': Probation, Enforcement and Legitimacy, *The Howard Journal of Criminal Justice,* 51(3): 300–316.

Robinson, G., McNeill, F. and Maruna, S. (2012) Punishment in Society: The Improbable Persistence of Probation and other Community Sanctions and Measures in Simon, J. and Sparks, R. (eds) *The Sage Handbook of Punishment and Society*, London: Sage.

Rotman, E. (1990) *Beyond Punishment: A New View of the Rehabilitation of Criminal Offenders*, New York: Greenwood Press.

Sedgwick, P. (1982) *PsychoPolitics*, London: Pluto Press.

Sentencing Guidelines Council (2004) *Overarching Principles: Seriousness – Guideline*, London: Sentencing Guidelines Secretariat, December.

Szasz, T.S. (1972) *The Myth of Mental Illness*, London: Paladin.

Szasz, T.S. (1974) *Ideology and Insanity*, Harmondsworth: Penguin.

Underdown, A. (1998) *Strategies for Effective Offender Supervision, Report of the HMIP What Works Project*, London: Home Office.

Ward, T. (2009) Dignity and human rights in correctional practice, *European Journal of Probation*, 1(2): 110–123.

Ward, T. and Maruna, S. (2007) *Rehabilitation*, London: Routledge.

Weaver, A. and Weaver, B. (2013) Autobiography, empirical research and critical theory in desistance: A view from the inside out, *Probation Journal*, 60(3): 259–277.

3

GOVERNING REHABILITATION

Politics and performance

> For much of the twentieth century, probation was a core institution of criminal justice. Extensively used, in the vanguard of penal progress, it was often regarded as the exemplary instance of the penal-welfare approach to crime control. In today's criminal justice world, probation occupies a position that is more conflicted and much less secure. Over the last thirty years, probation has had to struggle to maintain its credibility, as the ideals upon which it was based have been discredited and displaced. Under pressure from government it has tightened its procedures, highlighted its supervisory capacities, downplayed its social work affiliations, intensified its controls, and represented itself as a community punishment.
>
> *(Garland 2001: 177)*

Ideology, mezzo politics, personalities and events

David Garland's opening quote is, in our view, entirely accurate, but much has happened since the turn of the millennium to probation and the rehabilitative endeavour. The overall rationale for this chapter then is to use probation's experience of the past dozen years or more to illuminate the wider political and ideological drivers responsible not only for the reconceptualisation of the state, but also for the way in which social problems are currently defined and managed. These drivers are complex, multi-dimensional, ever-changing and contradictory, but our view is that the key context of the grand neoliberal enterprise – a combination of economic liberalism and social conservatism – developed remorselessly over the past forty years has had and continues to have a vice-like grip on the direction of the economy and the role of the state and thus, inevitably, on the more intricate operation of the criminal justice system (Bell 2011, Cole 2008: 85–90, Standing 2011, Whitehead and Crawshaw 2012). Its contradictions can be seen clearly in the management of corrections, whereby the current Coalition administration is radically deconstructing the direct role of the state whilst simultaneously increasing the frenzy of the political machinery in its bureaucratic oversight of the markets it creates. Another feature of neoliberalism within the United Kingdom is that it has become the accepted or mainstream model for economic and social development of the political parties. As Bell comments:

> Taking the example of Britain, it was an economic project in the sense that it aimed to 'free' the market from political and social constraints by retrenching the welfare state, creating a flexible labour market and promoting privatisation and deregulation. However, such an economic project also converged with the political project of Thatcherism to regain the centre-ground of British politics.
>
> *(2011:7)*

In this sense, there has been continuity in the overall thrust of all the New Labour administrations since 1997 and now the Coalition administration of Conservatives and Liberal Democrats in terms of the analysis and definition of crime and the delivery mechanisms for reducing re-offending. This can perhaps be exemplified by the fact that the privatisation of a substantial part of current probation resources is being undertaken by legislation placed on the statute books by New Labour in the form of the Offender Management Act 2007 (Burke 2013a).

We have commented elsewhere (Burke & Collett 2008: 9) that the post-Second World War period was one in which the Probation Service, certainly until the early 1970s, operated within what has been referred to as a *Butskellite* consensus around penal policy and the treatment of offenders. This old fashioned term (coined in 1954) essentially signified a loose agreement across the mainstream political parties that a relatively liberal approach to offenders should not be undermined by the pursuit of sectional interests for party political gain. Commentators are right to caution against the view that all was benign in the criminal justice environment during this period and Joe Sim, for one, argues that the *penal turn* – the move to harsher treatment of offenders – can be better understood as an intensification of law and order processes "already deeply embedded in the political and cultural institutions of the state and civil society" (2009: 15). However, from a probation perspective at the operational level, the re-emergence of punitive sanctions and expressive justice (Garland 2001: 8–9) could be felt from the early 1980s and by the 1990s the environment had developed into what Bottom's termed *populist punitiveness* (1995). Any institutional or establishment consensus about the treatment of offenders had disappeared or rather become less relevant in the environment of a *penal arms race* within which Conservative and Labour parties outbid one another so as to be seen tough on crime and criminals.

This process was aided and abetted by Home Secretaries like Jack Straw and Michael Howard who have looked westward for new ideas about corrections during a period of depressingly converging trends between Britain and the United States in terms of wider inequality (Wilkinson and Pickett 2010) as well as expanding levels of prison and probation (Teague 2011, Teague 2012). Whilst Teague is right to reflect that the relentless rise in penal sanctions in both the United States and the United Kingdom has occurred whoever has been in charge (2012: 72), it is also evident that political parties and within them, different administrations, have had differing impacts on the practice of criminal justice, certainly when played out at the local operational level. It is also the case that, in England and Wales at least, individual Home Secretaries and more latterly Justice Secretaries have impacted significantly on both the style and substance of criminal justice policy and operational practice (see Silverman 2012). Why wouldn't that be the case in such a highly charged political environment within which probation has become the focus of ambition for particular politicians? Getting tough, however, usually costs money and in a period of apparent austerity brought on by the international banking crisis of 2008, it is not just the ideological commitment to neoliberal definitions and solutions to social problems like crime that shape policy but the bottom line of cost. This, as we shall argue, impacts not only upon service delivery but also on the nature and extent of local democratic accountability.

In addition, as the introductory chapter outlines, we are clear that key events and occurrences in the criminal justice arena are used as touchstones and reflectors for the state of wider society and its institutions. When asked by a journalist what can blow governments off course, Conservative post-war Prime Minister Harold Macmillan is reputed to have responded – *events dear boy, events.* Our view is that, rather than being blown off course, the political process has become adept, certainly in the crime arena, of using criminal justice events to serve wider political needs and feed the longer-term fortunes of the political parties. The criminal actions of two 10-year-old boys, Jon Venables and Robert Thompson in 1993 (see Collett 1993), the failures of criminal justice agencies to protect the public from the murderous behaviour of released prisoners in the first decade of this century (HM Inspectorate of Probation 2006a, HM Inspectorate of Probation 2006b, Hill 2009, Fitzgibbon 2011, Fitzgibbon, 2012) or the English riots during August 2011 (Guardian/LSE 2011, Riots, Communities and Victims Panel 2012, Briggs 2012, Collett 2013) are significant but by no means exhaustive examples. In other words, events in the criminal justice world often allow politicians to gird their ideological loins and push forward to policy positions and operational approaches that would have been otherwise untenable. Events, in our estimation, can serve the ideological determination of politicians to both shape the definition of social problems and their management. They are also an important part of the mix in understanding how the role of the state and the definition of social problems, including crime, develops over time. However ideologically committed politicians and their intellectual gurus are to particular forms of social, political and economic organisation within so called liberal democracies, their deterministic intent is always mediated by the day-to-day rub of party political fortunes, personalities, events and even luck. From an operational perspective, we are confident in asserting that many civil servants, workers and managers with probation and the wider criminal justice system would attest to this.

In the opening chapter of *The Culture of Control* Garland identifies *12 indices – currents of change occurring over last thirty years of the century*. These encompass such things as the decline of the rehabilitative ideal, re-emergence of punitive sanctions and expressive justice, changes in the emotional tone of crime policy, the return of the victim, the protection of the public, politicisation and the new populism, the reinvention of the prison, the transformation of criminological thought, expansion of crime prevention and community safety, civil society and the commercialisation of crime control, new management styles and working practices and, finally, a perpetual sense of crisis (2001: 6–20). We are confident that most workers in the arenas of community justice and community safety would attest to the authenticity of these *currents*, some attenuated, others more exaggerated than at the turn of the century. The Culture of Control was published just as the National Probation Service for England and Wales (NPS) came into being and our job now is to consider how, within an enduring ideology of neoliberalism, the politics and events of the past fifteen years have constructed new ways of defining social problems and designing service delivery mechanisms for the purpose of delivering rehabilitation. Before embarking on that, however, we need to provide some background against which the NPS needs to be understood.

The 1991 Criminal Justice Act: Last chance to move centre stage?

Although our focus is ostensibly on the period of New Labour ascendency and beyond to the current Coalition government, a brief historical aside is required to set the context and provide what, from our perspective, was a highpoint in probation's recent history. From the early days following the 1907 Probation of Offenders Act until the late 1970s, the Probation Service was often lauded for its work but it remained a *Cinderella* service in terms of resources and influence (Mair and Burke 2012). Notwithstanding its traditional role within the criminal justice system, it was also important in the development of wider community-based services, including victim support schemes. In fact, probation supported and sometimes initiated a myriad of local voluntary organisations and groups that provided services to offenders and their families. Furthermore, individual probation officers, utilising the skills and knowledge built up through practice, left the Service to set up ground-breaking voluntary organisations to meet the needs of particular disadvantaged groups (for example see Wallich-Clifford 1974). Compared to what was to come, the governance arrangements were relatively loose and dependent upon oversight by a Probation Committee made up of local magistrates appointed from their local bench and local councillors appointed by their local authorities. There was, however, capacity at the local level to innovate, support and respond to social and community problems including the disturbances which occurred in England's major conurbations in the early 1980s (Scarman 1981, Gifford *et al.* 1989, Broad 1991, Collett 2013). Those same governance arrangements that allowed a good degree of latitude to interpret what constituted legitimate work were also characterised by close if sometimes fractious relations between probation staff and magistrates (see Parker *et al.* 1989). Magistrates were usually attached to individual offices in the form of case committees which provided a channel for Services to explain their work with offenders. Conversely, it enabled magistrates to raise issues and concerns about the supervision of offenders and services provided to the local magistrates' court. These exchanges varied tremendously both within and across probation areas and were often benign and mutually supportive but at their worst were characterised by paternalism and propriety on the part of the magistracy and a Service attitude bordering on patronising and arrogant. Magistrates were, in the eyes of some staff, there to be educated about the Service's work with offenders as well to receive varying messages across the decades including the shift from *treatment* and *rehabilitation* to *diversion from prison* through the provision of *alternatives to custody* (Vass 1990).

However, as political consensus began to break down during the 1980s, significant debates took place about the future of probation and even the criminal justice system itself. The Conservative administrations of this decade set about a significant reshaping of the landscape, beginning with the introduction of a *National Statement of Objectives and Priorities* to more clearly define the work of the Service (Home Office 1984). What followed was a concerted attempt to move the purpose of sentencing and the governance of the Probation Service forward in order to deliver punishment in the community (Home Office 1988a, Home Office 1988b, Home Office 1990a, Home Office 1990b, Home Office 1991). Amongst this flurry of publications, the White Paper, *Crime, Justice and Protecting the Public* (Home Office 1990c) and the outcome of the review of the parole system undertaken by Lord Carlisle (Home Office 1988c) provided the philosophical background to as well as the legislative intent for the seminal Criminal Justice Act (CJ Act) of 1991. This act, surprisingly liberal in its attempt to impact on the prison population, also signposted a very different future for probation. John Patten, the then Home Office minister with responsibility for probation, captured the dilemma facing the Probation Service in his assertion that a window of opportunity existed through which the Probation Service could move *centre stage* in the criminal justice system if it was prepared to rise to the challenge of delivering punishment and public protection (Patten 1998).

Central to Probation's future role would be its contribution to a new sentencing framework. Wasik and Taylor, in their guide to the 1991 Criminal Justice Act, argued that English and Welsh sentencing law lacked a clear rationale, ostensibly relying on a leading decision of the court of appeal advocating retribution, deterrence, prevention and rehabilitation as "the four aims of sentencing, without providing any explanation as to how these aims are to be reconciled or which is to prevail where there is a conflict between them" (Wasik and Taylor 1994: 1). In a number of respects it was this lack of rationale which often created friction between the magistracy and their *officers of the court,* with probation officers complaining of the lack of commitment by sentencers to rehabilitation and sentencers accusing Probation of being unrealistic in their recommendations for supervision (Parker *et al.* 1989: 94–95). Under the act, a *just-desserts* (sic-misspelt throughout the White Paper!) approach was introduced, arguing for proportionality in sentencing based on placing an offender under the appropriate level of *restriction on liberty* according to the seriousness of the offence. Tripwires or thresholds were built into the sentencing framework in order to try and restrict the use of imprisonment. As the White Paper had argued:

> For most offenders, imprisonment has to be justified in terms of public protection, denunciation and retribution. Otherwise it can be an expensive way of making bad people worse. The prospects of reforming offenders are usually much better if they stay in the community, provided the public are properly protected.
>
> *(Home Office 1990c: para 2.7)*

Probation was to become sentence in its own right and in relation to community sentences, paragraph 6 (2) of the act, sentencers were required to pass *the most suitable* one for the offender. This approach, reflecting a Home Office where "Oxbridge-educated mandarins such as David Faulkner held sway" (Silverman 2012: 7) received the support of Douglas Hurd, who as Home Secretary wanted to see coherent approaches to offender rehabilitation that reduced the dominance of imprisonment. Philippa Drew, an influential and highly regarded Head of the Probation Division, put it this way in an interview with Jon Silverman – the 1991 Act was "an attempt to create an intellectually coherent framework within which fewer prisoners would be sentenced to shorter terms" (Silverman 2012: 53)

It would be fair to say the response of the Service to Conservative overtures was tentative and varied from concern about some of the provisions (for example the introduction of curfew orders) to a cautious welcome for some of the substantive provisions (for example, see McLaren and Spencer 1992, Williams 1992). Additionally, a number of commentators encouraged Probation to engage for longer-term gains with what appeared to be "an uncharacteristically conservative commitment to reducing the prison population" (Nellis 2004: 118). Writing just prior to the publication of the White Paper, Howard Parker, a professor of social work at Manchester University and an influential if critical supporter of probation suggested that there was much to play for.

> Yet government rhetoric is now loosening up with talk of corporate strategies. This is a window of opportunity which the service and its friends must seize on. If a proportionate reduction in custody is to be achieved, it will have to involve greater accountability for the judges and magistrates, binding sentencing guidelines and slip resistant punishment in the community packages.
>
> *(1990: 15)*

In similar vein, in a *Probation Journal* special edition on the Criminal Justice Act 1991, Philippa Drew was invited (at the time of her transfer to the Prison Service) to make some valedictory comments. After describing both the strengths and weaknesses of the Service she went on to say that:

> The Service has a great future in both its criminal and its civil work. As regards the former the opportunity is there for the Service to use its strengths, its skills and its experience to show that offenders can be punished and rehabilitated much more effectively in the community than in prison.
>
> *(1992: 94)*

Put simply, the Service was asked to modernise and envision itself as a different type of organisation from the one that reflected its social work origins and its work with *clients*. If reluctant at first to embrace an identity that firmly placed it within the criminal justice system and the operational delivery of correctional punishments to offenders, the Service nevertheless rose to the challenge of working much more closely with the judiciary and magistracy. The implementation period between the passing of the act and its operational commencement was marked by significant common training for sentencers and probation staff and in some important respects, the sentencing framework of the 1991 Act provided Probation with the opportunity to improve its whole approach to advising sentencers.

In essence this *justice*-based or *just-deserts* approach to sentencing aimed to introduce a much clearer rationale for the use of punishments and imprisonment. By separating the *quantity* of restriction on liberty from the *quality* of the intervention – the *most suitable* for the offender in the words of the act – it gave Probation the opportunity to separate its traditional advising, assisting and befriending role from the control over individual offenders inherent within statutory supervision. In fact the care/control debate had exercised many practitioners and academics during the 1970s and 1980s (see Bryant *et al.* 1978, Bottoms and McWilliams 1979, Harris 1980, Senior 1984, McWilliams 1987) as had concern that the rehabilitative intent of criminal justice professionals was delivering unjustifiable intrusions in the lives of some offenders (see Hudson 1987: Chapter 1). Additionally, there was a growing body of evidence from academic research that *welfarist* approaches to sentencing, aided and abetted by probation and social work reports to courts, were having a harmful impact on particular groups of offenders (see Allen 1987, Carlen 1988, Worrall 1990).

The sentencing framework contained within the act helped refocus the attention of both workers and sentencers to the basic reason why men and women were before the court – because they had committed criminal offences and not because they were seen to be poor mothers or lazy fathers! (Buchanan *et al.* 1991, Collett and Stelman 1992). However, on a wider level, the ascendancy of *justice-based* approaches to sentencing during the 1980s was rightly contested by some who saw *just deserts* as a mechanism for perpetuating the inequalities experienced by those who appeared before the courts. Hudson, arguing that discretion is part of the very essence of criminal justice concluded that:

> … restricting it at one stage only enhances it at another, rather as tightening a belt does nothing to reduce body fat, merely displaces the bulge out at the midriff. What should be problematized is not discretion per se, but the use of discretion in discriminatory ways.
>
> *(1987: 128)*

This reflects a key issue for us in terms of the relationship between the importance of equality before the law, due process and wider social and economic equality to which we will return. However, we would defend the intent of the 1991 Act because it provided for a broader focus on proportionality and punishment. Indeed, it built into its provisions not only the concept of sentences being *the most suitable* for the offender, but within the guiding principles outlined in the White Paper it stated that "Each order should be tailored both to the seriousness of the offence and the characteristics of the offender. A comparatively short order may make severe demands on some offenders that more severe orders would on others" (Home Office 1990c: para 4.9) There was still, in Nellis's words "… considerable scope for rehabilitative work" (2004: 118) and although not fully realised at the time, certain provisions of the act would also have a significant impact on probation's future role.

- The *serious-enough* threshold for sentencers to utilise a community sentence meant that better off offenders were not to be fined as they would have been dealt with prior to the act, but placed under some form of community supervision. Probation's experience of supervising the poor and disadvantaged was now broadened to include a new set of offenders, often with significant but different offending-related needs.
- The act incorporated the recommendations of the Carlisle Report (Home Office 1988c) which included a significantly new structure for the post release supervision of offenders. Prior to the act, ex-prisoners could voluntarily approach Probation for help. Now individuals who received between

twelve months and four years would be subject to supervision and the effect of this, notwithstanding the additional workload, was exposure to a different group of offenders who had committed relatively more serious offences including sexual and violent attacks.

- The principle of *just deserts* and proportionate punishment was varied in one important respect. Section 1(2)(b) stated that "where an offence is a violent or sexual offence, that only such a sentence would be adequate to protect the public" implies that an individual can be sent to prison to protect the public even if the offence is not serious enough for a custodial sentence. When this provision is linked to Section 31(3) of the act, it becomes clear that the protection of the public relates to the potential for the commission of further offences. This approach meant the Service would have to increase in its organisational responsibility for public protection beyond parole and the conceptualisation of work around predicting risk, dangerousness and harm. As Faulkner and Burnett reflect, "It began the movement towards preventive sentencing, without regard for proportionality, which culminated in the indeterminate sentences for public protection introduced by 2003 Criminal Justice Act" (2012: 49).

The early signs for moving away from the use of imprisonment were positive even before the sentencing framework became operational in October 1992. A slow but fairly constant rise in the post-Second World War prison population was halted and between January 1992 and January 1993, it had fallen by some 4,000 to approximately 44,000 (Home Office 2003: 6). From an operational and practitioner perspective, the provisions of the legislative provisions were beginning to make sense and the act provided for a more rational and constructive exchange between Probation and sentencers. To the disinterested observer, these two factors might be taken as evidence of the successful implementation of a significant and complicated piece of legislation for once achieving its policy and operational aims. For Cavadino *et al.*, the 1991 Act embodied *punitive bifurcation*, whereby more offenders would be kept out of prison but at the cost of enhanced punishment and control – punishment in the community (2013: 27). On a wider ideological level, Garland argued, however, that the reappearance of *just deserts* " … also re-established the legitimacy of an explicitly retributive discourse, which in turn, has made it easier for politicians and legislatures to openly express punitive sentiments and to enact more draconian laws" (2001: 9).

We have sympathy with both these views and it is evidentially clear that community punishments have become laden with increasing levels of restriction under the rallying cry of successive administrations to make community penalties tough and credible in the minds of the public. However, we are also cautious in embracing an overly determinist view of the relationship between *just deserts* and punitive intent and we will consider this further and its practical and policy implications for the delivery of community sentences under successive administrations. Indeed, insofar as the 1991 Act was based on *just deserts*, its provisions were seen as supporting such a liberal approach to sentencing that it was soon to be emasculated and key provisions repealed. Downes and Morgan, writing in 2002 succinctly captured the politics of the period following implementation.

> Alarmed by their deteriorating position in public opinion polls, both in general and on crime, the Conservatives rapidly cast their previous and long-germinated penal policy to the winds and sought to regain lost terrain. First Kenneth Clarke, then Michael Howard, as new Conservative Home Secretaries after 1992, quickly dropped the key reforming clauses of the 1991 Act: unit fines (which linked the level of fines to disposable income) and the need normally to disregard previous convictions in sentencing. Michael Howard's notorious 'prison works' speech to the Tory Party Conference in 1993 was the climax to this somewhat panic-stricken shift.
>
> *(quoted in Mair and Burke 2012: 153)*

This accords with Faulkner and Burnett's view that despite concerns that criminal justice measures would lurch to the right to more punitive forms of treatment and condemnation of offenders following Thatcher's election in 1979, it didn't happen until John Major's tenure as Prime Minister, beginning in 1990 (2012: 5). The politics of the moment were defining ones for the future direction of the criminal justice system and the delivery of rehabilitation within it – as Cavadino *et al.* summed up the position:

> In terms of the philosophy of punishment, the conservative government then abandoned just deserts in favour of the assertion that 'prison works' by incapacitation and deterrence.
>
> *(2013: 55)*

In a number of important ways, Probation now had to face up to the realities of its continued existence as the rehabilitative arm of the correctional services, tentatively positioned on the centre of a stage that was being dragged ingloriously to the right with every public utterance from Conservatives – soon to be joined in that chorus by New Labour. A creeping realisation that the Service needed to modernise to survive was quickly replaced by disillusionment and concern that dancing to a politician's tune made very little difference to the long-term authority and standing of probation – a state of affairs that, as we shall argue, has been repeated with depressing repetition. Nellis, questioning whether the Service ever accepted its centre stage role, nevertheless captures the wider situation perfectly.

> The centre-stage offer was in any case rescinded in 1993, following a backlash against the 1991 Act's perceived liberalism by sentencers (and

> the tabloid media) and by an internal realignment in government which resulted in the Home Office adopting an *expressive* mode of penal action, exemplified by its persistent demonization of offenders as a class, and its 'prison works' strategy, loosely derived from America's penal incapacitation strategy.
>
> *(2004: 118)*

Notwithstanding the need as the Tories saw it to deal with the newly introduced sentencing framework, they were also busy scrutinising the organisational, governance and delivery arrangements of local probation services. Their intentions had been outlined within the Green Paper, *Supervision and Punishment in the Community* (Home Office 1990a) and a follow-up decision paper (Home Office 1991). The underlying themes emphasised Probation as a criminal justice agency, protecting the public and enforcing orders. A recurring theme of greater co-operation with partners was combined with the stated goal that for probation to be less an exclusive provider of services and more managers of supervision programmes, involving the voluntary and private sectors (see Mair and Burke 2012: chapter 7). In governance terms, creeping central control was the order of the day from the Home Office and the issuing of detailed guidance to areas soon followed in the form of National Standards (Home Office *et al.* 1992).

Thatcher's neoliberal project had begun to shape the future arrangements for the whole of the criminal justice system and Roger Statham's unpublished 1990 paper appears to be one of the first attempts by a serving chief officer to identify what privatisation and globalisation might mean for the Probation Service (Statham, 1990, Whitehead and Statham 2006: 266–270). The vision contained in the Green Paper and its decision document derivative was summarised by Mair and Burke:

> ... significant structural changes were suggested: the amalgamation of smaller probation areas, making probation committees more like management boards, giving the Home Office more control over senior appointments, moving to 100% funding by central government, changing the training system so that there would be greater emphasis on criminal justice issues and removing the need for probation officers to hold a social work qualification and – perhaps most controversially – introducing a national probation service.
>
> *(2012: 144)*

The authors add that whilst there were few signs of these being taken forward in the short term, within a decade New Labour had acted upon all of them! (2012: 144)

On the march with New Labour

In retrospect, the 1991 Act can be seen almost as an aberration by a government who realised their mistake and quickly went about making amends. In the wake of the murder of James Bulger and before his killers were brought to trial, the then prime minister, utilised all his skill for political opportunism through his utterance that we should *understand a little less and condemn a little more* (see Collett 1993). John Major followed that up with a comment in a 1994 speech that *crime is a decision not a disease* (quoted in Garland 2001: 198). The gloves were off and amongst practitioners at the time, there was a clear awareness of the accelerating demise of penal-welfarism. With the higher political and media profile given to crime, law and order during the last decade of the twentieth century, punitive crime control policies were increasingly viewed as a mechanism for securing electoral support for political parties beyond the actual instrumental intent of the proposals – it all seemed to set the mood music for hardening social and economic policy.

New Labour came into power in 1997 with a view that all crime should be met with punishment and that repeated offending (in contrast to the original intention of the 1991 Act) should be punished more severely. Faulkner and Burnett, in our view, accurately capture the developing sense that punishment is also to be seen as a mechanism for crime control – not just in terms of indeterminate sentences for public protection (eventually introduced by the 2003 Criminal Justice Act where a prisoner could be held beyond tariff because they could not prove that they were not a danger to the public), but also at the other end of the spectrum where anti-social behaviour orders, dispersal orders, civil-gang injunctions and other measures were introduced to control less well-defined behaviours (2012: 94–96). Joe Sim puts this approach to the *other end of the spectrum* in broader ideological terms arguing that Blair's speeches during the period 2004–2006

> contained a litany of his favourite ideas: respect, decency, community, the impact of global change and the need for summary powers to protect the decent, law-abiding majority from the ravages of the feral, atavistic minority. Once again, the context was modernisation, and specifically the need to reform the country's institutions to equip them to respond to the challenges generated by the economic and political demands of a free market, globalised economy …
>
> *(2009: 78)*

Furthermore, it was not just the hardening of attitudes toward crime but the hardening of a trend toward the demonisation of individuals who commit crime that could be detected in both old Tory and New Labour rhetoric. As the nature and extent of crime, particularly with the impact of drugs on those poor communities already suffering from the impact of Thatcherite de-industrialisation, was being transformed, so too was the language being used to describe those who appeared before criminal courts. In discussing the denigrating trends of managerialism and debasing language, Faulkner and Burnett remind us that the language deployed by tabloid journalists and their editors could also be found in government publications.

> Expressions like the 'war on crime', the war on drugs, 'vermin', 'feral' children and 'monsters' create an impression of an enemy who has to be defeated, of creatures of a different species, of people who are worthless and beyond redemption, or of a criminal class that has no place in a civilised society and have to be driven from it. Such dehumanising language serves to put them beyond the considerations normally extended to human beings; and the use of such expressions implies a justification of oppressive methods of law enforcement and of punishment, the removal of some of the protection that the criminal justice process is supposed to provide, and an arbitrary loss of liberty 'for the protection of the public'.
>
> *(2012: 34)*

These *denigrating trends* have continued unabated and as we shall argue in Chapter Seven have come to be utilised in the demonisation of wider and larger groups within mainstream society – often without any contact with the criminal justice system. In terms of delivering rehabilitation, however, besides acting as part of the justification for increasingly reactionary approaches to offenders and higher levels of incarceration, they also become self-defeating in terms of reducing re-offending. Faulkner and Burnett recognise exactly this point when they comment that such language also undermines efforts to bring about an offender's rehabilitation and reintegration into the communities from which they come and in which they live (2012: 34).

In this context then, Blair's often repeated mantra "tough on crime, tough on the causes of crime" (1993) can be viewed as a very clever mechanism for introducing ambiguity into public understanding of criminal justice policy approaches to rehabilitation. Although often quoted or referred to, the title of the article is rarely mentioned – in fact it appeared in the *New Statesman* under the title "Why *crime is a socialist issue*". Whilst most certainly *Old Labour language*, the phrase itself reflected Labour's concern with law and order and found its way four years later into a party's manifesto that was significantly New Labour. The Manifesto stated:

> On **crime**, we believe in personal responsibility and in punishing crime, but also tackling its underlying causes – so tough on crime, tough on the causes of crime, different from the Labour approach of the past and the tory policy of today.
>
> (*Labour Party 1997* emphasis in original)

In addition, it made this approach one of its ten key commitments in its *contract with the people,* oddly adding a specific target – "We will be tough on crime and tough on the causes of crime, and halve the time it takes persistent juvenile offenders to come to court" (Labour Party 1997: commitment 6). The choice of words seemed to be aimed at assuaging the liberal left and those who believe in the efficacy of rehabilitation, whilst also justifying increasingly punitive legislation and action to keep a supposedly sceptical electorate on side. As we shall argue, this dual intent of New Labour policy has had reverberations down the years of New Labour administrations and continuing into the early years of the current Coalition government approach to reducing re-offending.

In power and on the offensive

The election of a New Labour government in 1997 was seen by many within the Probation Service as marking a potential upturn in its fortunes within a more enlightened approach to law and order issues. In terms of its wider political vision, the party's manifesto made it clear that it, "had no intention or desire to replace one set of dogmas with another" and instead promoted an approach based on *pragmatism and eclecticism* (McLaughlin *et al.* 2001: 305) that offered a *third-way* between right-wing individualism and left-wing socialism (Giddens 1998). From the outset it was clear that the government's intentions towards the Probation Service would be located within a broader vision to modernise public services, although according to Hough, New Labour's approach was "presented not as a retreat from the provision of public services but as a change in the way that they are delivered. New Public Management is seen as the best way to drive up public sector performance, and thus improve social justice" (Hough *et al.* 2006: 2-3). New Labour's analysis, initially at least, was that crime and social problems in general were interrelated with a range of causes that could not be treated in isolation. Therefore, according to McLaughlin *et al.* at the heart of the government's modernisation programme was an "emphasis on developing and employing incentives and levers to promote strategic co-ordination and collaboration via 'joined-up' partnerships" (2001: 307).

Notwithstanding this broad approach, which is discussed in detail in Chapter Six, New Labour in opposition had given significant consideration to crime and punishment – probably more than any party in opposition before, and of course the Prime Minister in waiting had been shadow Home Secretary from July 1992 to October 1994. It seemed that Blair wanted to ensure that the law and order debate, which usually played into the hands of the Tory party, would not derail New Labour.

Silverman, in his analysis of *Crime, Policy and the Media* (2012), reminds us that Blair's original desire was to be Home Secretary and that either directly or through such mechanisms as the Prime Minister's Delivery Unity, he retained an influential role. Indeed one of Silverman's themes "is the way in which the Home Office, especially in New Labour's second term, often found itself dancing to the tune emanating from Downing Street" (2012: 2). Furthermore,

> In the pre-New Labour period, examples of significant pieces of legislation being actively developed by the Home Office that were stymied or even

> radically reshaped, as a result of interventions by Number 10 are scarce on the ground. But since 2001, it is equally hard to find crime-related or justice policies which do not bear some evidence of Downing Street's midwifery
>
> *(2012: 65)*

Blair, attracted by the concept of communitarianism pioneered by the American, Amitai Etzioni and searching for the *third way* in British politics seized upon the reductionist notion of rights and responsibilities. As Silverman says:

> Reduced to its core elements of 'rights and responsibilities' it found a welcoming home in a wide spectrum of the British press. But those who bothered to read Etzioni's original 'sacred text' ('The Responsive Community: Rights and Responsibilities' cited in *The Spirit of Community 1995*) might have had a foretaste of the punitive medicine which New Labour would prescribe when in government.
>
> *(2012: 19)*

The 1997 New Labour manifesto was clear on its areas for action – captured in phrases and references to poor conviction rates, violent crime, and unnecessary bureaucracy affecting the police and crown prosecution service, compulsory drug testing and treatment, zero tolerance to antisocial behaviour, enhancing the position of victims and driving forward statutory crime prevention. Probation isn't mentioned once by name but the warning signs were clear in Faulkner and Burnett's succinct summary of New Labour's analysis of what was wrong as they came into office in 1997:

- Inconsistent sentencing inadequate to protect the public and satisfy public opinion.
- Sentences were administered ineffectively with too little attention to punishment and enforcement and prevention of re-offending.
- Too much crime undetected and or unsolved.
- Juvenile crime was out of control – children needed to be brought with the scope of the criminal law and punished accordingly.
- Antisocial behaviour was a serious problem and should be brought within the scope of the criminal law rather than civil justice system.

(2012: 55)

Likewise, the authors capture the prominent features of the Labour government's policies for the criminal justice system:

- Overhaul of the youth justice system including the creation of the Youth Justice Board (YJB)and youth offending teams (YOTs).
- Reform and micromanagement of police services.

- Further legislation to increase severity of sentencing and improving rates of conviction (often referred to as closing the justice gap).
- Development of community safety structures based on a statuary duty for local authorities and chief constables to work together to formulate and deliver strategies to reduce crime and disorder in their geographical areas.
- Major campaign to reduce antisocial behaviour through the use of antisocial behaviour orders (ASBOs).

(2012: 56)

This overview of New Labour analysis and policy intent does not of course, indicate what New Labour had in store for probation, but the signs were there in Home Secretary, Jack Straw's initial attempt to bring the Prison and Probation Service together. *Joining Forces to Protect the Public* (Home Office 1998) did not muster sufficient support for Straw to plough ahead at the beginning of New Labour's first term (see Wargent 2002: 185). However, Probation's *public protection* credentials were emphasised and under the Criminal Justice and Court Service Act 2000, the names of the three main community orders supervised by probation were changed. Worrall and Hoy accurately reflect that the content of the orders was essentially the same as before, but the emphasis on words *community*, *rehabilitation* and *punishment* in their titles was intended to create a public perception that "a tough law and order agency was behind these changes" (2005: 93). This was further reinforced by ending probation's responsibility for family court welfare services by creating the Children and Family Court Advisory and Support Service (CAFCASS).

It would, however, be fair to assess the mood in Probation during the early years as one of tentative hope – probation practitioners, managers and leaders were hopeful, even expectant that the role of the state in the provision of services to help rehabilitate offenders would be given a significant boost by New Labour – *tough on the causes of crime* would become a reality, particularly in the light of *Reducing re-offending by exprisoners* – an important report from the Social Exclusion Unit (2002) which appeared to have the backing of key figures at the heart of government. Lifting New Labour's election slogan, Mair and Burke put it thus, "For many, and certainly in the probation service, there was an expectation that things could only get better" (2012: 159).

Enter the National Probation Service: Dancing to a different tune?

It is undeniable that the 1991 Criminal Justice Act created the conditions and the legislative responsibilities for the Probation Service to become more important within the overall criminal justice system. Probation had been put firmly on the stage, not at its centre perhaps, but the intensification of the breakdown in political consensus presaged a much more rampant politicisation of crime, disorder and antisocial behaviour. Throughout New Labour's opposition period significant thought and planning was evident in not only managing the political messages about crime, law and order, but also in detailing how a New Labour criminal justice would operate. During the initial period in government, Home Secretary Straw revealed his preference for the bringing together of the Prison and Probation Services and although he backed off at this juncture, there was nevertheless significant work being undertaken to transform both probation and the criminal justice landscape and on 1 April 2001, the National Probation Service (NPS) came into being.

Eithne Wallis, a former chief probation officer who had initially been appointed to manage the transition of fifty-five constitutionally separate probation services into the national service, was appointed to the National Probation Directorate (NPD) as its first National Director. Wholly funded by and responsible to the Home Office, the National Directorate and its forty-two areas were to be coterminous with the administrative structure of the Police Services, the Crown Prosecution Service (CPS) and Her Majesty's Court Service (HMCS). Co-terminosity with local authorities was achieved through grouping political administrations together but was complicated by the existence of two-tier authorities, usually in shire counties, where the county councils held sway over the major strategic and operational services (adult care, social services and education) but the Crime and Disorder Reduction Partnerships (CDRPs) were the responsibility of the district tier. The Prison Service sat outside these arrangements and was organised within the existing government Office regions (nine English and one Welsh). The National Probation Directorate appointed a regional probation manager to each of the regions, not only to make strategic links with the Prison Service but also with the Regional Government Offices responsible for crime reduction and other crime-related policies. The structure resulted in some large areas, notably London, where five former probation service areas were reduced to a single area, with an offender caseload comprising 23 per cent of the work in England and Wales (Morgan 2007: 97). Each probation area was administered by a Board of fifteen members, comprising independent members, a Lord Chancellor's representative (a Crown Court Judge), magistrates and community representatives. The Board appointed a treasurer and secretary and the chief officer (appointed by the Secretary of State and accountable to the Director General) was a full member of the Board. With the exception of the chief officer, the Board has responsibility for the employment of staff within their areas.

The intentions of New Labour were clear – they wanted to improve the business acumen of boards and strengthen the governance for delivering correctional services within the local area. Their push on geographical coterminosity presaged further changes to the key criminal justice players and was generally widely welcomed. However, the continuing failure to reform a prison service where the allocation of prisoners often far away from their homes was and continues to be a major frustration.

The National Director Eithne Wallis set out her strategy in a document called *A New Choreography* (National Probation Service 2001). It outlined a vision for the Probation Service which emphasised the concepts of *justice* and *protection of the public* and recognised *preventing victimisation* as an essential probation task. The document identified nine areas of practice that it was believed needed to be improved in the form of *stretch objectives* – a term new to the world of probation. These were:

- More accurate and effective assessment and management of risk and danger.
- More involvement of victims of serious sexual and other violent crime by giving them real information on the offender's release arrangement.
- The production and delivery of offender programmes which have a proven track record in reducing re-offending.
- Intervening early to take young people from crime.
- Enforcement.
- Providing courts with good information and pre-trial services.
- Achieving equality of opportunity for staff and users of NPS.
- Building an excellent organisation that is fit for purpose.
- Building an effective performance management framework.

(National Probation Service 2001)

Nellis and Gelsthorpe eloquently described the document as a classic piece of *utopian managerialism:*

> A New Choreography failed to take thinking about values forward in a coherent fashion. It promoted an eclectic mix of moral commitments (victim awareness, rehabilitation of offenders), scientific aspirations (empiricism) and organisational imperatives (partnership; continuous improvement).
>
> *(2003: 230)*

However, it is also right to reflect that staff saw in the forceful leadership and personal style of Wallis and her desire to commit to a vision of Probation's future, some sense that the Service was to be taken seriously. In essence, there was both goodwill towards the new arrangements and a sense of optimism. Wallis herself used the phrase – *strong centre, strong local* – to describe her overall vision for the operation of the Service, but almost inevitably tensions between central control and operational delivery within a highly localised, partnership-based culture of local governance soon appeared. Looking back on the introduction of the national service, Peter Raynor, for example commented that:

> It is tempting to speculate that the nationalisation of a service, which was formerly rooted in localities and at least to some degree in a sense of ownership by local sentencers may have made it more vulnerable to politically driven change: a single service based in London under the wing of the Home Office

> is a more obvious focus of political awareness and target for political gestures than 54 locally based services involving hundreds of influential magistrates.
>
> *(2004: 317)*

More specifically, Wallis was committed to the development of the *What Works* or the *Evidence-Based Practice* initiative (Underdown 1998), but became caught up in the pursuit of creating local enthusiasm for more effective ways of working with offenders whilst working with a treasury that would only provide resources for clearly identified outputs. Robinson captured this dilemma perfectly:

> The appropriation of 'what works' by the centre has confused the picture, arguably intensifying both positive and negative correlates of 'what works': that is, lending weight to the service's claims of effectiveness; but also introducing standardisation on a national level in the form of accredited programmes and the development of a national assessment system.
>
> *(2001: 248)*

Like Raynor, this author goes further to argue that the *What Works* could also be seen as "a powerful catalyst to the creation of a national service, arguably completing the process of rendering the service governable by the centre and thereby increasing the service's vulnerability to centrally-imposed changes in the ideological purpose of its work" (Robinson 2001: 248).

The crime control policies of New Labour in its first term were far more ambitious than those of the previous Conservative government and initially appeared to offer a more enlightened approach to tackling the social and economic causes of crime. In this respect, the early optimism felt by the Probation Service was perhaps justified in that it appeared to occupy a central place in the government's crime control policy – a role matched by increased investment and an enshrined separate identity after the rejection of a prison's probation review. The move toward a National Probation Service had the potential of providing a stronger national voice for probation at the centre of national policymaking. However, whilst Napo had initially welcomed the creation of the national service, concerns quickly emerged over the impact on the delivery of front-line services and in the autumn of 2002 voted to take industrial action. In particular the increased costs resulting from the growing bureaucracy at the centre (from under 90 staff to almost 300 in less than 15 months) and the privatisation of facilities (including cleaning, estate management and food preparation in approved premises) across areas was seen as the thin end of the wedge. The threat of industrial action in response to increased workloads was also prevalent during the early years of the new national service (Napo News October 2002). It was clear that workloads were increasing but at the local level, it could be argued that staff concern and misgivings about the new arrangements also reflected the more structured approaches to work with offenders which was seen as an attack on traditional officer autonomy, the threat of privatisation, annual uncertainties about local budgets and a burgeoning target culture that increasingly bore down on individual practitioners and their managers. Two contradictory features of the new environment were apparent. Firstly, as Enver Solomon noted "of all the criminal justice agencies, the Probation Service has had the largest real terms increase in spending. In cash terms, spending on probation tripled between 1998–1999 and 2004–2005, the equivalent of a real terms increase of 160%. The extra funding paid for an expansion in the probation workforce and organisational restructuring" (2007: 14). Secondly, Probation was still facing an overwhelming demand for its services to the extent that the Chief Inspector of Probation talked of the system of community punishments silting up probation (HMI Probation 2003: 5) and suggested that consideration should be given to private contractors taking over the supervision of low-risk offenders and individuals on community service because the Probation Service was stretched to capacity (HMI Probation 2003: 7). Although a highly respected figure, Rod Morgan's suggestion did not go down well in probation circles!

One thing is certain though, that in the creation of a National Probation Service, central government now had control over a set of previously relatively autonomous local area services and was intent on pursuing a top-down direction of correctional services, initially in line with the *What Works* initiative, but increasingly aligned to its desire to create an integrated local approach to crime and antisocial behaviour through the state. The central drive from the NPD reflected the burgeoning target culture of New Labour and in combination with the control of local governance arrangements, probation practitioners became increasing directed in terms of their practice, senior managers constrained by fear of withdrawal of budget and heavy handed interventions from a highly critical centre. In addition, boards expected to be involved in an unprecedented level of local governance. It is deeply ironic that those board members who were recruited from the private sector to modernise and inject free enterprise thinking were, in our experience, the very people who supported the service as a public sector agency whilst complaining about over-controlling governance arrangements imposed from the centre. As Faulkner and Burnett reflect, "Like other public services, criminal justice was to be run in accordance with the principles of modern public management (the New Public Management) based on targets, markets, competition and contracts" (2012: 55 and Chapter 9, see also Deering 2011: 19–25, Teague 2012). Probation was directly in the government's sights and by the time New Labour lost power, there was the most all-encompassing and rigid regulatory framework of targets, priorities, inspections, audit and governance arrangements which were squeezing the life out of probation. The situation was captured superbly in the publication by the Probation Association of *Hitting the Target, Missing the Point* (Probation Association 2011).

In the period of gestation leading to the introduction of the National Probation Service, probation chief officers had debated long and hard about the threats and potential for the new arrangements and eventually bought into the idea of a national service, believing that it would be able to exercise a national voice and be more authoritative in terms of the direction of national policy for the rehabilitation of offenders. The Association of Chief Officers of Probation (ACOP) was a major casualty of this thinking and was disbanded in 2001. However, it soon became clear that the National Director would not be allowed an independent voice by virtue of her role as a civil servant. It was also apparent that the service was not equipped in terms of knowledge, skill and experience to deal with the Whitehall interface with ministers and civil servants. It would be another seven years before probation leaders areas across the country galvanised themselves to form the Probation Chiefs Association (PCA).

Tough on crime: Sentence reform and system management

As the National Service commenced operation, the government instigated two reviews into the sentencing process in response to what it perceived as a lack of public confidence. The first by Sir Robin Auld was charged with reviewing the criminal courts system and looked at various ways in which efficiency might be improved (2001). Auld proposed a unified criminal courts system, in three divisions, to replace magistrates' and Crown courts although the recommendation to create a new intermediate court tier was not adopted in the ensuing White Paper. The second report was written by a senior civil servant, John Halliday (Home Office 2001), and entailed a wide-ranging review of sentencing policy. *Making Punishments Work: Report of a Review of the Sentencing Framework for England and Wales,* argued for a clearer but also more flexible framework for sentencing so that rehabilitation and reparation could play a larger role. Halliday advocated replacing the desert-based system enshrined in the 1991 Criminal Justice Act with one combining elements of both *desert* and *utilitarian* principles arguing that the erosion of the 1991 Criminal Justice Act had resulted in muddle, unnecessary complexity and a lack of clear purpose or philosophy in sentencing policy (see Lewis 2005: 121). He drew particular attention to the lack of post-release support for short-term prisoners, which as a result of the introduction of Automatic Unconditional Release (AUR) meant prisoners serving less than twelve months were released without any form of statutory post-release supervision. He recommended prison sentences under twelve months should be replaced by a new sentence of *custody plus*, whereby a short period in custody would be followed by a much longer period under probation supervision. The eventual outcome of both reviews was a White Paper, *Justice for All* (Home Office 2002), which recommended a broad range of reforms, once again using the language of modernisation. Extra expenditure was provided to modernise prisons and to improve information technology, all aimed at *joining up* the criminal justice system, together with the creation of a National Criminal Justice Board and a new Cabinet Committee to oversee reform.

Both Auld and Halliday gave impetus, initially under the direction of the National Criminal Justice Board, to the introduction of Local Criminal Justice Boards (LCJBs). Unlike the existing Local Criminal Justice Consultative Committees, usually chaired by a senior judge and from which LCJBs took over, the new arrangements allowed for both the cementing of local operational and strategic action to *narrow the justice gap* (the problem of attrition between reported crime and prosecution of individuals), increase public confidence, improve the efficiency of the local justice system and increasingly focus on reducing re-offending as the means for reducing local crime rates. Their operation capitalised on the coterminosity of forty-two criminal justice areas. Run as shadow boards for the 2002–2003 financial year, they formally came into being in April 2003.

LCJBs proved to be both popular and effective in developing and sustaining local partnerships. In a number of important respects, local probation areas were able to demonstrate that they could punch above their weight, particularly in relation to the police and it would be fair to say that boards generally respected the strategic leadership skills that probation chiefs could offer, as evidenced by the number of LCJBs chaired by probation. Besides facilitating partnership arrangements at all levels and across an increasingly significant number of non-criminal justice agencies, LCJBs were able to cement the work of managing dangerous offenders through the Multi-Agency Public Protection Arrangements (MAPPA) and dealing with persistent offenders through the priority and prolific offender (PPO) schemes required by operational policy driven by central government.

However, unable to trust *the local* despite its much repeated rhetoric of decentralisation, New Labour did to LCJBs what it invariably did to individual agencies and that was to impose central oversight and bureaucratic control through, in this case, a well-funded and resourced Office of Criminal Justice Reform (OCJR). Local targets and rigid performance management frameworks based on dubious and easily distorted measures of local performance were increasingly imposed. As a result, local criminal justice agencies felt thwarted in terms of what they were trying to achieve with non-criminal justice agencies. At the centre, the OCJR was charged with creating a coherent strategic vision across relevant government departments in order to deliver a coherent set of joined-up targets at the local level. It was partly successful but as with all attempts by the centre to manage the local, its resources were ultimately used to impose another layer of bureaucracy that would ultimately be seen to be counter-productive, unclear and behind the times. This approach to governance was not an isolated example within the criminal justice system or indeed across the public sector itself, as the Director of the Institute for Public Policy Research (IPPR), Nick Pearce, reflected:

> ... as its time in office wore on, Labour drifted into being instinctive centralisers (when it should have been the opposite), loaded more responsibility on to the state (when it should have sought to share the task of governing), and

> tended to rely on cash transfers and policy transactions (when it should have sought to build institutions and foster relationships). Even while workers' real wages were stagnating, these instincts left Labour open to the charge that it valued material more than moral worth.
>
> *(2013)*

Tough on the causes of crime: Reducing re-offending

The introduction of LCJBs was welcomed during the early part of New Labour's second term, not just as a means of bolstering local strategic and operational partnerships; local authorities welcomed the chance to move beyond traditional responsibilities for community safety, taking on the additional challenge of reducing re-offending. Indeed, this was ultimately reflected in the Policing and Crime Act 2009 which made Probation a statutory partner of Community Safety Partnerships (CSPs) and required local authorities to consider reducing re-offending in the exercise of all their duties (Ministry of Justice 2010c). However much these *system management* approaches were welcomed, many within the Probation Service and the wider criminal justice family had hoped being tough on crime would be balanced not only by the introduction of more focussed and effective approaches to the rehabilitation of individual offenders, but also to the deployment of a comprehensive approach to tackling wider social problems. The social and economic characteristics of most acquisitive offenders were well documented and in the nomenclature of a burgeoning academic field of desistance research, Probation's approach to enhancing personal capital required action to enhance access to and develop social capital as well if offenders were to desist from criminal careers. Optimism that New Labour would not forget its pledge to be tough on the causes of crime became manifest in the content of a Report of the Social Exclusion Unit (SEU), *Reducing re-offending by ex-prisoners* (2002). Surveying the immense financial as well as personal cost of re-offending to wider society, the report identified nine key factors (education and training, employment, drug and alcohol, mental and physical health, attitudes and self-control, institutionalisation and life skills, housing, benefits and debt and families). Although there was little mention in either the subsequent Carter Report (2003) or various consultation documents about the future of the correctional services, the work of the SEU was influential in its identification and reaffirmation of realistic and practical ways to reduce re-offending and it shaped the *Reducing Offending National Action Plan* (Home Office 2004a) and subsequent Regional Resettlement Strategies. In line with the SEU analysis, most of the pathways identified focused on the provision of practical services although the seventh was concerned with *Attitudes, Thinking and Behaviour.* According to Maguire and Raynor:

> Looked at in this way, the Reducing Re-offending National Action Plan seems to go beyond traditional 'welfare' approaches to resettlement (or 'after-care' or 'throughcare', as it was called in earlier incarnations) and to reflect a multi-causal explanation of offending, neither a purely deterministic view (external problems and forces acting on the helpless individual) nor one based entirely on individuals exercising 'free will' or 'agency' in choosing to offend. *(2006: 27)*

The new framework was to be overseen by a cross-governmental board of senior officials, chaired by Martin Narey, along with representatives from key government departments responsible for the complementary services involved in resettlement. Despite the *Reducing Offending National Action Plan* (which formulated over sixty action points to support the rehabilitation of offenders) and increased investment in resettlement services, there was a lack of commitment to fulfil the original vision of the SEU: Namely, that government departments would forge a united front in reducing re-offending by ex-prisoners through systematically addressing the social context of their resettlement needs and the high levels of homelessness, mental illness, poverty, family breakdown, drug misuse, and poor educational attainment of offenders. Despite the SEU report and the National Plan's call for government departments to work together, the reality was that the most politically acceptable and convenient actions have been promoted at the expense of the measures to tackle social exclusion. This approach was further compounded by political infighting between the relevant departments. Investigative journalist Nick Davies caught the bureaucratic and political context.

> The Treasury was interested in saving money by turning people away from prison, but it was not prepared to take any political risks, so Treasury officials backed the SEU's plans for more education and job advice for prisoners – they were politically easy to sell – but they would give nothing to the other causes of crime. Overwhelmingly, the Treasury's investment stayed with the prisons even though the SEU had found so much evidence of their failure ... Other government departments were even worse. The small Home Office team spent months trying to secure housing for released prisoners, waving the SEU evidence that a stable home cut reoffending by 20%. All they wanted was for the Office of the Deputy Prime Minister to tell local authorities to treat more prisoners as 'vulnerable' and, therefore, entitled to housing. The ODPM would have none of it. It said prisoners' housing was a job for the Prison Service. The Prison Service said that was fine but it didn't have any housing. The ODPM said it was no good coming back to it, because the law would not allow it to treat prisoners as 'vulnerable'. One of those involved said this was

> 'nonsense – they just didn't want to do anything'. The ODPM got its way: even if it did mean more crime, there was no effective priority on housing for released prisoners.
>
> *(quoted in Burke 2005: 38–39)*

In a number of important respects, the failure of an SEU inspired resettlement strategy reflected the inability of New Labour to balance the need for light touch national strategic direction balanced by local implementation reflecting local needs and problems. Ultimately, it became a responsibility for regional offender managers (ROMs) introduced in 2005 and their successors, the directors of offender management (DOMs) introduced in 2009 to direct Regional actions plans. This heavy-handed, remote and bureaucratic approach ultimately became counterproductive. The Prison Service was largely unable to deliver on placing prisoners close to home and at the local authority level, resources continued to be in short supply.

It is worth noting, however, that New Labour did set about reinvigorating interest in the operation of the Crime & Disorder Act 1998. From its inception, the act required local police services and relevant local authorities to consult with the public in developing strategic plans to deal with crime and disorder at the local level. Initially, local Crime and Disorder Reduction Partnerships (CDRPs) tended to focus on crime prevention measures (for example CCTV, fitting window locks, alley-gating and other forms reducing the opportunities for crime within the local environment). New Labour's focus on antisocial behaviour required cooperation between police and local authorities and from 1997 to the middle of the next decade, the development of police basic command units (BCUs) and neighbourhood policing, mirrored by probation's local delivery units (LDUs) and an increasing interest by local authorities in reducing re-offending, all aided by coterminous geographical and administrative boundaries, created more coherence at the local level. In fact the Local Government Association got in on the act, producing a well-received report – *Going Straight* (2005), picking up many of the themes within the SEU report and articulating very clearly why reducing re-offending was and should be the business of local authorities. Its recommendations (as much to its own members as to the wider criminal justice sector) were progressive and envisaged much greater integration between CDRPs, LCJBs and local authorities to deliver meaningful resettlement services and community-based supervision that would reduce the need for imprisonment. It was also the driving force behind a follow-up report produced by the Coalition on Social and Criminal Justice (2006) which argued that going straight could be achieved by going local. Supported by the Probation Boards Association (PBA), it was the last throw of the dice in a battle to shake off centralised control and let the local state determine its approach to reducing re-offending. With hindsight, the Local Government Association's vision can be viewed as highly progressive one in terms of both the partnership arrangements it advocated and the approach to working with both offenders and local communities.

As we shall see, however, the die had already been cast in the form of Patrick Carter's first report (Carter 2003). New Labour did develop a National Community Safety Plan 2008–2011 (Home Office 2007) but in reality the new strategy reinforced pre-existing arrangements between central government and local authorities rather than advocating anything truly groundbreaking. Faulkner and Burnett capture the essence of the plan in the following:

> This brought together a number of the governments Public Service Agreements – those concerned with improving children's safety and prospects, increasing the number of socially excluded people in more settled situations, reducing the harm caused by drugs and alcohol and building safer, more cohesive, empowered and active communities – and linked them to Local Area Agreements, The plan was essentially a 'top-down' initiative, with a large number of nationally prescribed indicators, but that the activities to be pursued at local level should promote the involvement and empowerment of local communities and should be related to local issues.
>
> *(2012: 71)*

Ultimately, local authorities were required under the Policing and Crime Act 2009 to give consideration to reducing re-offending in the exercise of all its duties, and Probation was made a *responsible authority* of the CDRPs – now renamed community safety partnerships (CSPs). A *National Support framework – Reducing Reoffending, Cutting Crime, Changing Lives* (Home Office/Ministry of Justice 2010), was published to support these new responsibilities and galvanise and integrate the many initiatives already running across local partner agencies. There was significant support for this approach but the irony of a different future for the management of the correctional services and one that would strike at the heart of local partnership working was not lost on the probation community even at this early stage in the long march to *Transforming Rehabilitation*.

The search for organisational perfection

Having undergone a wide-ranging, rapid and complex reorganisation in its first three years, the Probation Service was again faced with further transformation as Patrick Carter, at the behest of the Number 10 Policy Unit, began undertaking a review of correctional services. This culminated in *Managing Offenders, Reducing Crime: A New Approach* (Carter 2003). Like the Halliday Report (Home Office 2001), Carter stressed the need for *seamlessness* both in the management of offenders in custody and the community and in terms of the relationship between the courts, partner agencies and the public.

Despite immediate concern expressed about changes to structure and governance proposed by Carter (for example see Probation Boards Association

2004 and 2005), the report itself was in fact significantly concerned with sentencing policy and practice and the enforcement of sentences, aspects of which were judged, either explicitly or by implication, to be seriously flawed (Morgan 2007: 105). It identified the increases in the number of offenders sentenced to custody and community penalties as resulting from the increased severity of sentences, inconsistency in sentencing practice and the reduction in the use of fines, rather than an increase in crime or crime becoming more serious. It also found that sentences were often poorly targeted and ineffective, particularly short prison sentences, which had also been a concern for Halliday. The Carter Report and the immediate Home Office response (2004b) reflected a belief that if the recommendations to reduce prison numbers and re-offending were carried out, the prison population would rise to 80,000 (instead of the previously projected 93,000) by 2009 and the numbers of those under community supervision might rise to 240,000 (instead of 300,000). This was of course dependent upon a change in sentencing practice initiated by the Sentencing Guidelines Council, which was to be the mechanism for keeping sentencing practice and the capacity of the system in alignment.

The other major strand in the report was a perceived need to increase organisational effectiveness in the field of community and custodial services. The report proposed the creation of a new National Offender Management Service (NOMS) based on the belief that "a new approach is needed for managing offenders, to reduce crime and maintain public confidence" (Carter 2003: 4). The prison and probation services would be incorporated within this new organisation to *manage* offenders and commission various resources from the public, private and voluntary sectors as necessary, in effect, creating a market for offender-related services. Carter also believed that the quality of interventions would be improved by introducing an element of commercial competition – what he called *contestability* – which would allow other public sector, private or voluntary agencies to bid against prisons and probation for contracts to replace them. Contestability was seen as having the potential to bring both positive outcomes in terms of increased innovation and diversity in service delivery. In this respect the proposals contained within the Carter Report can be seen as the incisive application of New Public Sector Management into the world of probation.

Although the report was somewhat sketchy in terms of how contestability would be implemented, it was likely that Probation Areas would become providers bidding for contracts against the private, voluntary and community sectors to deliver services. This was somewhat different from its role as a purchaser or commissioner of services from these sectors, and contestability would therefore usher in a potentially different relationship between the Probation Service and the voluntary sector with a greater emphasis on competition than partnership. In this respect, Mike Nellis reflected that:

> The NOMS's model for contestability seems to derive far more from the prison service experience with contracting-out to commercial organisations than from the probation service's experience of 'partnership' with voluntary and community groups.
>
> *(2006: 55)*

Despite considerable unease amongst sentencers, prison and probation staff, criminal justice commentators and a variety of politicians toward what was viewed as poorly communicated and insufficiently developed plans for the creation of a correctional service in England and Wales (Oldfield and Grimshaw 2008), the recommendations contained within the Carter Report were accepted almost immediately by the government without consultation with the main stakeholders. As Rumgay has reflected:

> Carter reduced the accumulation, over nearly a century, of expertise in meeting increasingly complex, legislative obligations to a few lines that seemingly dispensed with all tiers of management, supervision and support.
>
> *(2005: 207)*

Nellis argued that this state of affairs indicated that Probation had become an *object* rather than a *partner* in policy development. He also suggested that the desire to merge the probation and prison services pre-dated the modernisation programme of the Labour government and was in reality a long-held aspiration amongst Home Office civil servants, of which the formation of the National Probation Service was merely a compromise position bringing Probation under the direct control of the Home Office (2004). Commenting on the haste with which the Carter debate was being taken forward, Raynor suggested that it "arose from a perceived political need for another eye-catching 'big idea' in criminal justice to maintain the government's stance of activism in relation to crime" (2004: 322).

At the same time as the Carter Report was published, the Criminal Justice Act 2003 (CJA 2003) received royal assent. A new *Community Order* had been devised with twelve possible requirements for sentencers to select from. Despite criticisms that the provisions replaced proportionality with a "smorgasbord" approach to sentencing aims (Von Hirsch and Roberts cited in Easton and Piper 2005: 89), subsequent research indicated that in reality the new Community Order has been used pretty much like the community sentences it replaced and in this respect had little diversionary impact on the use of short custodial sentences (Mair, Cross and Taylor 2007, Mair and Mills 2009). The CJA 2003 also introduced the term 'dangerous offenders' into legislation within the context of establishing a new sentencing framework based upon public protection. The act also made it easier to recall prisoners and lengthened the licence period for most offenders, ultimately increasing the prison population.

In February 2003 Martin Narey, formerly Director General of the Prison Service, became the first Commissioner for Correctional services in England and Wales, with responsibility for Prison and Probation Services plus oversight of the Youth Justice Board. The following year he became the first Chief Executive of the National Offender Management Service and as such it was he rather than the National Director of the National Probation Service who became the prominent publicly-visible manager of the Service. The National Director became accountable to Narey and in this way "the probation service was linked, as never before, with the prison service" (Worrall and Hoy 2005: 95).

In May 2004, NOMS published its preferred model to deliver the new organisational structure, splitting the purchaser and provider functions, with both accountable to the NOMS Chief Executive. There was no mention of the forty-two Probation Areas and boards, which on the provider side were replaced by a *Director of Public Sector Interventions* working to a National Management Board. On the purchaser side, ten Regional Offender Managers (ROMs), each with a Commissioning Advisory Board and a Regional Management Board, were to oversee commissioning and offender management respectively. It was envisaged that an estimated 70 per cent of probation staff would be line-managed by the ROMs (Morgan 2007: 107), and those in the *Interventions* part of the service would be due to come under a separate employer, initially a national employer under the Director of Public Sector Interventions. There was clearly significant friction within the upper echelons of the Home Office as Eithne Wallis stepped down as director of the NPS in 2004 and a new post, National Offender Manager, was filled by a former Greater Manchester Chief Officer, Christine Knott. Widespread concerns expressed in the responses to the consultations regarding the new structure forced the government to take a more cautious approach to some aspects of the change programme such as the creation of regional boards and the separation of probation staff into offender management and intervention functions. However, its commitment to the establishment of end-to-end management, and the introduction of greater contestability, initially using the existing structure of the forty-two Probation Boards and current legislation was reaffirmed. A leaked document to *The Guardian* in November (Travis 2004) claimed that there were real concerns within Whitehall regarding the implementation of NOMS, including a warning that the size of the project and its complexity resulted in a loss of confidence among ministers, staff and unions. Despite these warnings, in a November meeting between Martin Narey and Tony Blair, the Prime Minister reasserted his desire to see faster progress toward contestability and insisted that the split between offender management and interventions be ready for piloting by April 2005.

Notwithstanding the more political and ideological arguments about the role of the public sector, a key criticism of the proposals was that the commissioning and purchasing of services would add layers of bureaucracy and expense. One interpretation/implication of the 'Preferred Model' was that at a regional level (and sub-regional level) there would be a Prison Service structure, an Offender Management structure and a Public Interventions structure. This would duplicate, overcomplicate and spread confusion amongst partner agencies. An additional regional structure would inevitably add to costs, bureaucracy, and potentially create new *silos* (Burke 2005: 21). Additional and attendant criticisms concerned fragmentation of service delivery and the loss of accountability at the local level both to local communities but also to key stakeholders and particularly sentencers. As we shall argue in later chapters, these exact same criticisms resurface under the *Transforming Rehabilitation* proposals of the Coalition administration

A differentiated marketplace, it was argued, could lead to a loss of rigour and coherence in the assessment and management of serious, dangerous and highly persistent offenders. The Probation Boards Association argued the point that "Probation is a virtual monopoly provider for good reason. It is a strength which helps protect communities against risk" (2004: 12). Whilst there are clear overlaps between the work of the probation and prison services, aligning them more closely together underplays the complex network of relationships with other agencies (police, health, housing, local authorities) in responding to the public protection agenda; together they offer better offender supervision in the community. Indeed, looked at through a different prism, the difference between the organisational and operational cultures of prison and probation could be viewed as entirely positive. Hindpal Singh Bhui, for example warned that a merger between the prison and probation services could undermine Probation's distinctive and relatively progressive journey toward race equality (2006: 186).

The ten ROMs were appointed in the autumn of 2004, although Home Office plans to transfer Probation Area staff to be line-managed by the ROMs had been abandoned as the legality of such a move was questionable. Instead, a new approach was forged. Probation boards would be abolished, to be replaced by trusts, and instead of moving across to be line-managed by the ROMs, Probation staff, whether involved in offender management or the delivery of interventions, would likely move between whichever providers, public, private or voluntary sector, successfully tendered to the ROMs or the National Offender Manager for contracts or service level agreements. In October 2005, the Home Office published a consultation paper *Restructuring Probation to Reduce Re-offending* (Home Office 2005a). Amongst its key proposals was the replacement of local probation boards by smaller business-focused bodies appointed directly by the Home Secretary, who would hold the power to contract for Probation Services with the aim of driving greater value for money through competition.

Martin Narey resigned at the end of 2005 and was replaced, though without permanent secretary status, by Helen Edwards, formerly Director of the National Association for the Care and Resettlement of Offenders (NACRO). According to Nellis and Goodman, Edwards was a "quietly efficient administrator without [Narey's] messianic zeal for NOMS" (2008: 214). Nevertheless, as Morgan observed, "the new locus of influence was preserved" (2007: 99), with policy continuing to be driven by NOMS rather than the National Probation Directorate. In March 2006 the government published *Working with Probation to Protect the Public and Reduce Re-offending* (Home Office 2006a), emphasising a shift from a central directorate, with new larger trusts replacing boards. In effect, the National Probation Directorate would cease to exist and its functions subsumed within NOMS, whilst the prison service would continue to have a Director General, the Probation Service would not. Napo claimed that of the over 750 responses received only 4 could be termed as broadly supporting the plans (Napo News Feb 2006).

In August 2006 the government published its long-awaited prospectus on how contestability would be introduced into the provision of Probation Services, *Improving Prison and Probation Services: Public Value Partnerships* (Home Office 2006b). Among its proposals was the introduction of a 5 per cent target for probation boards to spend on sub-contracting in 2006–2007, increasing to 10 per cent in 2008. This was never going to be enough and during 2006, the Home Secretary, John Reid was reported to have described the Probation Service as "poor or mediocre" (Travis 2006), and that it was his intention to privatise up to a third of its £800 million budget. As The Offender Management Bill progressed through Parliament "the National Probation Directorate was quietly dissolved and its functions dispensed into NOMS's internal structures" (Nellis and Goodman 2008: 216). The Offender Management Act of 2007 duly embedded commissioning and contracting out into the framework of probation.

In her 2008 McWilliams lecture, outgoing General Secretary of Napo, Judy McKnight, assiduously brought together seven *organograms* describing evolution and change from the original Carter Report of 2003 to the NOMS organisational chart of 2008 (McKnight 2009). For those who were engaged in making sense of these shifting organisational sands and concomitant, almost continuous sense of uncertainty and crisis during this period, we can only agree with her observation that there was a frequent lack of support, indeed even attacks on Probation from the government side:

> ... has also enabled it to justify its never-ending structural reforms, undertaken to enable contestability and competition to be introduced. Continuous structural reform over recent years has also taken its toll, not only on the confidence of the Service but also on its ability to have a spokesperson at a senior level, whose advice Ministers will heed.
>
> *(McKnight 2009: 332–333)*

Further internal changes occurred within the Home Office under Reid's watchful eye and subsequently in January 2008 Jack Straw, Labour's Justice Secretary, announced yet another structural change at the Ministry. In its new form NOMS would have *agency* status and be implemented effective the beginning of April 2008. Phil Wheatley, former Director General of the Prison Service, was appointed chief executive of the new organisation tasked with reducing duplication and making savings from the centre. Commissioning was to be replaced by service level agreements and the ROMS incorporated into the Prison Service Area Manager structure. The post of Director of Probation was retained but only until the move to trust status for all forty-two areas had been achieved. Directors of Offender Management (DOMs) were appointed to each of the nine English regions and to Wales beginning in April 2009. Although regionally-based and responsible for all prison and probation expenditure and performance within each region, they were effectively senior civil servants operating as part of NOMS. Yet again these highly expensive appendages to a national bureaucracy were to last only a year before plans were afoot to ultimately disband the structure, as all Probation Areas successfully gained trust status, albeit with some amalgamations (at the end of the trust process, forty-two Area Boards had been conflated into thirty-five trusts).

Running scared: New Labour and the media

As Ken Clarke settled into his Coalition job as Justice Secretary, concerns reached a head. In a survey of probation chiefs carried out by Channel 4 News and supported by the Probation Chiefs Association, it was clear that the majority of chiefs believed that neither prisons nor probation had the capacity to keep up with the levels of offenders entering the criminal justice system, and most importantly area services were so stretched any further cuts to budgets would make it impossible to protect the public *all of the time.*

> Most are agreed that resources have been spread too thinly, there is universal agreement that the current commissioning system isn't working (a "mess" said one chief), and nearly half admitted that they were not able to offer the full range of community orders they are supposed to.
>
> (*Channel 4 News* 2010)

Reacting to the survey, one of the current authors (then vice-chair of the Probation Chiefs Association) told Channel 4 News on 31 August 2010 that this survey was a "wake-up call" for the new Coalition and called for more resources. He said,

> We have over the last five years been operating within an increasingly complicated, bureaucratic and ever-changing environment and certainly for the last two years, we've been delivering services against reducing budgets.
>
> (*Channel 4 News* 2010)

We consider this to be an accurate view of how Probation chiefs and their managers were frustrated working within the increasingly volatile world of corrections. In addition, operational staff bore the brunt of responding to changes in operational priorities and fluctuating staffing levels. What particularly peeved staff was the continual sniping at Probation by politicians despite the fact that nationally, the service was hitting or exceeding all its targets, successfully navigating their way through the government's own trust programme. By the time New Labour lost power at the May 2010 General election, many in Probation felt largely disillusioned by a government that had offered hope of constructing a rational and progressive approach to crime and its causes, but had delivered bureaucratic confusion, complexity and deep uncertainty about the future of Probation within the shifting sands of structural reform. The ideological and political nostrums for Probation and the constant requirement to find new structures to deliver neoliberal approaches to public sector management made little sense to those who thought probation had delivered everything asked of it by successive administrations. In addition, the constant uncertainty about resources not only made it impossible to plan operational delivery from year to year, but raised the key issue of operational capacity to protect the public.

However, there is another story regarding how the impact of personalities and events affected public preconceptions of offender rehabilitation. By both accident and design, an unholy alliance of media interests and political design ensured that specific events were used to their maximum potential to shape policy and enhance the egos of key politicians. In 2012, Jon Silverman provided a fascinating account of how the multi-faceted relationship between crime, the media and policy played upon the differing personalities of successive Home Secretaries. In the 1990s, he argues that there was a discernible move away from upholding the individual liberty of the citizen to an emphasis on community. This was work, he argues, that Michael Howard sketched in outline and was developed more fully by Blair and Straw, resulting in the redrawing of the contours of civil rights around the notion of community:

> … faced with rising crime levels and mediatized pressure, a new equation of liberty was modified for the 1990s. In the hands of Howard, Straw and Blair, it can be defined as the right of the community to be protected from the activities of the aberrant or suspect individual. It is evident in the Criminal Justice and Public Order Act 1994; achieves fuller expression in the Crime and Disorder Act 1998; and flowers exuberantly after 2000 with the Regulation of Investigatory Power Act, the Terrorism Act (Section 44) of that year, and the Proceeds of Crime Act 2002 and a host of other legislation throughout the decade.
>
> *(Silverman 2012: 21)*

During the first decade of this century, the relationship between New Labour and Probation turned up-close and personal. We have already mentioned the interplay between political utterances and policy development in relation to key events such as the murder of James Bulger in 1993, but our contention is that specific events during the height of New Labour's period in office helped to advance the onslaught on Probation as a public sector agency and played into the attritional approach to defining rehabilitative services within the ideology precepts of *New Public Management*. Unlike the police and prison services that are seen to represent the thin blue line between the *law abiding public* and the *criminal classes* and therefore require regular acts of visible political support, Probation has struggled to find champions within the political elite. If one set of circumstances highlights this so starkly it is the volte face that John Reid performed in relation to the carefully developed role of approved premises in accommodating dangerous offenders including those who had committed offences against children. Over ten years, the Approved Premises estate (in total some 100 individual hostels) had moved from providers of general support and accommodation for those released from custodial institutions and those sentenced to restrictive community sentences, to a key resource in the management of high risk of harm (dangerous) offenders. This was welcomed by practitioners who were often faced with the almost impossible task of managing the risk posed by offenders who have few roots in the community and whose lifestyles and offending behaviour make existing and future victims highly vulnerable. Approved Premises offered a supervision lifeline to local agencies, particularly through Multi-Agency Public Protection Arrangements (MAPPA) for the initial management of dangerous offenders before longer-term plans could be put in place. As Home Secretary John Reid, however, was unable to support the policy of his own department and of his own officials. As a highly placed official within the NPD said to Silverman,

> The *News of the World* told the Home Secretary that it had obtained details of the locations of bail hostels and was prepared to publish them unless he took action to remove sex offenders. The NPD view was: 'let them go ahead and publish'. It might result in a few bricks through windows but that happens anyway in the normal course of events. We were sure we could handle the fallout. But there was no appetite on the political side to stand up to the paper. Of course John Reid dressed this up by saying 'we've taken a principled stand on this' – but you can draw your own conclusions.
>
> *(2012: 36 interview with author, 4 September 2008)*

In the absence of any evidence that the use of Approved Premises for the initial management of child sex offender represented an enhanced risk to local children, local staff were left to fill the void by the use of less robust measures for those offenders who had to be released into the community under the terms of their custodial sentence. Reid's decision to cave in to the *News of the World* represented a serious threat to public protection measures at the local level and put local services on the back foot, many of whom had spent inordinate time convincing local authorities and communities that it was in their interests to support this specialised role for Approved Premises.

Probation Services felt let down and unsupported, particularly when perceived mistakes in their supervision of dangerous offenders were, quite rightly, subjected to intimate scrutiny and review. During early months of 2006, Probation Service was subjected to ongoing negative media attention following several alleged failings. The attacks followed the criticism by the Chief Inspector of the Probation Service following the murder of the Chelsea banker, John Monckton by Damien Hanson and Elliot White, both of whom were under statutory supervision at the time of the offence (HM Inspectorate of Probation 2006b). Vital details about Hanson's violent personality were not included in his parole report and as a result he was not deemed to be a high risk. This led to the subsequent suspension and reinstatement of four members of the London Probation Area and subsequently an approach to David Scott, then chief officer of Hampshire Probation Area, to take over the London service, which he did in 2005. In May 2006 another HM Inspectorate of Probation report (2006a) was published, investigating the circumstances surrounding the murder of Naomi Bryant by Anthony Rice – a discretionary lifer released after sixteen years in prison. The then Home Secretary, Charles Clarke, was reported as describing the Probation Service as "the dagger at the heart of the criminal justice system undermining public confidence in criminal justice as a whole" (Daily Telegraph, 21 March 2006, cited in Allen and Hough 2007: 566). As Silverman himself comments:

> The Naomi Bryant case also, rather than being about human rights, was essentially about the management of risk. As were, to a greater or lesser degree, other high profile murders such as that of the Nottinghamshire jeweller, Marian Bates in September 2003; the Chelsea banker, John Monckton, in November 2004: and the torture, rape and murder of 16-year old Mary-Ann Leneghan in Reading in May 2005. Quite properly, all these cases received exhaustive media attention, not merely for the nature of the crimes themselves but for the flaws they exposed in the supervision of dangerous offenders by the probation service and the competence of decisions taken on release by the Parole Board.
>
> *(2012: 38)*

With the murder of two French students, Laurent Bonomo and Gabriel Ferez in June 2008, London Probation Services (and the wider probation community) braced itself, as one of the accused murders was Dano Sonnex, subject to post-release probation supervision. The prison service, police and Probation Area all bore varying degrees of responsibility for the tragedy, but the most high profile casualty was the Chief Officer of Probation for London, David Scott, who resigned in February 2009 after Jack Straw made it clear that he wanted his scalp. The case had parallels with Baby P and the treatment of Sharon Shoesmith as head of Children's Services in the London Borough of Haringey, who was sacked by Ed Balls, Secretary of State for Children, Schools and Families in December 2008 (see Fitzgibbon 2012).

There were significant failings in the overall management of Sonnex (Hill 2009) but what became clear very quickly was that the fallout would be far-reaching and that political opportunism would determine how the circumstances of the case would be dealt with at the highest level. David Scott, the chief officer of London Probation put it this way in an interview with John Silverman,

> I have no doubt that Straw was in a kind of bidding war with Ed Balls (over how quickly he could get rid of me). He was posturing and sabre rattling. And the thing which caused me most offence – and still does – was that there was no attempt to balance or mediate a number of complex issues which played a part in the case.
>
> *(2012: 46 interview with author, October 2010)*

One of the *complex issues* related to the resources that London Probation had to deploy at the local (Borough) level and any one of us in leadership positions understood the context within which continuing uncertainty about resources made it almost impossible to plan their deployment beyond a year-by-year basis. Under both the NPD and later NOMS it was almost always the case that the determination of annual budgets occurred at the last moment and on one occasion after the commencement of the financial year. Under treasury rules, areas were not allowed to carry through underspends from one year to the next except under stringent and continually changing rules. Like most other Probation Areas, London Probation had underspent its 2008–2009 budget of £154 million by £3.5 million. This was not just deft housekeeping but reflected the requirement of the then National Probation director, Roger Hill, to maximise underspends. Silverman is therefore entirely accurate when he comments that "David Scott and other senior probation figures maintain the reason was that the National Offender Management Service (NOMS) had taken a decision in October 2008 to encourage all probation boards to maximise under-spends to help them through a tougher financial settlement in the year 2009–10" (2012: 47).

Straw was not going to accept this and so became personal, making comments to Silverman that David Scott was paid a lot of money, "He had made himself, or been made chairman, of the Association of Chief Probation Officers and it meant that his eye was off the ball. He had not got a grip" (2012: 47 Interviews with the author 21 September 2010). Furthermore, close reading of the Justice Secretary's statement to the House of Commons demonstrates how personal the issue of London Probation and the murder of the two French students had become (see Hansard 2009). What is deeply ironic and mischievous in Straw's sideswipe at David Scott is that in 2006, the incoming Permanent Secretary at the Home Office, Sir David Normington, expressed surprise both in meetings with the probation leadership and directly to David Scott about the absence of a leadership forum. Furthermore, Home Office minister, David Hanson was very supportive of chief officers' efforts to form the PCA. The truth was that Scott was supported unanimously by his chief officer colleagues to lead the PCA.

In a comment piece for the *Probation Journal*, published before the interview with Silverman, Scott had bravely accepted that he had decided to resign "because something had gone gravely wrong. Two innocent young men died terrible deaths at the hands of Sonnex and another individual. Failings by the service I led and the wider criminal justice system contributed to their deaths" (Scott 2010: 292–293).

> However nothing had prepared me for the duplicity of the agency nor, more shockingly, the posturing of the then Justice Secretary in the national media. Why the Justice Secretary should state that I had been suspended when I had not remains a mystery to me. His assertion that I would have been sacked (prejudging any hearing) is deeply ironic coming from the head of the Ministry of Justice.
>
> *(2010: 293)*

Probation in general and David Scott in particular were left to carry the can, despite the Justice Secretary accepting, in his statement to the press on the 4 June 2009, that the fact that Sonnex was free to kill "…was the consequence of very serious failures across the criminal justice system that he had not been arrested and incarcerated some weeks before" (Ministry of Justice, 2009: 1). As Scott himself said,

> You have the power and media influence of the police. You have the Prison Governors Association made up of seconded governors, paid for and accommodated by the prison service. And alongside them, you had a Probation Service, which had no national leadership. The irony is that I had only just been appointed chair of the Probation Chiefs Association to be the public voice of the service when the Sonnex crisis broke. At the time, I was vice-chair of the London Criminal Justice Board and the Met police's attitude was 'we are all in this together, this was a bad case and nobody comes out of it well'. But when you look back at the wreckage, you see the smoking ruins of the probation service and not the police.
>
> *(2012: 50 interview with author, 26 October 2010)*

In fact, the only agency to apparently come out of the situation without blame according to the Justice Secretary was the NOMS. In his Commons statement, Straw reflected that NOMS, of course a New Labour creation, was "the one agency to come out of this properly" (Hansard 2009: column 528), referring to a straightforward administrative task of dealing with the eventual recall of Sonnex into custody. Not only did some who were working in senior leadership positions at the time consider NOMS to be highly dysfunctional (Collett 2013: 164), but in elevating a relatively straightforward task to an indicator of bureaucratic effectiveness underlined the Justice Secretary's inability or refusal to acknowledge the complexities of managing dangerous offenders within both complex multi-agency arrangements and a failing host environment. It came as no surprise to those in the probation industry that David Scott, a highly experienced senior manager appointed by his peers in 2008 to lead the Probation Chiefs Association, would accept responsibility for mistakes that had happened in the Sonnex case. As he stated in a lengthy *Guardian* article, "My resignation was evidence of the responsibility I felt for the mistakes that had allowed these acts of barbaric savagery to occur. It had happened on my watch and I fully accepted that I was accountable" (Scott 2009).

The Justice Secretary refused to countenance the idea that resources or rather the perpetual uncertainty about resource allocation was part of a disabling environment that New Labour had created through the implementation of NOMS, but Scott articulated what many within probation knew to be the reality.

> Workload pressures, poor accommodation and failing information systems were recurrent themes among frontline staff, and they wanted senior managers, myself included, to listen more to these concerns. Those with senior private sector experience on our excellent governing body viewed our operational environment with dismay and disbelief.
>
> *(2009: 2)*

Whilst Scott accepted that the reality for public sector organisations will always be the challenge to manage within overstretched resources, he was scathing about the failure of command and control, the modus operandi of NOMS and the political style of New Labour at the time, "For organisations to learn lessons (just as with people) there has to be a willingness to face up to what has gone wrong, however unpalatable" (Scott 2010: 293).

In her telling account and analysis of social work and probation in the light cases like Sonnex and baby Peter, Wendy Fitzgibbon comments that political life declines in quality precisely as government by media has risen to become a major driving force (2012: 94). Playing to the media and utilising critical incidents to prove political toughness and shift the blame may send out messages to the wider public about the intent of a government to tackle crime and reform the public sector, but if a reasoned analysis of the weaknesses of policy and the fragility of practice in complex environments is ignored, it ultimately puts the public at further risk. Straw got his man but at what cost?

Enter the Coalition: Breaking the cycle and breaking probation

Following the election in May 2010, there was a faltering flurry of activity focussed around the notion of delivering a *Rehabilitation Revolution,* but it seems to us that the Coalition had simply quickened the pace of what New Labour had either put in place or aspired to before their electoral defeat. Ken Clarke, as the newly appointed Justice Secretary, inherited the legislative framework of the Offender Management

Act 2007, which had introduced Probation Trusts and laid the basis for the future relationship between the Secretary of State and those thirty-five trusts. Competition was clearly going to be the order of the day and in December 2010, plans for a *Rehabilitation Revolution* were outlined in the form of the Green Paper, *Breaking the Cycle* (Ministry of Justice 2010a) and an accompanying Evidence Report (Ministry of Justice 2010b). The Justice Secretary's oral statement to the Commons talked of bringing forward *a revolutionary shift in the way rehabilitation is financed and delivered*, based on more local and professional discretion, fewer targets and less proscription, greater competition and a system of Payment by Results (PbR) applied to all providers by 2015. This aspect of the Green Paper was followed up by the publication of a competition strategy (Ministry of Justice 2011a).

Whilst economic fortunes had been radically transformed between the latter days of New Labour and the new government as a result of the 2008 global banking crisis, there was also the shroud of David Cameron's *Big Society* hanging over the early days of the Coalition plans. Our view, elaborated in Chapter Five, is that the *Rehabilitation Revolution,* far from promoting or supporting Cameron's vision, instead took advantage of economic circumstances to continue to push further the interests of a neoliberal economy. As a Treasury insider informed the Financial Times before the 2010 Spending Review, "Anyone who thinks the spending review is just about saving money is missing the point. This is a once-in-a generation opportunity to transform the way that government works" (quoted in Garside 2012: 10). Notwithstanding immediate and deep concerns about what the *Rehabilitation Revolution* would hold for the future structure and governance of probation, there was some sense, even optimism, that under Clarke's stewardship, a refocussing on community penalties might take place.

In his response to the consultation process, Clarke made it clear that community orders were not to be seen as alternatives to short prison sentences, but as the means to stopping offenders from re-offending: "Punishment is our first and most important response to crime, but is not sufficient to prevent offenders from re-offending" (Ministry of Justice 2011b: 6). The consultation process attracted some 1200 responses (Ministry of Justice 2011b: 3) and despite major misgivings across the criminal justice sector, it was clear that payment by results and the privatisation would shape the future world of corrections:

> We will pioneer a world first – a system where we only pay for results, delivered by a diverse range of providers from all sectors. This principle will underpin all our work on reoffending. This is a radical shift.
>
> *(Ministry of Justice 2011b: 7)*

The next part of the overall consultation process was the publication of two documents entitled *Punishment and Reform* – one dealing with *Effective Probation Services* (Ministry of Justice 2012a) and the other *Effective Community Sentences* (Ministry of Justice 2012b). Essentially, *Effective Probation Services* brings emphasis to the provisions of the Offender Management Act 2007 and the 'competition strategy'. Competition is seen as a means of raising the quality of public services which should be financed by the taxpayer, but delivered by whoever is best suited to do so (Ministry of Justice 2012a: 3). A comprehensive *Payment by Results* (PbR) approach is envisaged for the future and Probation Trusts are to be developed as commissioners of services with separate local entity bidding for work in order to create a purchaser/provider split:

> Under my plans, the public sector will continue to have a major and well-defined role – as the safety of the public is our priority. In keeping with the model of competition already applied elsewhere in the penal system, my plans envisage that responsibility for monitoring offenders who pose the highest risk, including the most serious and violent offenders will remain the remit of the public sector. The proposals in the consultation suggest opening to the market the management of low risk offenders. The public sector will also retain responsibility in the case of all offenders for taking certain public interest decisions including initially assessing levels of risk, resolving action where sentences are breached, and decisions on the recall of offenders to prison. Our proposals also exclude probation advice to court from competition. This advice is principally concerned with identification of the most appropriate sentences for offenders and prosecuting their breaches – which must remain reserved to the public sector.
>
> *(Ministry of Justice 2012a: 3)*

Although there is some inevitable overlap, the second consultation paper, *Effective Community Sentences* (Ministry of Justice 2012b) aimed to consult on the development of existing and future provision envisaged in the Legal Aid, Sentencing and Punishment of Offenders Bill (which received royal assent on 1 May 2012). The consultation document, whilst containing some welcome sections on the treatment of women offenders and the development of reparative and restorative justice measures, was largely a rehash and reaffirmation of the importance of credible community sentences, rigorously enforced to punish offenders as well as to reform them. The paper reiterated the government's position that community orders were not there to replace short-term custody (Ministry of Justice 2012b, para. 20). It argued the case for a punitive element in every community order, the introduction of intensive community punishments (interestingly for those at the cusp of custody), more flexible use of fines and innovations in the deployment of electronic monitoring, and the piloting of the alcohol abstinence and monitoring requirement provided for within the Legal Aid, Sentencing and Punishment of Offenders Act.

Taken together, these two papers, with seventeen and forty-five questions, respectively, posed for consultation, had the feel of a vision for the privatisation of punishment and reform that could not answer the practical and policy questions that such an ideologically-driven approach raised. As a key example, the role of probation is described as the *vital glue that holds services together for offenders* (Ministry of Justice 2012a, para 70) and envisaged the Service's continued accountability for MAPPA, Safeguarding and Community Safety Partnerships, but simultaneously countenances a reduction in the number of trusts to provide economies of scale for competition and the future possibility of transferring accountability from the Secretary of State to local authorities or Police and Crime Commissioners.

The penal arms race was to continue apace, but the question now became one of who is to deliver what? David Faulkner, in a letter to *The Guardian,* urged the government to provide "a clear principled sense of direction based on prevention, rehabilitation, problem solving and restoration ..." which would be consistent with the older traditions of the Conservative Party, but he brilliantly captured our current predicament when he concluded that the debate on criminal justice had already relapsed into "the *dreary language of punishment and competition*" (Faulkner 2012: 31, italics added).

When Ken Clarke was replaced by Chris Grayling as Justice Secretary in September 2012, it was evident that the pace and ideological intent of the rehabilitation reforms would intensify. January 9 2013 saw the publication of another consultation paper, entitled *Transforming Rehabilitation: A Revolution in the Way we Manage Offenders* (Ministry of Justice 2013a). This attracted some 598 responses (Ministry of Justice 2013b) and supposedly shaped the basis of the government's final position encapsulated in *Transforming Rehabilitation: A Strategy for Reform* (Ministry of Justice 2013c). The document summarises the intended reforms in the following manner:

> By fundamentally reforming the system, and finding efficiencies to extend rehabilitation to more offenders, we can start to make a difference. The reforms we will implement include:
>
> - **For the first time in recent history, new statutory rehabilitation** extended to all 50,000 of the most prolific group – offenders sentenced to less than 12 months in custody;
> - A fundamental change to the way we organise the prison estate, in order to put in place an **unprecedented nationwide 'through the prison gate' resettlement service**, meaning most offenders are given continuous support by one provider from custody into the community;
> - Opening up the market to a diverse range of **new rehabilitation providers**, so that we get the best out of the public, voluntary and private sectors, at the local as well as national level;
> - **New payment incentives** for market providers to focus relentlessly on reforming offenders, giving providers flexibility to do what works and freedom from bureaucracy, but only paying them in full for real reductions in reoffending;

- A **new national public sector probation service**, working to protect the public and building upon the expertise and professionalism already in place.

(*Ministry of Justice 2013c: 6–7* emphasis in original)

In other words, Probation would become a residual public sector organisation dealing with the most difficult and dangerous offenders and the remaining offenders who constitute about 70 per cent of probation's workload will be supervised in future by private sector organisations, in conjunction with those voluntary sector organisations who wish to form commercial alliances. Local Probation Trusts will disappear as services are commissioned on the basis of some twenty-one *contract package areas*. This simple description, of course, does not capture the complex web of relationships and partnerships that exist at the local level. These range from those built up over years of informal engagement and commissioned activity to meet local needs to partnerships enshrined in law and binding on local Probation Trusts. An initial attempt by the Ministry of Justice to clarify partnership arrangements under future structures (2013d) already highlights the potential for wasteful duplication and the danger of blurred accountability and governance that would currently be the responsibility of the local Probation Trust.

The move towards the privatisation of Probation has been relentless under the Coalition government and despite its apparent commitment to almost continuous consultation, the process has exposed the centre's lack of understanding about, amongst other things, the complex world of *the local*, of working partnerships, local accountability, perverse incentives, the volatile nature of offender risk and ultimately the cultural strengths of Probation as an organisation and the professionalism of its staff. Consultation offered a process through which civil servants attempted to find solutions to the major problems these reforms would create – as such the outcomes of the consultations read like endorsements of the proposals and the *Transforming Rehabilitation* live events were seen by many experienced managers as nothing more than road shows to demonstrate the government's intent.

Summary: Neoliberalism, *new public management* and beyond

> After more than one hundred years of work with offenders, often with little encouragement or recognition for their efforts, a small island of decency and humanity in the criminal justice system may be disappearing.
>
> (*Mair and Burke 2012: 181*)

With its origins in the philanthropic and religious movements of the late nineteenth century, Probation offers a fascinating historical and contemporary insight to wider social, economic and political thinking, whilst crime itself provides a prism through which social and political elites, the media, local communities and individual victims are able to voice their concerns, not just about crime, but what it represents or reflects about society and its institutions. In this sense, the work of probation and its rehabilitative role has become increasingly politicised and its values contested and challenged. In 2004, in an article presciently entitled "Into the Field of Corrections: the End of English Probation in the Early 21st Century?" Mike Nellis wrote:

> So the future is indeed as bleak as Garland envisages it at the end of *The Culture of Control,* although – metaphorically speaking – more the 'scorched earth' of remorseless managerialism and permanent revolution than the 'iron cage' of a petrified, cumbersome bureaucracy. Either way, humanistic values, the only standpoint from which one might resist the onslaughts of managerialism, and the debasements which follow, are ceasing to have credibility and leverage in criminal justice.
>
> *(2004: 133)*

We began by outlining Garland's twelve *indices of change* and our analysis suggests that from a Probation perspective, whilst all remain relevant, we have attempted to highlight politicisation, new management styles and a perpetual sense of crisis as indicative of New Labour and now the Coalition's approach to offender rehabilitation. We would add another – blaming Probation – which has come to the fore not just in relation to individual failures in supervision, but more insidiously to wider social problems and the management of particular groups (see Chapter Seven). It can, therefore, be argued that Probation's enhanced utility and instrumental importance following the implementation of the 1991 Criminal Justice Act within a highly politicised environment has come with a heavy cost as it has been accelerated down a correctional path. It did not have to be that way and we would defend the *just deserts* provisions within the 1991 Act, the real problem was that the act did not fit with the burgeoning political designs of those who cared little for understanding the wider causes of crime and wanted to move wider societal thinking down a narrow punitive channel.

Whilst it is possible to identify a particular emphasis in each of New Labour's three terms in office (see Burke and Collett 2010), it seems to us that James Treadwell captured New Labour's overall approach to probation in his observation that "The creation of the National Offender Management Service (NOMS) can be regarded as the culmination of a move toward meticulous regulation of both those within the probation service and the offenders with whom they work" (Treadwell 2006: 3). Under this *meticulous regulation* the probation service increasingly became a law enforcement agency to which the offender reported in order for their court imposed punishment to be administered. Despite the best efforts of its workforce, Probation has become increasingly narrow in its focus and removed from *the local.* As we have argued elsewhere:

> A correctional framework driven by the unseeing requirements of public service modernisation encourages technicist and rigid responses to situations rather than real engagement with individual offenders, their families and their

> community networks. Whether its command and control or the mechanism of commissioning and contestability, a magic bullet for solving crime does not exist.
>
> *(Burke and Collett 2008: 10)*

To put it bluntly, the ability to assess, help, manage and if necessary control offenders has been made more difficult when the reality and context of offender's lives and the resources and networks available to support individuals within their own communities are not understood. In essence, New Labour could not square its desire to control probation from the centre through increasingly bureaucratic and perverse performance management ideology with its apparent commitment to localism, the development of civil society (see Chapter Six) and the role of the local state in tackling both crime and antisocial behaviour. It underestimated the complexity of the criminal justice environment which, we would argue, requires a legislative framework of clear and intelligible criminal justice provisions to deliver individual justice within an integrated environment of local state resources and expertise. The initial push to tackle the causes of crime was lost within an environment where reducing the use of imprisonment for less serious offenders was sacrificed on the high alter of media driven political expediency and the price for this was an ever increasing prison population driven by a myriad of poorly reasoned sentencing and enforcement initiatives.

We began this chapter by stating our position that *ideology, mezzo politics, personalities and events* all have their place in shaping social responses to crime in an environment that is complex, multi-dimensional, ever changing and contradictory. Rob Reiner captures this superbly in his analysis of the early days of the Coalition government and its approach to rehabilitation:

> After a few brief salad days during which the Coalition appeared to burnish its liberal criminal justice credentials, there has been a rapid return to form as the government has reverted to tough law and order. This has been facilitated by some unforeseeable events and personality clashes, but is more fundamentally the predictable unfolding of the consequences of its quintessentially neoliberal economic strategy.
>
> *(2012: 29)*

However, like Reiner, we cannot escape the reality that it is the ideological imperatives of the grand neoliberal economic strategy that has ultimately determined Probation's experience over the recent past. To simply concentrate on the immediate political environment, the interplay of party politics, public opinion, electoral success and service delivery mechanisms, without considering the wider ideological and political forces at play, makes understanding of policy direction and innovation in delivery mechanisms somewhat perplexing, particularly when they fly in the face of evidence about what is effective in reducing re-offending. The great irony in this entire onslaught on Probation is that as an arm of the state it has done all that has been asked of it and more despite the mesmerising cultural revolution of perpetual change and challenge. From the early days of the NPS, when some area services were found wanting, Probation has responded to demands for changes in delivery, governance and management. As trusts are abolished and those staff who do not lose their employment wander into the fragmented environment of either a truly national service or a private sector organisation, it must be especially galling that under the 2012–2013 annual performance ratings (National Offender Management Service 2013) all thirty-five Trusts were rated good (31) or exceptional (4). This is on top of the service being awarded the British Quality Foundation Gold Medal for Excellence in 2012 (Burke 2013b). The service has consistently implemented significant and complex change whilst improving re-offending rates, sometimes spectacularly in the context of local Integrated Offender Management schemes. The 2013 Compendium of re-offending statistics shows, for example, that community orders significantly reduce both the level and intensity of re-offending compared to matched offenders serving less than twelve months imprisonment (Ministry of Justice Statistical Bulletin 2013).

Furthermore, the highly effective work Probation undertakes through multi-agency public protection arrangements (MAPPA) is rarely given much public prominence except when, in exceptional cases, things go badly wrong. In the case of the murder of the two French students, Laurent Bonomo and Gabriel Ferez, it allowed Jack Straw to show us what he was made of, but where was he or his successor, Ken Clarke, when the outcome of an independent review by Sir David Omand of the supervision of Jon Venables, one of the killers of James Bulger, concluded:

> Having examined in great detail the local and national records of this case and interviewed many of those most directly involved, I believe the public would be reassured to know of the dedication and professionalism of all concerned. It is very reassuring to see the efforts that were made over a long period to uphold the safety of the public and the interests of justice.
>
> *(Omand 2010: 87)*

The reconstruction of the public sector begun under the Thatcher administrations from 1979 and continued under New Labour; now the Coalition administration has moved from pressing for efficiency and effectiveness within the state sector to the potential achievement of those aims through segmentation of service delivery and the invisible hand of the market. The price of creating this tension, when driven by those with an obsession for market solutions, has been the utilisation of very significant resources, both financial and intellectual, in a morale-sapping and increasingly dysfunctional operation of NOMS. This is the inevitable consequence of playing the only game in town – the pursuit of a neoliberal ideology that prizes above all the privatisation of all before it. Viewed from this vantage point of an all-embracing ideology, the modernisation of public services including the Probation Service makes sense in terms of the demanding hegemony of neoliberalism and the willing handmaiden of *new public management* (NPM) – competition and the construction of markets, the transfer of management models from private sector, the separation of policy from operations and purchasing from providing, an emphasis on the measurement of and control of inputs and outputs and on performance management and the assessment and management of risk.

As a corollary, the role of professionals has been downgraded by New Labour and the Coalition government who have both been generally suspicious of professional or service cultures, regarding them as working to promote the services' own interest and resist change. David Faulkner and Ros Burnett have commented whilst there may be some force in that argument "... cultures can also work to promote professional pride and standards that are more deeply rooted than the performance measures of NPM" (2012: 175). This is an argument supported by Rob Mawby and Anne Worrall, who conclude their study of probation culture by arguing that:

> ... probation cultures are complex but, if properly understood, do not undermine the objectives of offender management nor need they be feared by management, the government or the media. However, attempts to dismantle or dilute these cultures by fragmenting probation work and parcelling it out to the lowest bidder, may be counter-productive by loosening the 'ties that bind' probation workers to what was described to us as an 'honourable profession' and thus devaluing their commitment to their core universal value of reducing crime by working with offenders who are conditionally at liberty.
>
> *(2013: 154)*

David Garland wrote in *The Culture of Control* that the management of risks and resources has displaced rehabilitation as the organisation's central aim (2001: 177). As a high-level description of developments this may be accurate, but those engaged in the world of practice and interaction with offenders on the day-to-day level do not necessarily and completely absorb the such ideologically driven developments. From his research with probation practitioners, John Deering concluded that:

> In terms of the broad themes discussed in the literature, there was little to indicate the influence of the new penology on practitioner behaviour. Whilst obviously very much aware of risk, they continued to work with individuals based on their continuing assessment of risks and needs rather than work in any generalised manner aimed at simply managing risks; clearly their aim was transformative. Punishment was acknowledged, but rather as a result of an individual's withdrawal of consent, rather than as anything *they* did as part of their role.
>
> *(2011: 180)*

Governance in the sense of controlling, managing and making accountable the performance of probation to the wider community will change further and dramatically under the Coalition's *Rehabilitation Revolution*. Our experience with probation tells us that each generation of Probation workers have defined their own golden age, but we also agree with the argument that features of a moral economy, defined by Whitehead and Crashaw (2013: 589) as the assertion of the primacy of human interests over economic ones, have consistently and historically been reflected in the Probation Service through respect for all people, belief in the capacity of the individual to change and the importance of human relationships in helping individuals lead crime-free lives. These features of work within an *honourable profession* may yet offer some hope:

> Paradoxically, the neoliberal state that eyes the main chance in a competitive and marketized environment may inadvertently offer opportunities to re-scope its mission, which takes account of moral economy. One cogent reason for pursuing this is that the moral economy of human relationships informed by the doctrine of personalism, facilitates effective practice.
>
> *(Whitehead and Crawshaw 2013: 597)*

However, it is not just about the importance of values in the relatively narrow sense of what works in reducing re-offending and promoting rehabilitation, but the wider utility of those values as an expression of the aspirations of our communities. As Rob Canton reminds us:

> Yet whatever its achievements and potential, it is not only in these terms that probation should be understood and valued. Its value lies too in what it stands for, the values it expresses – conspicuously the values of social inclusion and a belief in the possibility of change.
>
> *(2011: 225)*

Herein lies the rub for Probation – having been beaten up and demoralised by New Labour and now facing a defining putsch by the Coalition government that will effectively reduce it to a residual public protection agency, will it also lose its capacity to reflect and promote society's vision and values toward the treatment of offenders? In the next chapter we consider the impact of these developments on the occupational culture and working practices of Probation staff tasked with the delivery of rehabilitation.

References

Allen, H. (1987) *Justice Unbalanced: Gender, Psychiatry and Judicial Decisions*, Milton Keynes: Open University.

Allen, R. and Hough, M. (2007) Community penalties, sentencers, the media and public opinion in Morgan, R. and Gelsthorpe, L. (2007) *Handbook of Probation*, Cullompton: Willan.

Auld, Lord Justice (2001) A Review of the Criminal Courts of England and Wales, London: The Stationary Office.

Bell, E. (2011) *Criminal Justice and Neoliberalism*, Palgrave Macmillan: London.

Bhui, H.S. (2006) Anti-Racist Practice in NOMS: Reconciling Managerialist and Professional Realities, *The Howard Journal of Criminal Justice,* 45(2): 171–190.

Blair, T. (1993) 'Why crime is a socialist issue', *New Statesman*, 29(2): 27–29.

Bottoms, A.E. (1995) The Philosophy and Politics of Punishment and Sentencing, in Clarkson, C. and Morgan, R. (eds) *The Politics of Sentencing Reform*: 17–49, Oxford: Clarendon Press.

Bottoms, A.E. and McWilliams, W. (1979) A non-treatment paradigm for probation practice, *British Journal of Social Work*, 9(2): 159–202.

Briggs, D. (ed.) (2012) *The English Riots of 2011: A summer of Discontent*, Hampshire: Waterside Press.

Broad, B. (1991) *Punishment under Pressure: The Probation Service in the Inner City*, London: Kingsley.

Bryant, M., Coker, J., Estlea, B., Himmel, S. and Knapp, T. (1978) Sentenced to Social Work, *Probation Journal*, 25(4): 110–114.

Buchanan, J., Collett, S. and McMullan, P. (1991) Challenging practice or challenging women? Female offending and illicit drug use, *Probation Journal*, 38(2): 56–62.

Burke, L. (2005) From Probation to the National Offender Management Service: Issues of Contestability, culture and Community Involvement, *Issues in Community and Criminal Justice Monograph 6*, London: Napo.

Burke, L. (2013a) Innovation and probation, *Probation Journal*, 60(3): 223–226.

Burke, L. (2013b) Grayling's Hubris, *Probation Journal*, 60(4): 377–382.

Burke, L. and Collett, S. (2008) Doing with or doing to: What now for the probation service? *Criminal Justice Matters*, 72: 9–11.

Burke, L. and Collett, S. (2010) People are not things: What New Labour has done to probation. *Probation Journal*, 57(3): 232–249.

Canton, R. (2011) *Probation: Working with Offenders*, Abingdon, Oxon: Routledge.

Carlen, P. (1988) *Women, Crime and Poverty*, Milton Keynes: Open University.

Carter, P. (2003) *Managing Offenders, Reducing Crime: A New Approach*, London: Home Office.

Cavadino, M., Dignan, J., and Mair, J. (2013) *The Penal System: An Introduction*, London: Sage.

Channel 4 News (2010) *Probation chiefs' public protection warning*, 31 August. http://www.channel4.com/news/probation-chiefs-public-protection-warning (Accessed 18 November 2013).

Coalition on Social and Criminal Justice (2006) *Neighbourhood by neighbourhood: Local action to reduce re-offending*, London: Local Government Association.

Cole, M. (2008) *Marxism and Educational Theory: Origins and Issues*, London: Routledge.

Collett, S. (1993) Beyond reason and understanding: The everyday understanding of crime, *Probation Journal*, 40(4): 184–187.

Collett, S. (2013) Riots, Revolution and Rehabilitation: The future of Probation, *The Howard Journal of Criminal Justice,* 52(2): 163–188.

Collett, S. and Stelman, A. (1992) From SIRs to PSRs: All change or nothing new? *Probation Journal*, 39(2): 63–69.

Davies, N. (2005) Lifeline that failed victim of system, *The Guardian*, 22 June.

Deering, J. (2011) *Probation Practice and the New Penology: Practitioner Reflections*, Farnham: Ashgate.

Downes, D. and Morgan, R. (1994) "Hostages to Fortune?" The politics of law and order in post-war Britain in Maguire, M., Morgan, R. and Reiner, R. (eds) *The Oxford Handbook of Criminology*, 1st edn, Oxford: Clarendon Press.
Drew, P. (1992) The Probation Service: A Few Valedictory Comments, *Probation Journal,* 39(2): 92–94.
Easton, S. and Piper, C. (2005) *Sentencing and Punishment: The Quest for Justice*, Oxford: Oxford University Press.
Faulkner, D. (2012) Harsh lessons for the Coalition (Letters Page), *The Guardian (letters page),* 8 May.
Faulkner, D. and Burnett, R. (2012) *Where Next for Criminal Justice?* Bristol: Policy Press.
Fitzgibbon, W. (2011) *Probation and Social Work on Trial: Violent Offenders and Child Abusers*, London: Palgrave Macmillan.
Fitzgibbon, W. (2012) In the eye of the storm: The implications of the Munro Child Protection Review for the future of probation, *Probation Journal*, 59(1): 7–22.
Garland, D. (2001) *The Culture of Control*, Oxford: Oxford University Press.
Garside, R. (2012) Criminal Justice and social justice at a time of economic crisis in Silvestri, A. (ed) (2012) *Critical reflections: social and criminal justice in the first year of the Coalition government*, London: Centre for Crime and Justice Studies.
Giddens, A. (1998) *The Third Way: The Renewal of Social Democracy*, Oxford: Wiley–Blackwell.
Gifford, L., Brown, W. and Bundey, R. (2009) *Loosen The Shackles – First Report of the Liverpool 8 Inquiry into Race Relations in Liverpool*, London: Karia Press.
Guardian/LSE (2011) *Reading the Riots: Investigating England's Summer of Disorder*, London: Guardian/LSE.
Hansard (2009) Sonnex case, Commons debate, 8 June: cols 517–528.
Harris, R. (1980) A changing Service: The Case for Separating 'Care' and 'Control' in Probation Practice, *British Journal of Social Work*, 10: 163–184.
Hill, L. (2009) *Investigation into the Issues Arising from the Serious Further Offence Review: Dano Sonnex*, London: National Offender Management Service.
HM Inspectorate of Probation (2003) 2002/2003 *Annual Report*, London: HMIP.
HM Inspectorate of Probation (2006a) *An Independent Review of a Serious Further Offence Case: Anthony Rice*, London: HMIP.
HM Inspectorate of Probation (2006b) *An Independent Review of a Serious Further Offence Case – Damien Hanson & Elliot White*, London: HMIP.
Home Office (1984) *Probation Service in England and Wales: Statement of National Objectives and Priorities*, London: Home Office.
Home Office (1988a) *Punishment, Custody and the Community*, London: HMSO.
Home Office (1988b) *Tackling Offending – An Action Plan*, London: Home Office.
Home Office (1988c) *The Parole System in England and Wales: Report of the Review Committee (Carlisle Committee)*, London: HMSO.
Home Office (1990a) *Supervision and Punishment in the Community: A Framework for Action*, London: Home Office.
Home Office (1990b) *Partnership in Dealing with Offenders in the Community*, London: Home Office.
Home Office (1990c) *Crime, Justice and Protecting the Public: The Government's Proposals for Legislation*, London: HMSO.
Home Office (1991) *Organising Supervision and Punishment in the Community: A Decision Document*, London: Home Office.
Home Office (1998) *Joining Forces to Protect the Public: Prisons-Probation, A Consultation Document*, London: Home Office.

Home Office (2001) *Making Punishments Work, The Report of a Review of the Sentencing Framework for England and Wales (Halliday Report)*, London: Home Office.

Home Office (2002) *Justice for All*, White Paper, London: Home Office.

Home Office (2003) *Prison Statistics England and Wales 2002*, London: Home Office.

Home Office (2004a) *Reducing Re-offending National Action Plan*, London: Home Office.

Home Office (2004b) *Managing Offenders: Changing Lives*, London: Home Office.

Home Office (2005a) *Restructuring Probation to Reduce Re-offending*, London: Home Office.

Home Office (2005b) *Managing Offenders, Reducing Crime – The Role of the Voluntary and Community Sector in the National Offender Management Service*, London: Home Office.

Home Office (2006a) *Working with Probation to Protect the Public: Summary of Responses to Restructuring Probation to Reduce Re-offending*, London: Home Office.

Home Office (2006b) *Improving Prison and Probation Services: Public Value Partnerships*, London: Home Office.

Home Office (2007) *National Community Safety Plan, 2008–2011*, London: Home Office.

Home Office, Department of Health and Welsh Office (1992) *National Standards for the Supervision of Offenders in the Community*, London: Home Office.

Home Office/Ministry of Justice (2010) *National Support Framework: Reducing Reoffending, Cutting Crime, Changing Lives – Guidance on New Duties for Community Safety Partnerships in England and Wales*, London: Home Office/Ministry of Justice.

Hough, M., Allen, R. and Padel, U. (eds) (2006) *Reshaping Probation and Prisons: The New Offender Management Framework*, Researching Criminal Justice Series Paper 6, Bristol: Policy Press.

Hudson, B. (1987) *Justice Through Punishment: A Critique of the 'Justice' Model of Corrections*, London: Macmillan.

Labour Party (1997) *New Labour because Britain deserves better*, Labour Party.

Lewis, S. (2005) Rehabilitation: Headline or footnote in the new penal policy? *Probation Journal*, 52(2): 119–135.

Local Government Association (2005) *Going straight: reducing re-offending in local communities*, London: Local Government Association.

Maguire, M. and Raynor, P. (2006) How the resettlement of prisoners promotes desistance from crime: or does it? *Criminology and Criminal Justice*, 6(1): 17–36.

Mair, G. and Burke, L. (2012) *Redemption, Rehabilitation and Risk Management: A History of Probation*, London: Routledge.

Mair, G., Cross, N. and Taylor, S. (2007) *The use and impact of the Community Order and the Suspended Sentence Order*, Centre for Crime and Justice Studies, Kings' College: London.

Mair, G., and Mills, H. (2009) *The Community Order and the Suspended Sentence Order Three Years On: The views and experiences of probation officers and offenders*, Centre for Crime and Justice Studies, Kings' College: London.

Mawby, R. and Worrall, A. (2013) *Doing Probation work, Identity in a criminal justice occupation*, London: Routledge.

McLaren, V. and Spencer, J. (1992) Rehabilitation and CJA 1991: A world still to win, *Probation Journal*, 39(2): 70–73.

McLaughlin, E., Muncie, J. and Hughes, G. (2001) The Permanent Revolution: New Labour, New Public Management and the Modernization of Criminal Justice, *Criminology and Criminal Justice*, 1(3).

McKnight, J. (2009) Speaking up for Probation, *The Howard Journal of Criminal Justice,* 48(4): 327–343.

McWilliams, W. (1987) Probation, pragmatism and policy, *The Howard Journal of Criminal Justice,* 26: 97–121.

Ministry of Justice (2009) News Release – Justice Secretary Jack Straw Statement, 4 June: 80.

Ministry of Justice (2010a) *Breaking the Cycle: Effective Punishment, Rehabilitation and Sentencing of Offenders*, London: Stationary Office.

Ministry of Justice (2010b) Green Paper Evidence Report, *Breaking the Cycle: Effective Punishment, Rehabilitation and Sentencing of Offenders*, London: Stationary Office.

Ministry of Justice (2010c) *Statutory changes to Community Safety Partnerships (CSPs): Probation Instruction 05/2010*, London: National Offender Management Service.

Ministry of Justice (2011a) *Competition Strategy for Offender Services*, London: Ministry of Justice.

Ministry of Justice (2011b) *Breaking the Cycle: Government Response*, London: Ministry of Justice.

Ministry of Justice (2012a) *Punishment and Reform: Effective Probation Services*, London: Stationary Office

Ministry of Justice (2012b) *Punishment and Reform: Effective Community Sentences*, London: Stationary Office.

Ministry of Justice (2013a) *Transforming Justice: A revolution in the way we manage offenders*, London: Stationary Office.

Ministry of Justice (2013b) *Transforming Justice: Summary of Responses*, London: Ministry of Justice.

Ministry of Justice (2013c) *Transforming Justice: A Strategy for Reform*, London: Stationary Office.

Ministry of Justice (2013d) *Statutory Partnerships and Responsibilities*, London: Stationary Office.

Ministry of Justice (2013e) *The arrangements for statutory partnerships in Transforming Rehabilitation*, www.justice.gov.uk (Accessed 9 February 2014).

Morgan, R. (2007) Probation, governance and accountability in Morgan, R. and Gelsthorpe, L. (eds) (2007) *Handbook of Probation*, Cullompton: Willan.

Napo News (October 2002) Issue 143, London: Napo.

Napo News (February 2006) Issue 176, London: Napo.

National Offender Management Service (2013) *Probation Trust annual performance ratings 2012/13*, NOMS Agency: London.

National Probation Service (2001) *A New choreography: An Integrated Strategy for the National Probation Service for England and Wales: Strategic framework 2001–2004*, London: Home Office.

Nellis, M. (2004) Into the Field of Corrections: The End of English Probation in the Early 21st Century? *Cambrian Law Review*, 35: 115–133.

Nellis, M. (2006) NOMS, contestability and the process of technocorrectional innovation in Hough, M., Allen, R. and Padel, U. (eds) (2006) *Reshaping Probation and Prisons: The New Offender Management Framework*, Researching Criminal Justice Series Paper 6, Bristol: Policy Press.

Nellis, M. and Gelsthorpe, L. (2003) Human rights and the probation values debate in Chui, W.H. and Nellis, M. (eds) *Moving Probation Forward: Evidence, Arguments and Practice*, Harlow: Pearson.

Nellis, M. and Goodman, A. (2008) Probation and Offender Management in Huckleby, A. and Wahidin, A. (2008) *Criminal Justice*, Oxford: Oxford University Press.

Oldfield, M. and Grimshaw, R. (2008) *Probation Resources, Staffing and Workloads 2001–2008*, NAPO/Centre for Crime and Justice Studies, London: Kings' College London.

Omand, D. (2010) *The Omand Review: Independent Serious Further Offence Review: The Case of Jon Venables*, London: Sir David Omand GCB.

Parker, H. (1990) Soft–Packaging Penal Reform, *Social Work Today*, 25 January.

Parker, H., Sumner, M. and Jarvis, G. (1989) *Unmasking The Magistrates*, Milton Keynes: Open University Press.

Patten, J. (1988) A 'New World of Punishment': The view from John Patten's window of opportunity, *Probation Journal*, 35(3): 81–84.

Pearce, N. (2013) Labour must engage with the problems of real life, *The Guardian*, 14 February.

Probation Association (2011) *Hitting the Target, Missing the Point, A constructive Critique of the Regulatory Framework for Probation Trusts*, London: Probation Association.

Probation Boards Association (2004) *Managing Offenders, Reducing Crime and Managing Offenders, Changing Lives: The Government's Plans for Transforming the Management of Offenders – Outline Response from the PBA*, February, London: PBA.

Probation Boards Association (2005) *Managing Offenders, Reducing Crime and Managing Offenders, Changing Lives: The Government's Plans for Transforming the Management of Offenders – Full Response from the PBA*, February, London: PBA.

Raynor, P. (2004) The Probation Service "Pathfinders": finding the path and losing the way? *Criminal Justice*, 4: 309–25.

Reiner, R. (2012) Return Of The Nasty Party in Silvestri, A. (ed) (2012) *Critical reflections: Social and criminal justice in the first year of the Coalition Government,* London: Centre for Crime and Justice Studies.

Riots, Communities and Victims Panel (2012) *After the Riots: The Final Report of the Riots, Victims Panel*, London: Riots, Communities and Victims Panel.

Robinson, G. (2001) Power, Knowledge and 'What Works' in Probation, *The Howard Journal of Criminal Justice,* 40(3): 235–254.

Rumgay, J. (2005) COUNTERBLAST: NOMS Bombs? *The Howard Journal of Criminal Justice,* 44(2): 206–208.

Scarman, L. (1981) *The Scarman Report: The Brixton Disorders 10–12 April 1981*, Harmondsworth: Penguin.

Scott, D.M. (2009) Arrested Development, *The Guardian*, 10 June.

Scott, D.M. (2010) Who's protecting who? *Probation Journal*, 57(3): 291–295.

Senior, P. (1984) The Probation Order: Vehicle of Social Work or Social Control, *Probation Journal*, 31(2): 64–70.

Silverman, J. (2012) *Crime, Policy and the Media: The Shaping of Criminal Justice 1989–2010*, London: Routledge.

Sim, J. (2009) *Punishment and Prisons: Power and the Carceral State*, London: Sage.

Social Exclusion Unit (2002) *Reducing re-offending by ex-prisoners*, London: Office of the Deputy Prime Minister.

Solomon, E. (2007) Labour's criminal justice, the ten-year audit, *Criminal Justice Matters*, 67 (14), Centre for Crime and Justice Studies.

Standing, G. (2011) *The Precariat: The New Dangerous Class*, London: Bloomsbury.

Statham, R. (1990) The *Probation Service in a market driven world* (unpublished paper).

Teague, M. (2011) Probation in America: Armed, private and unaffordable, *Probation Journal,* 58(4): 317–332.

Teague, M. (2012) Neoliberalism, Prisons and Probation in the United States and England and Wales in Whitehead, P. and Crashaw, P. (2012) *Organising Neoliberalism: Markets, Privatisation and Justice*, London: Anthem Press.

Travis, A. (2004) Taking no prisoners, *The Guardian*, 17 November, http://www.guardian.co.uk/society/2004/nov/17/guardiansocietysupplement.crime (Accessed 24 November 2004).

Travis, A. (2006) Reid wants a bigger role for the private sector in probation service, *The Guardian* 8 November, http://www.guardian.co.uk/politics/2006/nov/08/ukcrime.prisonsandprobation (Accessed 2 December 2006).

Treadwell, J. (2006) Some Personal Reflections on Probation Training, *The Howard Journal of Criminal Justice,* 45(1): 1–13.

Underdown, A. (1998) *Strategies for Effective Offender Supervision*, Report of the HMIP What Works Project, London: Home Office.

Vass, A. (1990) *Alternatives to Prison: Punishment, Custody and the Community*, London: Sage

Von Hirsch, A. and Roberts, J. (2005) Legislating sentence principles – the provisions of the Criminal Justice Act 2003 relating to sentencing purposes and the role of previous convictions, in Easton, S. and Piper, C. (2005) *Sentencing and Punishment – The Quest for Justice*, Oxford: Oxford University press.

Wallich–Clifford, A. (1974) *No Fixed Abode*, London: Macmillan.

Wargent, M. (2002) The New Governance of Probation, *The Howard Journal of Criminal Justice*, 41(2): 182–200.

Wasik, M. and Taylor, R.D. (1994) *Blackstone's Guide to The Criminal Justice Act 1991*, London: Blackstone.

Whitehead, P. and Crashaw, P. (2012) *Organising Neoliberalism: Markets, Privatisation and Justice*, London: Anthem Press.

Whitehead, P. and Crashaw, P. (2013) Shaking The foundation: On the Moral Economy of Criminal Justice, *British Journal of Criminology*, 53, 588–604.

Whitehead, P. and Statham, R. (2006) *The History of Probation: Politics, Power and Cultural Change 1876–2005*, Crayford: Shaw & Sons.

Wilkinson, R. and Pickett, K. (2010) *The Spirit Level: Why More Equal Societies Almost Always Do Better,* London: Allen Lane.

Williams, B. (1992) Criminal Justice 1991: Implications for work with prisoners, *Probation Journal*, 39(2): 74–77.

Worrall, A. (1990) *Offending Women: Female Lawbreakers and the Criminal Justice System*, London: Routledge.

Worrall, A. and Hoy, C. (2005) *Punishment in the Community: Managing Offenders, Making Choices*, Cullompton: Willan.

4

PROVIDING REHABILITATION

Occupational culture and professional identity

> People start to believe that they can successfully change their lives when those around them start to believe they can.
>
> *(Maruna and LeBel 2010: 76)*

> An overemphasis on standards of conduct (conditions, expectations, etc.) without both a humanistic perspective on the process of the human condition and human change and a theory of the probation officer role in this brave new world has resulted in more revocations, and more attention to the failure of the offender to change.
>
> *(Taxman cited in McNeill et al. 2010: 9)*

Changing the occupational culture of probation

Probation work has never attained as strong an identity within the public imagination as other criminal justice agencies have done (Mair and Burke 2012). This is partly because much of its work is undertaken in confidential settings and involves the encouragement of longer-term change processes in individuals that do not sit easily with demands for *quick fixes* (see Chapter Two). There have recently been attempts to increase the visibility of some community sanctions such as unpaid work (Casey 2008), much of which takes place behind closed doors. Probation staff operate in an environment in which "rewards can be few and setbacks common" (Shapland *et al.* 2014a: 149) and as such the personal qualities required of and the professional skills deployed by Probation staff in their work are often underestimated and unappreciated. Mawby and Worrall in their comprehensive analysis of Probation's occupational culture describe probation as *dirty work,* that is, work necessary for society but which does not retain status or public trust (2013). Despite this and alongside the work of Mawby and Worrall, other research studies have consistently alluded to the existence of a strongly developed sense of identity amongst Probation staff and a high degree of homogeneity in the attitudes and values they hold to their work (Deering 2011, Phillips 2014a). Moreover, as Bourdieu has highlighted, how practitioners make sense of the external environment is often a product of socialisation and established practices (1980). These in turn are reflected in what he termed "habitus" to describe the individual's "internal set of dispositions that shape perception, appreciation, and action" (Page 2013: 152). As the opening quotes to this chapter indicate, there is also increasing evidence that "offenders (like everyone else) assess and respond to certain moral qualities of those that have authority over them" (McNeill 2009a: 6).

It is for these reasons, we would contend, that an appreciation of the key policy and practice developments outlined in the preceding chapter would be incomplete without taking into account the ways in which those delivering rehabilitation make sense of and operationalise the responsibilities assigned to them by the state, its various institutions and the wider community interests. Such considerations raise a number of key questions: What are the skills and personal qualities utilised by Probation staff in their work? How do they implement the policies and practices of the organisation? How do Probation staff define *quality* in their interactions with offenders and how do they reconcile potential conflicts between their own personal values, those of individual offenders and the broader organisational and policy goals? How do they balance the helping and supporting aspect of their work with an appropriate use of authority? How do they interact with other criminal justice actors within the penal-criminal justice complex?

Drawing on Bourdieu's insights into how social practices are constructed, Fergus McNeill *et al.* note:

> Such modes of enquiry and analyses need to be directed towards advancing our understandings not just of penality in-practice but of *how and why* penal-professional cultures, practices and habituses change and resist change.
>
> *(2009a: 436)*

Workplace social practices reflect and confirm organisational cultures and sometimes lead to change and challenge. Liebling and Crewe define organisational culture as "a collective construction of social reality: shared habits of thought, attitude and language, consisting of 'working rules' but also of emotional frameworks or sensibilities that might explain those working rules" (2014: 155). Organisational cultures can be a unifying force, particularly in periods of change because "naturally, in these circumstances practitioners look to familiar roles, routines and shared language to bolster their sense of self, and consequently change in the norms around practice and culture tends to be gradual and perhaps uneven, prompted by new procedures, technology or the physical environment over time" (Robinson 2013: 95). However they can also be characterised by entrenched behaviour and attitudes, exclusionary practices and therefore become an obstacle to change. This is particularly true within the police service, for example, were there has been a strong sense of a *cop culture* which Reiner (2000) describes as a "subtle and complex intermingling of police officers sense of mission, action-orientated behaviour and cynicism" (cited in Foster 2003: 200).

Over the years, much attention has been given to Probation's occupational identity, the values it encompasses and what is sometimes referred to as its *mission* – a term that harkens back to its origins in the religious and philanthropic endeavours of Victorian society (see McWilliams 1983). Although grounded in structures of local service delivery and systems of local accountability, Probation has historically had a strong sense of its own identity as a national system of offender rehabilitation or perhaps more precisely, as a service replicated at local level across England and Wales. This partly reflects its operational base within national criminal justice legislation (particularly sentencing powers) and the role of the *probation officer* as an *officer of the court* (McWilliams 1981). It is also a manifestation of the historically directive role of the Home Office in matters of finance, policy direction, record keeping and training. It has also helped that, unlike social service departments whose responsibilities were extensive across all areas of social work need, Probation has, notwithstanding its role in civil work until 2001, always retained a focussed interest in offenders and the work of the criminal courts.

In the third of his influential quartet of essays on the history of the Probation Service, McWilliams describes the early development of Probation in terms of a move from a *diagnostic* to a *treatment* phase in probation practice, based on a transformation from "a service devoted to the saving of souls through divine grace to an agency concerned with the scientific assessment and treatment of offenders" (1986: 241). Subsequently, in the twentieth century the ascendancy of penal-welfarism (which asserted rehabilitation over punitive measures where possible) provided the organizing principle, intellectual framework and value base that bound together the criminal justice system and made sense of it for practitioners (Garland 2001). Central to this was the role of the professional worker providing expert judgment based upon the accumulated experience of social work and a growing body of theory from the social sciences. In short, under penal-welfarism the *bark and bite* of sentencers, to use Garland's phrase, was counterbalanced by the *treatment and help* provided by social workers and Probation staff. Professionalism, in this sense, was understood as the exercise of discretion.

However, probation work (as we have argued in Chapter Three) does not exist in a political, social or cultural vacuum and the wider social changes affecting the field of penality so well articulated by Garland in *The Culture of Control* (2001) meant that those welfare discourses and techniques that previously provided the rationale for rehabilitative work ultimately lost their political and cultural purchase.

As a result, a key feature of the contemporary reform and modernisation agenda has been the search by political decision-makers and their bureaucratic servants within Probation for a new or more explicit identity for probation. This fitted in with the government's wider reform and modernisation agenda to search out efficiency and effectiveness in supposedly improving public services. From the mid-1990s this has been couched within the language of reducing re-offending. The reconfiguration of probation practice along apparent *What Works* lines was characterised by a creeping emphasis on managerialism, centralised control and a performance culture based upon national standards for supervision and targets set by the Treasury (see Chapter Three). It could be argued, with justification, that the priority given toward risk management and public protection and a move toward accredited programmes as part of the *What Works* initiative, also further served to diminish the practitioner's voice in Probation policy and practice. According to Nellis it also meant that Probation's *humanistic sensibilities* were somewhat eroded in the process (2007).

After many years of being subjected to new public management and before the final move to marketise probation, many within the service would agree with Vanstone's withering description that in organisational terms, Probation had been moved from

> ... being an organic or adaptable organisation (characterised by personal involvement, achievement orientation, continual adjustment, shared group tasks, lateral and vertical communication, and consultation) to a mechanistic or bureaucratic one (characterised by 'impersonality', ascribed roles and rules, rational efficiency, rigid hierarchical structure, mainly vertical communications, specialisms of tasks and expectations and expectations.
>
> *(2010: 29)*

Changing the language of rehabilitation

The language within which probation work is framed has perceptibly changed over the past thirty years to convey a qualitatively different response or approach to the rehabilitative endeavour. The *client, probationer* or *service user* in old language has now been replaced by the uniform and ubiquitous *offender.* As Fitzgibbon (2012) has observed, the ascendency of public protection and punishment over rehabilitation has legitimised the deconstruction of the individual under Probation supervision into a bundle of risks. Although balancing the care and control aspects of supervision has always been a part of probation work, the adoption of a risk-based approach is a double-edged sword for probation practitioners. On the one hand, probation officers attained the status of *risk experts* (Nash 2008) within the Risk-Need-Responsivity (RNR) model of offender supervision and through involvement in the MAPPA and MARAC structures (discussed in Chapter Six), probation became "strategically important in its own right as well as often being the vital oil in the machinery of the local criminal justice system" (Burke and Collett 2008: 10). On the other hand, whilst it has heightened expectations about the efficacy of risk management, the inevitable apparent failures to protect the public have become high profile public and media events which have pointed the finger at probation whilst more powerful partners remain protected from the inevitable fallout.

Within the overall discourse of offender management, probation supervision can be seen, as Deering argues, mainly concerned with "assessing and managing risks, enhancing offenders' motivation to attend accredited programmes, gatekeeping access to services to address certain criminogenic needs and enforcing orders rigorously" (2010: 452). Those offenders assessed as lower risk can then be allocated to non-specialist probation staff with larger caseloads and under *Transforming Rehabilitation* ultimately supervised by a range of voluntary or private sector providers. There is though, within this mechanistic approach to the categorisation of individuals, a danger that the tiers of risk may also fragment expertise and experience within the organisation. Furthermore, the term *offender management* has been criticised for implying a depersonalisation or objectification of those individuals subject to supervision (Grapes 2007) and the *offender manager* role relegating the practitioner to little more than a sequencer of interventions, responsible for enforcement but providing little or no "offending work" (Raynor and Maguire 2006 in Deering 2010: 453). In other words, the programme of classification and structured intervention (not necessarily provided by the Probation Service) rather than the individual and their relationships, strengths and networks of resources have become the main agents of change. As practice has become more specialised, offenders in essence become "*portable entities*, and in which staff are obliged to engage in a '*pass-the-parcel*' style of supervision" (Robinson 2005). The increased emphasis on delivering programmes has also resulted in a retreat into more office-based practices (Bottoms 2008) in which a greater proportion of practitioners' time is spent interacting with computers rather than face-to-face work with those under their supervision. This, in turn, has led to a distancing of probation from local communities which has been compounded by a rationalisation of the probation estate into fewer but much larger offices. Phillips has recently described how changes to the physicality of Probation offices into open plan areas, designated by their specialist functions with enhanced security, not only reflects the broader managerially and risk-focussed policy landscape but has provides an additional lens through which to conceptualise contemporary probation practice (2014b).

Still, whilst the language and artefacts of supervision may have changed, those individuals with whom probation works remain largely the same (Canton 2011). Ultimately, Probation practitioners work through direct engagement with people who have offended and who, in many cases, live at the margins of society in terms of their access to social and economic goods. Such relationships are mediated through the worker's own personality, values, knowledge and skills. Engaging with moral complexity is thus part and parcel of probation work but it does not take place in a vacuum and is subject to a range of competing and sometimes contradictory influences (Burke and Davies 2011). Within neoliberal marketisation and modernisation strategies, public service provision is conceptualised as a dilemmatic space (Honig 1996) where professionals and street-level bureaucrats strive to balance colliding value systems, managing the tensions that are inherent in public life (Lipsky 1980). However, the use of neoliberal market mechanisms to improve efficiency, together with greater emphasis on centrally-imposed performance targets have led to tighter controls over activities which were previously the province of an individual Probation professional's personal judgement. Robinson and Ugwudike note in respect of the *New Choreography document* which set out the vision of the newly created National Probation Service "offenders are not the only group constructed and understood as rational actors or 'amoral calculators': so, too, are probation managers – albeit that for them incentives (in the form of extra resources) rather than disincentives to compliance were promised" (2012: 305). It could be further argued that as the National Probation Service was subsumed within the burgeoning control of NOMs, an organisation dominated by the *command and control* hierarchical structures of the prison service, it was effectively silenced before it was dispatched under the provisions of the 2007 Offender Management Act.

Searching for credibility

As we have indicated, for us the main drivers impacting upon the occupational culture and practices of Probation staff during the past two decades have been the challenges presented by the demands of neoliberalism, in all its economic and governance dimensions, and the perceived need for enhanced credibility and public support. The separation of probation training from social work in the mid-1990s was seen as one of the precursors of modernisation and as a means of presenting the Service as a more effective and thus credible agency of criminal justice/enforcement. In truth, such notions were based on a false dichotomy that characterised the social work role as one of caring and helping and probation as of one of control, thus ignoring the coexistence of humanitarian and disciplinary concerns in both (Millar and Burke 2013). Treadwell, who was himself a trainee on one of the Diploma in Probation Studies programmes, warned that probation training had become aligned to the worst excesses of authoritarian managerialism due to its overly vocational nature and that although the programme was not intended to create an unquestioning enforcement mentality, a number of trainees he observed did just that (2006). However, other later studies have found that in very broad terms their respondents had come into the job as probation officers to offer help and support in order to guide/assist/facilitate or even teach those under their supervision to overcome personal and structural issues that were at the root of their offending (Annison *et al.* 2008, Deering 2010). Findings from these latter studies would appear to indicate that, generally speaking, trainees remained committed to a more humanistic, person-based approach traditionally adopted by the Probation Service which was somewhat at odds with the government political putative agenda. Though the trainees had undoubtedly taken on the language of evidence-based practice, public protection and enforcement, this was overlaid by a commitment to an individualised approach to assessment and intervention that has its roots in traditional social work practice. Similar findings have been noted in other countries. In Bauwen's study of changes to the Belgium Probation Service, the author also found a level of ambivalence amongst workers toward the organisational changes that had taken place and the workers had retained a strong ethos based on social work values which had mitigated against attempts to move toward a more prescriptive and technicist approach to their practice (2009). Although in a note of caution, both the Treadwell (2006) and Deering (2010) studies found a potential strain between personal and organisational values which individuals had to find a way to reconcile.

> The increasingly bureaucratic case management role that probation services have adopted was not seen as compatible with the perception of the job held by many of those with whom I trained. They envisaged their role as being person centred. They were not naive in the belief that probation work was de facto social work. They believed they would work within a complex frame of care and control, incentive and instruction, but they did not believe that this would be a bureaucratic task first and foremost.
>
> *(Treadwell 2006: 4)*

More recently, the Diploma in Probation Studies has been replaced by the Probation Qualification Framework (Ministry of Justice 2009) in England and Wales. What is distinctive about this new development is that it is aimed at probation *service* officers (a paraprofessional grade) and not just those training to become qualified probation officers. This reflects a broader organisation change which has seen a significant increase in the deployment of probation service officers (PSOs) to deliver frontline services. Between 1998 and 2008, the number of PSOs had increased by 177 per cent compared to a 7 per cent increase in probation officers; by the latter date, PSOs accounted for 46.4 per cent of the Probation workforce (Mills *et al.* 2010).

Another significant organisational change has been what some commentators have termed the *feminisation* of probation (Annison 2007, Mawby and Worrall 2013). Prior to 1990 the Probation Service was dominated by male staff, but the latest Ministry of Justice figures show a 67/33 split in the ratio of female to male staff (Skinner and Goldhill 2014: 48). This might be partly a result of the changes to the training arrangements noted above, as the first intake of the Diploma in Probation studies had an approximate split of 30 per cent men to 70 per cent women (Annison 2007: 151). This trend might seem surprising given that, as we have noted, the

New Labour governments made significant strides in attempting to align Probation more closely with the police and prison service, both of which are unequivocally male-dominated organisations. As such, as Annison notes, attempts to impose a more masculinised ideology within Probation has not in reality materialised (2007).

What then has been the overall impact of these changes upon the occupational cultures within the Probation Service? Mawby and Worrall's comprehensive research with existing or former probation workers (2013), grouped interviewees into *lifers, second-careerists* (who had significant work lives or careers before joining the Probation Service), and *offender managers*. This latter group had trained under the Diploma in Probation Studies arrangements and were characterised as being predominantly female, more conversant with administrative systems and technology, but showed less awareness of community and social-structural conditions than the other two groups. Compared to the more vocational orientation of *lifers* and *second-careerists,* they also took a more pragmatic view of their work-life and valued aspects of their job such as security, status and salary.

Adopting, adapting, resisting

As we have noted, faced with marginalisation by the Home Secretary Michael Howard following his *prison works* speech, Probation tried during the late 1990s to transform itself rapidly, through a centralised managerial strategy, into an evidence-driven service informed by a *what-works* philosophy (Raynor *et al.* 2014). As Robinson has observed though, the development of *What Works* in the mid-1990s was something of a mixed blessing for whilst increasing the credibility of the service, it also increased the more technical and routinised aspects of the work (2002). The original evidence-based approach to offender supervision championed by Cedric Fullwood, then Chief Officer of Greater Manchester Probation Service and Graham Smith, Her Majesty's Chief Inspector of Probation (see Underdown 1995), saw structured and treatment-focused interventions within a much broader social context, where the realities of offenders' lives in terms of housing, employment, health and community ties would be acknowledged and dealt with. However, as it came to be implemented in England and Wales, *What Works* became entangled within broader public sector reforms which were concerned with cost savings and reducing the power of the professions as part of the managerialism and mechanisation of human services (McNeill *et al.* 2010: 6). The need for developing and utilising appropriate staff skills and techniques which was implicit in the research studies that kick started the *What Works* initiative were largely ignored. Practice became defined in terms of the development of prescriptive structured group work programmes which in the main were based on cognitive behavioural techniques. No comparable research was undertaken into the correlation between the role of practitioners in influencing the outcomes of individual supervision (Raynor *et al.* 2014) and this remained *a black box* (Bonta *et al.* 2008) in terms of enhancing our understanding of the supervisory process. Ioan Durnescu describes this process as a form of *probation industrialisation* in that

> practice became more and more focused on objectivizing its techniques and therefore only what was external, measurable and objective was promoted in mainstream policy and practice (e.g. skills, programmes). By contrast what was perceived as subjective, non-replicable and impossible to measure was assumed non-professional and therefore rejected from the mainstream policy and practice (e.g. staff characteristics).
>
> *(2012: 211)*

A study by Phillips (2011) based on fieldwork observations of probation staff explored the tensions inherent in these developments, particularly in respect to the introduction of targets, audits and risk-assessment tools and their impact on the occupational culture of probation. The author found that many staff had internalised managerialist approaches and although targets were seen as a mechanism for legitimising decisions taken, concerns were also expressed regarding the negative impact this was having on the contact time they were able to spend with those they supervised. Furthermore, whilst the introduction of targets had increased accountability, they also contributed to a culture of fear. This is particularly pertinent to the management of high risk cases, where it could be argued that political duplicity and deceit along with a wider blame culture (see Chapter Three for a detailed discussion) has not only undermined the Probation Service's work but also highlights the individual personal costs borne by those in positions of authority when things go wrong.

Ultimately, the stance adopted by staff toward targets, audits and risk assessment tools has tended to be one of either pragmatic acceptance or ambivalence. This would seem to give some credence to the view expressed by Causer and Exworthy (1999) that to present *New Public Management* as a divisive mechanism to assert the power of the manager over the worker is an exaggeration as many professionals have embraced these changes in order to safeguard or facilitate their own career aspirations and progression and ignores the fact that that many staff undertake both managerial and professional tasks in their roles (cited in Deering 2011). An alternative analysis is provided by Robinson and Burnett who suggest that probation staff who have been in the service for several years are accustomed to working within an organisation that is undergoing reform. Indeterminate change is the norm: it is a defining characteristic of their professional existence (2007: 332). Recent research by Worrall and Mawby has also challenged the notion that workers experience stress as a result of having to balance the welfare and punishment aspects of their work:

> We did not hear many about the withholding of effort. However disillusioned our participants might have been with the organization, they saw themselves as having a higher loyalty to offenders. They would work long hours and endure the tedium of spending 70 per cent of their time in front of computers if they could justify it as being in the interests of their 'clients'.
>
> *(2013: 111)*

Of course, it cannot be taken for granted that policy intentions will be adopted and operationalised as intended or that they will be either universally or uncritically accepted by staff. Occupational responses to political change are evident in terms of the power of professional cultures to assert rehabilitation as a moral enterprise rather than merely the instrumental delivery of outcomes. Studies into occupational cultures suggest that workers often continue to do what they have always done in the past regardless of an organisation's agenda, and that their practices are not necessarily based on research evidence "but rather are formed from gut-level, intuition, informal team socialisation processes, training or a lack of training, learned behaviours, lacking resources, and so forth" (Rudes *et al.* 2014: 19). As Canton notes though:

> It would be a mistake to see this necessarily as obduracy or as deliberate defiance. It may be better seen as a collision, when policy, thought through but often in abstract, encounters the complexity and vicissitudes of real life – a collision which practitioners try to manage with variable ratios of pragmatism and principle as they apply 'policy' to real working challenges. Nor should managers ever forget, in their commitment to put policy into practice, that there is a significant sense in which the policy of the organisation is less what they prescribe than what practitioner staff actually do.
>
> *(2011: 200)*

It may also be, as Smith claims, that increased workplace surveillance (through performance indicators and targets) and managerialism have made it more difficult for probation staff to resist overtly and collectively, effectively individualising resistance practices and pushing them *underground* (2007). More recently, Mawby and Worrall (2013) have employed the concept of edgework – which involves a form of controlled risk-taking – to explain how frontline probation staff mediate policies and guidelines with their established practices and values, working within competing demands and resources. This involves probation officers *putting their skills to the test* in ways which are sometimes tolerated by their organisation though not officially approved because there is a tacit recognition that such practices are desirable and achieve positive outcomes, even if they do not accord with official policies and guidelines:

> Through taking risks and being creative, probation workers regain agency and achieve feelings of authenticity and self-actualization. They are being true to themselves and their occupation and 'making a difference', realizing some of the motivations and hopes that led them into the career in the first place.
>
> *(Worrall and Mawby 2013)*

It could be argued, with some conviction, that it is in the area of enforcement practices that personal values and policy imperatives are most likely to collide. As Robinson and Ugwudike have highlighted, addressing what was perceived as inconsistent and lax enforcement became a central part to Probation's claim to legitimacy from the late 1990s onward and a means "through which to communicate Probation's preparedness to deliver penalties with a genuine 'penal bite' and, at the same time, to demonstrate an appropriately 'disciplined' workforce" (2012: 301). Drawing on the work of Bottoms, Robinson and McNeill make the helpful distinction between *formal* and *substantive* compliance. The former is signalled by behaviour that technically meets the minimum requirements of the order whereas the latter involves the active engagement and cooperation of those under supervision with their order (2008). Ugwudike found that in order to attain compliance, the probation staff in her sample were sensitive to the practical problems that might impinge upon supervision and attempted to manage them within the policy requirements of their work (2011).

These findings suggest that acknowledging the complexity of probation work does not mean encouraging unfettered discretion, which in itself can lead to discriminatory and unfair practice, but that "best practice results from both high accountability and wide (though not unbounded) discretion as opposed to the constrained practice of high accountability and narrow discretion, where, in reality, managers and front line staff have found themselves in recent years" (Eadie 2013: 16).

The return of *the relationship*

There is an increasing recognition that *how* Probation interventions are delivered and *by whom* is equally if not more important than *what* is being delivered in terms of affecting positive outcomes. One of the central themes emerging from the desistance literature is that "Practitioners have a crucial role to play in conveying hope – by communicating their belief in the individual, by recognising and reinforcing their efforts to change, and by developing and supporting access to opportunities for change" (Weaver 2014: 194). As Shapland *et al.* point out "People do not simply desist, they desist *into* something" (2012: 23). In this respect they need the *motivation* to change, the *capacity* to be and to act differently, and the *opportunities* to do so (McNeill 2009b).

In his review of the research literature on skills and personal attributes of probation staff, Durnescu identified what he termed *supportive skills* such as empathy, authenticity, reasonableness, good communication skills, an interest in people, a belief in the capacity for change; these were not only most valued by both practitioners and probationers alike, but were also most likely to have a positive impact on further offending (2014: 189). Moreover, in their study of probation staff, Bonta and colleagues found that the amount of time spent discussing probationers' needs as opposed to the conditions of probation in their meetings was positively associated with recidivism reductions (2008). Similarly, Petersilia and Turner's examination of intensive supervision programs found that when such programs emphasised monitoring and surveillance at the expense of treatment and rehabilitation, failure rates were high and programs displayed no effect on recidivism (1993). Durnescu also identified other approaches such an effective use of authority, role clarification, and cognitive behavioural interventions, which though apparently less valued by probation staff and probationers, also had a positive impact in reducing re-offending. Other skills or practices were less effective in terms of reducing re-offending but achieved different objectives such as for example securing compliance, and building motivation (2014).

Recent policy directives in England and Wales have once again stressed the importance of professional judgement and offender engagement in facilitating effective practice. This has included the relaxation of the *National Standards for the Management of Offenders* (2011). Whilst this has been universally welcomed by probation staff, there is also a view that the relaxation of national standards is merely a clever step on the road to privatisation – a way of making offender supervision more attractive to the private sector and voluntary agencies by reducing contractual requirements. More positively, there has been the roll-out of the *Offender Engagement Programme* (OEP) and the *Skills for Effective Engagement and Development* (SEED) training, which encourages practitioners to work collaboratively with those under their supervision. An initial evaluation of the SEED training found that it was well received by practitioners because the approach taken reinforced what they traditionally had perceived as good practice, although it was too early to establish whether or not the methods employed led to positive outcomes (Shapland *et al.* 2014).

In a corresponding study of the quality of Probation supervision (Shapland *et al.* 2014), the authors found that there was significant consensus on what staff saw as quality in terms of best practice. However, quality did not comprise a single concept but included a number of factors. These included the importance of the relationship between probation staff and the offender; the provision of adequate resources; an individual and flexible approach to supervision; having clear goals and outcomes of supervision such as reducing risk, seeing progress and producing a good outcome (this was likely to be a slow, gradual process involving realistic goals undertaken collaboratively between the supervisor and offender). Another important consideration is the attitudes, skills and values which staff brought to their supervision practice. It involves enabling service users to explore and develop their own narratives, to acknowledge their strengths as well as their problems and deficits, and developing new ways of coping with difficult situations. Those probation staff interviewed acknowledged that quality supervision was not delivered alone by one supervisor, but required support from colleagues and other agencies, and in this respect working with offenders was not seen as an exclusively one-to-one affair but needed to involve others with different abilities, resources and skills. The authors concluded that in this respect, collaborative working has become "part of the normal cultural fabric of probation practice in England and Wales" (Shapland *et al.* 2014: 144). It remains to be seen as to whether the *Transforming Rehabilitation* agenda involving "a plurality of providers with different histories, working practices, priorities and skills" (Fitzgibbon 2013: 87) will lead to new and innovative working relationships, or if it will fragment and undermine these positive developments? What ethos and practices will be maintained and sustained within the newly formed National Service (NPS) and the twenty-one Community Rehabilitation Companies (CRCs) will be a key issue.

Professional values or market-driven logic?

> In the next few weeks we will be 'automatically assigned' to a new role. This, in my opinion, will either be as an automaton, inputting data, regimented risk assessment, adherence to a plethora of targets and processes, onto new computer systems as civil servants with no capacity to say, 'Stop, this is not right'. Or alternatively, I will be assigned to an, as yet unknown, organisation that cares only to maximise shareholder profits. My esteemed colleagues and I are being treated as commodities, our clients as commodities, not for the public good but for shareholder profit maximisation.
>
> *(Anonymous probation officer 2013: 206)*

In September 2013, the Ministry of Justice published a target operating model for the *Transforming Rehabilitation* programme. It announced that the existing probation trusts would be disbanded on 31 March 2014 (subsequently amended to 31 May 2014) and probation staff reallocated before then into the new organisational arrangements by 31 January 2014. A new National Probation Service (NPS) is to be established as a directorate of the National Offender Management Service (NOMS) and will remain in the public sector with direct responsibility for high risk offenders and overall public protection. Twenty one Community Rehabilitation Companies (CRCs) will also be created to deliver local probation services to low and medium risk offenders. These will be set up as new companies, initially publicly owned from 1 April, but thereafter sold with the expectation that these new companies will operate from October 2104. In this respect, "CRCs will begin to operate as standalone businesses allowing for testing of some of the arrangements governing the 'border' between low/medium-risk and high-risk offenders" (National Audit Office 2014: 24). The same report estimates that around 46 per cent of staff would be allocated to the NPS and 54 per cent to the CRCs.

Whilst those working in the CRC will initially be staff transferred from the probation trusts, they will be operating within the context of competition and payment-by-results mechanisms which have become the defining characteristics of this new marketplace of service provision. As Kevin Robinson notes:

> In the first instance, they will be largely populated by workers who are knowledgeable about the probation service and may still feel the grip of loyalty to their old employer. But inevitably, over time, there will be greater separation and these practitioners who remain with the CRC will forge a stronger identification, distinguishing their new roles and identities from probation through co-creating narratives with other employees from non-probation backgrounds.
>
> *(2013: 96)*

Clearly then, in the short term, given that many of the potential bidders for the prime contracts are essentially outsourcing companies with limited experience of probation work, they will need the professional expertise of those former probation staff working in the CRCs (Senior 2013). Freed from the bureaucratic shackles of NOMS, there may even be scope to *think outside the box* (Robinson 2013: 5). In the longer term though, bringing together a diverse range of practitioners and mangers in the delivery of rehabilitative services is likely to lead to both creativity and tensions. Achieving an appropriate blend of skills and experience will be a major challenge. It is unclear what training these private sector companies will provide or what skill sets, values and overall competences staff will have in the future. Well qualified staff come at a price and the question must remain as to what these private sector companies will be prepared to pay for. If the experience of those engaged in the privatisation of Unpaid Work in the London Probation Trust is anything to go by, then reduced codes and conditions and staff redundancies are more likely to be the order of the day.

It is also a concern that the existing Probation Qualifying Framework (PQF) will only apply to the National Probation Service. The newly formed CRCs are only required "to maintain a workforce with appropriate levels of training and competence" (Ministry of Justice 2013: 41). The danger as Robinson points out is that there might be significant training investment in some areas of specialised practice, but that the majority of staff will receive training that is focused only on their current roles and functions (2013). Whilst there might be pockets of innovation within the CRCs, the majority of services will be aimed at the processing of offenders, especially given that caseloads will be inflated by the addition of the 50,000 short-term prisoners released on licence under the newly legislated provisions of the Offender Rehabilitation Act 2014, an undertaking for which no additional funding is provided. The watering down of training combined with a significant reduction in resources available to work with individuals who often have disorganised lives must raise concerns that this new rehabilitative endeavour will result in a *race to the bottom*. Staff remaining in the NPS, on the other hand, will benefit from a higher level of training and greater job security, but their role will be fundamentally one of public protection with little room for margin of error or innovative practices. There would appear to be little scope here for the kind of *edge work* described by Mawby and Worrall (2013). Given that they will become crown servants it will be difficult for them to challenge the dominant ideologies of the day. The 'institutionally silencing' of senior probation mangers that has already occurred during the *Transforming Rehabilitation* consultation period does not bode well in this respect.

How then will standards of practice be maintained in this brave new world? The establishment of the Probation Institute has been an interesting byproduct of the *Transforming Rehabilitation* agenda. The Institute is a joint venture between the Probation Chiefs Association (PCA), the Probation Association (PA), Napo and Unison, working with the Ministry of Justice to "provide a framework for unifying the probation workforce as a whole by providing professional leadership" (The Probation Institute 2013: 3). According to its prospectus, the Probation Institute would be

> ... an independent, not-for-profit Company Limited by Guarantee, aiming to become a recognised centre of excellence on probation practice, applying rigorous standards to the assessment of research and other evidence and its implications for the delivery of services that protect the public and rehabilitate offenders.
>
> *(2013: 3)*

It could be argued that those representing Probation's interests have at times failed to speak with one voice and in this respect the Institute is a welcome development although it will undoubtedly face significant challenges if it is to achieve its ambitions. Not least amongst these is the fact that the Institute is being established within a political environment that seeks to increase competition and achieve significant cost savings. Frances Crook has observed that:

> Perhaps the real regret is that it has taken the Transforming Rehabilitation reforms to see this Institute being set up, with the unavoidable sense that it is an afterthought to the primary goal of privatising the probation service.
>
> *(2013: npn)*

As membership of the Institute is voluntary it will rely on the cooperation of those involved and that they do the right thing. However, market conditions and the pursuit of profit might militate against this and undermine the reciprocity and trust which are necessary if the Probation Institute is to flourish.

The ties that bind

In this chapter we wanted to highlight the fact that the probation culture is neither one-dimensional nor unduly resistant to change. Throughout its history, the Probation Service has had to balance society's expectations and in recent years has experienced unprecedented organisational changes. Unsurprisingly, the pre-eminence of managerially-driven processes, risk management and acute resource constraints have narrowed the focus of probation supervision to a predominantly office-based encounter in which the amount of time available for face-to-face work has diminished. The community dimension of probation work has been increasingly neglected despite consistent findings from desistance literature that real and lasting change "can only be achieved by offenders working actively in and finding support from key others in their social environment" (Robinson *et al* 2014: 15). Yet despite these external pressures, the basic tenets of probation work still hold true and research has found a remarkable consistency amongst both practitioners and service users about what is important in the supervisory relationship, even if official ideas of what constitutes *quality* in these interactions might have changed (Shapland 2012). Successive research studies have suggested that rather than harking back to a mythical *golden age* of practice, probation staff are acutely aware of the importance of the responsibilities inherent in their risk management and public protection roles, even if they are sceptical of the contemporary methods used to achieve them.

The dominant culture within probation has remained remarkably resilient even though inevitably it has had to change and adapt to a wide variety of policy narratives. Nor has there been much evidence of the emergence of a new breed or generation of staff with different orientations and motivations despite changes to the demographic of the workforce. The essence of probation work remains a rational one located in a belief that professional relationships can be a powerful tool in stimulating and supporting positive personal change, even if the means of achieving this is contested. As Robinson *et al.* note, it is "the combination of essentially humanistic motivations for entering the field *and* the inescapably relational context in which the work is necessarily located that produces both the essence and the durability of the probation habitus" (2014: 15). Moreover, as Rob Mawby and Anne Worrall's research into probation occupational cultures has highlighted, Probation staff often achieve best outcomes in their work when practicing *on the edge* – when they are able to utilise their professional skills and judgement in the interests of individuals and the wider communities in which they are located (2013). Probation work

> … inevitably involves a willingness to work holistically and optimistically, though not naively, with uncertainty, ambivalence and (to a degree) failure.
>
> *(Mawby and Worrall 2013: 154)*

Whether practitioners will still be able to do this under *Transforming Rehabilitation* is questionable as such behaviours would seem to sit uneasily within a risk-averse environment and highly prescribed contractual arrangements.

Delivering quality services that rehabilitate individuals is ultimately about the attitudes, motivations and enthusiasm of the staff involved. It remains to be seen how Probation staff will respond to a new set of arrangements to which they seem overwhelmingly opposed both in principle and practice. Notwithstanding the professional and ideological opposition to the Coalition's plans, the speed with which the provisions contained within *Transforming Rehabilitation* are being implemented will almost inevitably intensify the *initiative confusion* and *change fatigue* that many frontline practitioners have experienced since the advent of NOMS (Robinson and Burnett 2007). An internal assessment conducted by the Ministry of Justice gave a maximum score to the probability that there would be a "reduction [in] performance" and increased the "potential for service delivery failure" (Doward 2013: npn). If the intentions of *Transforming Rehabilitation* are realised it could result in a loss of experienced Probation staff (and there is emerging evidence that this is already happening) who are able or willing to challenge the dominant ideology of marketisation which we discuss in the next chapter. In this respect we would do well to heed Mawby and Worrall's prescient warning that, "attempts to dismantle or dilute probation cultures, however, could be counter-productive by loosening the 'ties that bind' probation workers to an 'honourable profession'" (2011: 27).

References

Annison, J. (2007) A gendered review of change within the Probation Service, *The Howard Journal of Criminal Justice*, 46(2):145–161.

Annison, J., Eadie, T. and Knight, C. (2008) People first: Probation officer perspectives on probation work, *Probation Journal*, 55(3): 259–27.

Anonymous Probation Officer (2013) Dear Mr Grayling, *British Journal of Community Justice*, 11 (2/3): 205–206.

Bauwens, A. (2009) Probation officers' perspectives on recent Belgium changes in the probation service, *Probation Journal*, 56(3): 257–268.

Bonta, J., Rugge, T., Scott, T. L., Bourgon, G. and Yessine, A. (2008) Exploring the black box of community supervision, *Journal of Offender Rehabilitation*, 47: 248–70.

Bottoms, A.E. (2001) Compliance with community penalties in Bottoms, A.E., Gelsthorpe, L. and Rex, S. (eds), *Community Penalties: Change and Challenges*, Cullompton: Willan.

Bottoms, A.E. (2008) The community dimension of community penalties, *The Howard Journal of Criminal Justice*, 47(2): 146–169.

Bourdieu, P. (1980) *The Logic of Practice*, Palo Alto, CA: Stanford University Press.

Burke, L. and Collett, S. (2008) Doing with or doing to: What now for the probation service? *Criminal Justice Matters*, 72: 9–11.

Burke, L. and Davies, K. (2011) Introducing the occupational culture and skills in probation practice, *European Journal of Probation*, 3(3) 1–14.

Canton, R. (2011) *Probation: Working with offenders*, Abingdon, Oxon: Routledge.

Casey, L. (2008) *Engaging Communities in Fighting Crime: A Review* (Casey Report), London: Cabinet Office.

Causer, G. and Exworthy, M. (1999) Professionals as Managers Across the Public Sector in Exworthy, M. and Halford, S. (ed) *Professionals and the New Managerialism in the Public Sector*, Buckingham: Open University Press.

Crook, F. (2013) *Professionalising the Probation Service*, http://www.howardleague.org/france-scrookblog/professionalising-the-probation-service/ (Accessed 8 January 2014).

Deering (2010) The purposes of supervision: practitioner and policy perspectives in England and Wales in McNeill, F., Raynor, P. and Trotter, C. (eds) (2010) *Offender Supervision: New directions in theory, research and practice*, Cullompton: Willan.

Deering, J. (2011) *Probation Practice and the New Penology: Practitioner reflections*, Farnham: Ashgate.

Doward, J. (2013) Probation privatisation plans will put 'public at higher risk', *The Observer*, Sunday 15 December 2015. http://www.theguardian.com/society/2013/dec/15/probation-reforms-put-public-at-higher-risk (Accessed 7 April 2014).

Durnescu, I. (2012) What matters most in probation supervision: Staff characteristics, staff skills or programmes? *Criminology and Criminal Justice*, 12(2): 193–216.

Durnescu, I. (2014) Staff skills and characteristics in probation history: A literature review in Durnescu, I. and McNeill, F. (eds) (2014) *Understanding Penal Practice*, Abingdon, Oxon: Routledge: 181–193.

Eadie, T., Wilkinson, B. and Cherry, S. (2013), Stop a minute': Making space for thinking in practice, *Probation Journal*, 60(1): 9–23.

Fitzgibbon, W. (2012) In the eye of the storm: The implications of the Munro Child Protection Review for the future of probation, *Probation Journal*, 59(1): 7–22.

Fitzgibbon, W. (2013) Risk and Privatisation, *British Journal of Community Justice*, 11 (2/3): 87–91.

Foster, J. (2003) Police Cultures in Newburn, T. (2003) *Handbook of Policing*, Cullompton: Willan.

Garland, D. (2001) *The Culture of Control*, Oxford: Oxford University Press.

Grapes, T. (2007) Offender Management in Canton, R. and Hancock, D. *Dictionary of Probation and Offender Management*, Cullompton: Willan.

Honig, B. (1996) Difference, Dilemmas, and the Politics of Home in Benhabib, S. (ed) *Democracy and Difference: Contesting the Boundaries of the Political*, Princeton, NJ: Princeton University Press.

Liebling, A. and Crewe, B. (2014) Staff-prisoner relationships, moral performance, and privatisation in Durnescu, I. and McNeill, F. (eds) (2014) *Understanding Penal Practice*, Abingdon Oxon: Routledge. pp. 153–167.

Lipsky, M. (1980) *Street-level Bureaucracy: Dilemmas of the Individual in Public Service*, New York: Russell Sage Foundation.

Mair, G. and Burke, L. (2012) *Redemption, Rehabilitation and Risk Management: A History of Probation*, Abingdon, Oxon: Routledge.

Maruna, S. and LeBel, T.P. (2010) The desistance paradigm in correctional practice-from programmes to treatment in McNeill, F., Raynor, P. and Trotter, C. (eds) (2010) *Offender Supervision – New directions in theory, research and practice*, Cullompton: Willan. p. 65–89.

Mawby, R.C. and Worrall, A. (2011) *Probation workers and their occupational cultures*, Leicester: University of Leicester. (Summary report of ESRC project findings).

Mawby, R.C. and Worrall, A. (2013) *Doing Probation Work: Identity in a Criminal Justice Occupation*, Abingdon, Oxon: Routledge.

McNeill, F. (2009a) Probation, rehabilitation and reparation, *Irish Probation Journal*, 6: September.

McNeill, F. (2009b) What works and what's just? *European Journal of Probation*, 1(1): 21–40.

McNeill, F., Burns, N., Halliday, S., Hutton, N. and Tata, C. (2009) Risk, responsibility and reconfiguration-Penal adaptation and misadaptation, *Punishment & Society*, 11(4): 419–442.

McNeill, F., Raynor, P. and Trotter, C. (eds) (2010) *Offender Supervision: New directions in theory, research and practice*, Cullompton: Willan.

McWilliams, W. (1981) The probation officer at court: from friend to acquaintance, *The Howard Journal of Criminal Justice*, 20: 97–116.

McWilliams, W. (1983) The mission to the English police courts 1876–1936, *The Howard Journal of Criminal Justice*, 22: 129–147.

McWilliams, W. (1986) The English probation system and the diagnostic ideal, *The Howard Journal of Criminal Justice*, 25(4): 241–260.

Millar, M. and Burke, L. (2013) Thinking beyond utility: Some comments on probation practice training, *The Howard Journal of Criminal Justice*, 51(3): 317–330.

Mills, H., Silvestri, A. and Grimshaw, R. with Silberhorn-Armatrading, F. (2010) *Prison and Probation Expenditure 1999–2009*, London: Centre for Crime and Justice Studies.

Ministry of Justice (2009) *Probation Qualifications Framework Review, Consultation Paper CP(L) 9/09*, London: MOJ/NOMS.

Ministry of Justice (2013) *Target Operating System: The Rehabilitation Programme*, September, Ministry of Justice: London.

Nash, M. (2008) Exit the 'polibation' officer? De-coupling police and probation, *International Journal of Police Science & Management*, 10(3): 302–312.

National Audit Office (2014) *Probation: landscape review*, HC1100 Session 2013–14, 5 March, London: National Audit Office.

Nellis, M. (2007) Humanising justice: the English Probation service up to 1972 in Gelsthorpe, L. and Morgan, R. (eds) *Handbook of Probation*, Cullompton: Willan.

Page, J. (2013) Punishment and the Penal Field in Simon, J. and Sparks, R. (eds) (2013) *The SAGE Handbook of Punishment and Society*, London: SAGE. p. 152–167.

Petersilia, J. and Turner, S. (1993) Intensive probation and parole in Tonry, M. (ed) *Crime and Justice: An Annual Review of Research*, Chicago: University of Chicago Press.

Phillips, J. (2011) Target, audit and risk assessment cultures in the probation service, *European Journal of Probation*, 3(3): 108–122.

Phillips, J. (2014a) Understanding 'the relationship' in English probation supervision in Durnescu, I. and McNeill, F. (eds) (2014) *Understanding Penal Practice*, Abingdon, Oxon: Routledge. pp. 122–139.

Phillips, J. (2014b) The architecture of a probation office: A reflection of policy and an impact on practice, *Probation Journal*, (awaiting publication).

The Probation Institute (2013) *The Probation Institute: A Prospectus for Comment by Stakeholders*, London: The Probation Chiefs Association (PCA), the Probation Association (PA), Napo and UNISON. http://probation-Institute.org/ (Accessed 4 January 2014).

Raynor, P., Ugwudike, P. and Vanstone, M. (2014) The impact of skills in probation work: A reconviction study, *Criminology and Criminal Justice*, 14(2): 235–249.

Robinson, A. (2013) Transforming rehabilitation: Transforming the occupational identity of probation workers? *British Journal of Community Justice*, 11(2/3)/ Winter: 91–103.

Robinson, G. (2002) Exploring risk management in probation practice: Contemporary developments in England and Wales, *Punishment & Society*, 4(1): 5–25.

Robinson, G. (2005) What works in offender management? *The Howard Journal of Criminal Justice*, 44(3): 307–318.

Robinson, G. and Burnett, R. (2007) Experiencing modernization: Frontline probation perspectives on the transition to a National Offender Management Service, *Probation Journal*, 54(4): 318–337.

Robinson, G. and McNeill, F. (2008) Exploring the dynamics of compliance with community penalties, *Theoretical Criminology*, *12*(4): 431–449.

Robinson, G. and Ugwudike, P. (2012) Investing in 'Toughness': Probation, Enforcement and Legitimacy, *The Howard Journal of Criminal Justice*, 51(3): 300–316.

Robinson, G., Priede, C., Farrall, S., Shapland, J. and McNeill, F. (2014) Understanding 'quality' in probation practice: Frontline perspectives in England & Wales, *Criminology and Criminal Justice*, 14(2): 123–142.

Rudes, D. S., Viglione, J. and Taxman, F. S. *et al.* (2014) Professional ideologies in United States probation and parole in Durnescu, I. and McNeill, F. (eds) (2014) *Understanding Penal Practice*, Abingdon, Oxon: Routledge. pp. 11–30.

Senior, P. (2013) Probation: Peering through the uncertainty, *British Journal of Community Justice*, 11(2/3)/ Winter: 1–9.

Shapland, J., Bottoms, A., Farrall, S., McNeill, F., Priede, C. and Robinson, G. (2012) *The quality of probation supervision: A literature review*, The University of Sheffield: Centre for Criminological Research.

Shapland, J., Sorsby, A., Robinson, G., Priede, C., Farrall, S. and McNeill, F. (2014) What quality means to probation staff in England in relation to one-to-one supervision in Durnescu, I. and McNeill, F. (eds) (2014) *Understanding Penal Practice*, Abingdon, Oxon: Routledge. pp. 139–153.

Skinner, C. and Goldhill, R. (2014) Changes in Probation Training in England and Wales: The Probation Qualification Framework (PQF) Three Years On, *European Journal of Probation*, 5(3): 41–55.

Treadwell, J. (2006) Some Personal Reflections on Probation Training, *The Howard Journal of Criminal Justice*, 45(1): 1–13.

Ugwudike, P. (2011) Mapping the interface between contemporary risk-focused policy and frontline enforcement practice, *Criminology and Criminal Justice*, 11(3): 242–258.

Underdown, A. (1995) *Effectiveness of Community Supervision: Performance and Potential*, Manchester: Greater Manchester Probation Service.

Vanstone, M. (2010) Creative work: An historical perspective in Brayford, J., Cowe, F. and Deering, J. (eds) *What Else Works?* Cullompton: Willan.

Weaver, B. (2014) Co-producing desistance: Who works to support desistance? in Durnescu, I. and McNeill, F. (eds) (2014) *Understanding Penal Practice*, Abingdon, Oxon: Routledge. pp. 193–205.

Worrall, A. and Mawby, R. (2013) Probation worker responses to turbulent conditions: Constructing identity in a tainted occupation, *Australian & New Zealand Journal of Criminology*, 46(1): 101–118.

5
COMPETING REHABILITATION
Markets, profits and delivery

> Only in a valueless world would the concept of justice itself become just another commodity to be priced and transacted.
>
> *(Neilson 2012: 422)*

Going private on public goods

A significant feature of the impact of the rise of neoliberalism outlined in the previous chapters has been the transformation in the role of the state from a provider of public services to that of a facilitator of market solutions (Bell 2011). Moreover, it is not just the radical transformation of the service delivery mechanisms from public to private that impacts on the practice of criminal justice and the rehabilitative endeavour but the way in which the relationship between communities and offenders are affected. Neilson's reference to values challenges us to question the impact of *commodification* in a more profound and far reaching way. We cannot and should not ignore this challenge because the rehabilitative endeavour is about more than delivering instrumental outcomes for individual offenders. It is also about society's expression of how we should treat troubled and troublesome individuals.

The *Transforming Rehabilitation* proposals (Ministry of Justice 2013) can be seen as the culmination, or at least a significant tipping point, on the journey toward the commercialisation of justice and the marketisation of rehabilitative services. According to Pat Carlen:

> … governments have increasingly distanced themselves from policy delivery and instead repositioned themselves as indirect consumers of penal products via agencies operating to get the best deal for them and their electorates who

> nowadays have been taught to think of themselves more as customers of government agencies than as participants in government.
>
> (2005: 426)

Certainly, throughout the period covered by this book, there has been a growing political consensus that competition and privatisation are the best mechanisms to increase innovation and improve efficiency. Furthermore, the political promotion of market competition can be viewed as part of a broader ongoing commitment since Thatcher, through the New Labour period and now the Coalition administration, to not only curtail but to discipline the public sector. In essence, we have seen since the beginning ofThatcher's administrations in the late 1970s, the loss of a commitment to post-war Keynesian economics, a mixed-ownership economy and a supportive welfare state, in favour of monetarism, privatisation, lower taxation for higher income earners and a reduced social state (Crouch 2011: 16). As Seymour (2012) has highlighted, the privatisation of public goods has been attractive to the Conservatives for a number of reasons. By opening the public sector to profit and by reducing the power of public sector workers (who have traditionally provided a basis for *Labourist* politics), it suppresses wage pressures, in theory making investment more appealing. Moreover, in emphasising the market-based principles of resource allocation, it inevitably favours those who are strongest in their control of the market and who also happen to represent the social basis of conservatism. From this perspective, the attack on the post-war consensus can be understood as having less to do with a fundamental flaw in the ideas behind that consensus and more to do with the declining social power of the classes whose interests it promotes. Conversely, those institutions that stood to gain most from neoliberalism – the global corporations and the financial sector – have become increasingly powerful and more or less unchallenged (Crouch 2011: 1).

Thatcher and the discipline of the market

> A frontal attack upon this situation is not recommended. Instead the group suggests a policy of preparing the industries for partial return to the private sector, more or less by stealth. First we should destroy the statutory monopolies; second we should break them up into smaller units; and third, we should apply a whole series of different techniques to try and edge them back into the private sector.
>
> *(The Ridley Report 1977: npn)*

During the first Thatcher administration (1979–81), privatisation was initially subordinate to other policy concerns such as inflation, but there was an increasing realisation that the privatisation of profitable public utilities could be a valuable mechanism to raise revenues and thus reduce public-sector borrowing. This led to experimentation with some large public sector companies such as British Aerospace and Cable & Wireless. However, amid the recessionary period of the early 1980s, the *discipline* of the marketplace was increasingly extolled as the means to make the large nationalised utilities more efficient and productive, and thus the British economy more competitive. Most of the industries in state ownership were seen as natural monopolies and therefore difficult to subject to normal market competition, and so different means of introducing limited competition were utilised. In the case of the railways, for example, services were divided up into smaller units and sold to rival firms. Water authorities, on the other hand, were handed over to what were effectively private monopolies subject to neither competition, regulation or marketplace competition. Those services which had considerable public support, such as health and education, were a more difficult nut to crack and the introduction of privatisation into these services did not really develop strongly until the turn of the millennium. This led to compromise positions, such as contracting out of public services to private providers with government itself the customer, or public-private partnerships in which government continued to provide the service but the infrastructure (buildings, equipment etc.) was owned by a private company and leased back to government on a rental basis. All of these mechanisms for service delivery were backed up by the principles of *New Public Management* which emphasised service users as *customers* (Crouch 2011: 20). From this largely instrumental and pragmatic origin, the notion of privatisation took on a much more *philosophic accretion* (Drakeford 1988) as part of a broader cultural shift intended to reengineer public support away from social democracy and to embrace enterprise. This *popular capitalism* vaunted by Thatcher involved extending the opportunities available for larger numbers of the electorate to have a stake in private companies and under the *right to buy* scheme, access to home ownership for council house tenants.

In criminal justice terms, it was only during the Conservative government's third term that a serious intent to privatise began to take shape as the then Home Secretary, Douglas Hurd, "... moved from dismissing the idea of privatisation of prisons as unacceptable, to announcing that he had no objection in principle to a private company running a remand centre'" (Lilley and Knepper 1992: 181). The Green Paper, *Private Sector Involvement in the Remand System* (Home Office 1988d), signalled the beginning of the move from principle to practice of involving the private sector in the direct provision of correctional services. The spectre of privatisation which had been given concrete form in this Green Paper was further emphasised by the Audit Commission in the following year:

> The Probation Service is therefore at a critical point. It can either move to the forefront of the government's penal policy; or it could find that another agency is given responsibility for new community options and, perhaps, part of its existing workload.
>
> *(1989a: 6)*

Then in 1990, the Green Paper, *Supervision & Punishment in the Community: A Framework for Action,* bluntly spelt out the government's belief that:

> ... the disciplines of the market place can often serve as an effective guarantee of quality and value for money in the provision of public services. Government departments and local authorities have made substantial gains in efficiency by contracting out a wide range of services either to private sector suppliers or to the voluntary sector.
>
> (*Home Office 1990a: 37*)

The government had started to create the conditions for a criminal justice marketplace. Three private remand centres were established along with the introduction of the privately run Prisoner Escort to Courts Service (PECS). At the same time, exploratory discussions examined potential areas of policing that might take advantage of privatisation. In relation to the Probation Service however, Ryan and Ward's hypothesis was that the main function of privatisation talk was to coerce the Service into complying with the government's desire to turn it into a deliverer of community punishment (1991). These were far from empty threats, The Conservative government's prison privatisation programme strengthened its belief that commercial organisations could run penal institutions, and when electronic monitoring was introduced in the late 1980s it was the private sector rather than the Probation Service that was given responsibility for its management and delivery.

The success of Thatcherism lay in its capacity to recruit support from sections of the working and lower middle classes with a simple and accessible story, which offered an imaginary exit from their traditional expectations. This was encapsulated in the slogan, *property-owning democracy,* where the meaning of democracy was recast from popular control and equal citizenship and dressed up in the vernacular of *Sid* – the *man (sic) in the street* who could join the hitherto exclusive club of shareholders by participating in the sell-off of state assets with the inducement to buy at a discount the council house he rented. This connected an abstract neo-classical economic ideology to concrete and familiar circumstances and a compelling aspiration to freedom (Wilson and Bloomfield 2011: 9). Thatcherism thus appealed much more effectively than Labour to the idea of individualism, while the old institutions, reflecting a philosophy of a collectivism premised on a homogeneous working class, were in decline. Privatisation led in the main to private and unaccountable monopolies and the hoovering up of individual shares into conventional concentrations, while council-house sales in the absence of reinvestment left growing housing needs unmet. However, it was testimony to the hegemonic capacity of Thatcherism that *New* Labour implicitly accepted its key slogan (Wilson and Bloomfield 2011: 9).

New Labour: Compromise, PFI and contestability

> Born of dogma, reared on deceit, this privatisation is now exposed for what it is and always has been, private prejudice masquerading as public policy.
>
> *(Tony Blair speaking in the Commons, 12 December 1988)*

In opposition, the Labour Party had made electoral capital out of its opposition to privatisation, but once elected did little in government to reverse this trend. Promises to bring those prison establishments contracted to the private sector back under public control were quickly reneged upon. A further nine prisons were built, financed and operated under the Private Finance Initiative (PFI) between 1997 and 2010 in addition to the two contracted under the previous Conservative government (Bell 2011: 182). This change was no doubt prompted by the political reality that reversing 25-year contracts would be exorbitant, but it was also increasingly seen as an attractive opportunity "to reduce the capacity of the Prison Officers' Association to block progress and defend outdated practices" (Raynor & Vanstone 2007: 78).

In New Labour's first term, market-based strategies were scaled back and central direction in key public services increased. According to Hough, the New Labour variant of modernisation was "presented not as a retreat from the provision of public services but as a change in the way that they are delivered" (2006: 2). Nevertheless, the rewriting of clause four of the Labour Party constitution and specifically its commitment to *the common ownership of the means of production* was an important statement of intent that New Labour would not be tied to the dogma of the past, paving the way as Bell argues, for the extension of "corporatisation and commodification of the state-owned sector" (2011: 143).

According to Hough, New Public Management (NPM) was seen as the most effective way to drive up public sector performance and thus improve social justice (2006: 2). From this perspective, problems of poorly performing public service professions were best addressed through performance targets and managerial control rather than strengthening professional commitment and values. In this respect, it could be argued that New Labour was less ideologically driven in terms of privatisation and more concerned with driving up standards through the creation of a *mixed economy* of service providers. As a result, the Labour government adopted something of a compromise position aimed at fostering an entrepreneurial culture through mechanisms such as PFI which had the advantage of attracting short-term revenues without recourse to raising taxation. Indeed part of the rationale for the creation of NOMS – discussed in Chapter Three – was to deliver a system of *contestability* that initially aimed to put market tension into the monopoly of community-based corrections with the avowed intention of improving the quality and effectiveness of public provision. It was continually stressed by politicians and senior civil servants alike that contestability was not privatisation!

In the later Blair years, attempts were made to harness consumer power in various forms to challenge bureaucracy and increase competition and the second and third New Labour administrations pressed aggressively for further state downsizing and privatisation, mixing what one commentator termed "penal populism with commercial competition" (Bennett 2007: 10). The notion of contestability, originally proposed in the Carter Report (2003) was increasingly promoted within the correctional services. Carter believed that the quality of interventions would be improved by allowing other public sector, private or voluntary agencies to bid against prisons and probation for contracts. Contestability was seen as having the potential to bring both positive outcomes in terms of increased innovation and diversity in service delivery. Although the Carter Report was somewhat sketchy in terms of how contestability would be implemented, it envisaged that probation areas would have to bid for contracts against the private, voluntary and community sectors to deliver services (many of which it already held statutory responsibility for). This was somewhat different from its role as a purchaser or commissioner of services from these sectors. Contestability brought the promise of a potentially different relationship between the Probation Service and the voluntary sector, with a greater emphasis on competition than partnership. In this respect, Nellis reflected that "The NOMS's model for contestability seems to derive far more from the prison service experience with contracting-out to commercial organisations than from the probation service's experience of 'partnership' with voluntary and community groups" (2006: 55).

In October 2005, the Home Office published a consultation paper, *Restructuring Probation to Reduce Re-offending* (Home Office 2005). Among its key proposals was the replacement of local probation boards by smaller business-focused bodies, appointed directly by the Home Secretary, who would maintain the power to contract for Probation Services with the aim of driving greater value for money through competition. It was intended that these bodies would initially hold contracts to facilitate the transfer to the new regime and avoid mass transfers of staff. The following year, the government published its long awaited prospectus on how contestability would be introduced – *Improving Prison and Probation Services: Public Value Partnerships* (Home Office 2006). In his introduction, the Home Secretary warned that "where a whole probation area is failing to deliver expected levels of performance we plan to put the whole offender management function out to competition" (cited in Napo News Sept 2006). Among its proposals was the introduction of a 5 per cent target for Probation Boards to spend on subcontracting in 2006/2007 and 10 per cent in 2008. At the same time, according to Napo, NOMS was facing a cash deficit of at least £40 million (Napo News October 2006). Later in the same year, Home Secretary John Reid was reported to have described the Probation Service as *poor or mediocre* (Travis 2006), stating that it was his intention to privatise up to a third of its £800 million budget.

The Offender Management Act 2007 embedded commissioning and contracting out into the framework of probation. Commissioning was to take place on a national, regional and local level. Regional commissioners would manage these activities within their respective regions, commissioning some activities regionally, while others would be commissioned more locally by a *lead provider.* In the guidance to the act it proposed that so long as their performance met the requirements, the lead provider in a Probation Area would be the Probation Trust (Home Office 2007). Although initially the trusts appeared similar to the boards they were replacing, it was made clear that they were intended to be much more business-focussed and their continued existence would depend on winning business from newly appointed Regional Offender Managers (ROMs) and subsequently Directors of Offender Managers (DOMs) to whom their performance would be accountable. Any probation areas whose performance did not qualify for trust status by then would have their services opened up to competition from other trusts or providers. Under the 2007 Act, the Secretary of State was ultimately responsible for ensuring that probation services were provided either directly or indirectly. NOMS would set out its annual commissioning intentions and could choose to contract from Probation Trusts or any other provider from the private and voluntary sectors to deliver a specified set of services, with the exception of providing advice and assistance to the courts. By the time it left office in 2010, New Labour had abandoned its commitment to public provision based on the belief that the public service professional ethic provided a better motive to the provision of public goods than the maximisation of profits. Instead the perceived inadequacies of public services, such as probation, were seen to be the fault of the organisations themselves and the professional interests of the professional groups within them.

The Coalition's move from contestability to privatisation: A perfect storm?

> We will introduce a 'rehabilitation revolution' that will pay independent providers to reduce re-offending, paid for by the savings this new approach will generate within the criminal justice system.
>
> *(Coalition agreement 2010)*

The Conservative and Liberal Democrat Coalition government that took office in 2010 presented the crisis of global capitalism as a crisis of public sector borrowing, which in turn necessitated unprecedented cuts in public spending. Insinuated within this analysis was another key policy strand related to making the economy more competitive, entrepreneurial and innovative. Going forward, it was assumed that the private sector was inherently more productive than the public sector. In his 2010 budget speech, the Chancellor, George Osborne, accused the public sector of *crowding out* the private sector thereby providing an additional justification for contracting state services beyond the need to reduce the deficit (cited in Mazzucato 2011). For large private corporations, the 2008 financial crash had restricted the avenues for private investment and delivering new goods and services. Consequently, public sector services provided new opportunities for increasing profit margins out of existing provision. At a time when markets in general were becoming increasingly competitive globally, public contracts were attractive to private multinationals because it enabled them to provide services for which there was a guaranteed demand. This heady mix of economic austerity, disinvestment in the private sector by the banks and political ideology created a perfect storm which enabled the Coalition to accelerate New Labour's vision for a mixed economy of service provision and extend the reach of privatisation to parts of the state that had traditionally been seen as off limits.

The Conservative Party, had spelt out their plans for a *Rehabilitation Revolution* in their policy Green Paper, *Prisons with a Purpose* (Conservative Party 2008). As senior partners within the Coalition, they were well placed to move on the implementation of their plans. Based upon a belief (rather than any hard evidence) that the private sector had raised standards and brought about efficiencies within the prison system, *Prisons with a Purpose* argued that:

> The old monopolies in the prison and probation system need to be opened up to create a far more diverse range of suppliers of criminal justice services.
>
> *(Conservative Party 2008: 49)*

In order to achieve this, it was proposed that the *payment by results* (PbR) approach, which had already been introduced into other areas of public provision, such as health and employment services, be extended to rehabilitative services. The idea was that a basic tariff would be set to reflect the amount of money currently spent to secure and rehabilitate an individual offender with a particular re-offending profile. Prisoners who were deemed harder to help or more likely to re-offend would attract a higher payment. This payment would be made at regular intervals to providers and was intended to provide a strong incentive to reduce operating costs. It was argued that this approach could result in savings of up to £259 million a year by 2017 or £2,500 for every released prisoner (Conservative Party 2009: 15). In addition, providers would be able to earn a premium tariff payment which would only be paid if the individual did not re-offend for two years after their release from custody. It was envisaged that Probation Trusts would carry out the rehabilitation activities themselves or enter into contracts with other providers from the public, third and private sectors and pass all or part of the premium tariff on. This approach was seen as having the potential to bring new money into the system, for example, through greater philanthropic and social investment, and to improve performance by providing a greater focus on specified outcomes, potentially yielding cost saving by weeding out inefficiency (Justice Affairs Select Committee 2011). However as Grover points out in relation to employment services, there is a certain irony in the premise "that markets can create solutions for a phenomenon (worklessness) that itself is a consequence of failures in 'free' market activity" (2009: 496).

The *Breaking the Cycle: Effective Punishment and Rehabilitation and Sentencing of Offenders* Green Paper (Ministry of Justice 2010) subsequently set out the government's vision for reform. Whilst it was envisaged that a reformed and significantly slimmed down NOMS would retain central oversight for commissioning in the short term, it was intended that this would be devolved to local commissioners over time (2010a: 40). Six PbR projects were commissioned to test and develop the approach. The pilots were intended to explore different models for managing contracts, measuring impact and rewarding successful providers. Pilot schemes were to focus on short-term prisoners serving sentences of less than twelve months. A pilot PbR programme, begun under the previous Labour administration and already running at HMP Peterborough, targeted the release of prisoners serving sentences of twelve months or less. Investors were invited to pay into a Social Impact Bond (SIB) to be used to finance the work of the service providers to reduce re-offending rates amongst the target group. If these services achieved the outcome of reducing re-offending by 7.5 per cent over six years, then the investors would receive a return on their initial investment. Service providers were thus shielded from financial risk, all of which was to be borne by the investors (Hayes 2010: 4). Whilst there was some evidence that the Peterborough SIB initially introduced some new funding into the system and thus transferred the risk away from government to non-governmental investors, it has also been claimed that the Peterborough scheme has siphoned off money from organisations which would previously have been given the same resources in the form of grants (Gelsthorpe and Hedderman 2012).

HMP Doncaster, working in partnership with Serco, became the first prison to be contracted on a payment-by-results basis, with a proportion of its contract value dependent on the level of reduction in re-offending amongst prisoners serving twelve months or less who were released from the institution. Although these initiatives were focussed on a group who were not subject to statutory supervision by the Probation Service, it was clear that the government's intention was to expand the PbR approach into other areas of probation work. The government initiated *community pilots* with two Probation Trusts – Wales and Staffordshire & West Midlands – to work with individuals under community sentence and a third set of pilots related to projects initiated in July 2011 in Greater Manchester and five London boroughs operating according to *justice reinvestment* principles. PbR principles have also been utilised in four youth custody pathfinders, which were intended to encourage local authorities to use community-based interventions in place of custody. The Ministry of Justice also co-commissioned eight drug and alcohol recovery pilots with the Department of Health. It is clear, therefore that the government's longer-term aim was to apply PbR principles to all providers by 2015 with the exception of high risk offenders.

The *Competition Strategy for Offender Services* document (Ministry of Justice 2011a) reaffirmed the Coalition's intention to support the use of alternative delivery models, including joint ventures and social enterprises. It also announced that work was being undertaken to assess the potential for allowing public sector staff to form mutual or employee-owned enterprises "where this would add value and where there is currently no viable market for provision" (2011a: 12). In order to facilitate a marketplace of potential providers, the Ministry of Justice *2011–2015 Business Plan* indicated that rehabilitation services would no longer be directly provided without testing beforehand if the voluntary or private sectors could provide them more effectively (Ministry of Justice 2011b). This, in effect, fundamentally changed the role of the Probation Service from an almost exclusive monopoly provider of community sentences to just another provider (Mair and Burke 2012).

The earlier *Capacity and Competition Policy for Prisons and Probation* document (NOMS 2009) had contained an intention to market-test 25 per cent of community payback and in January 2011 the Ministry of Justice announced a competition to deliver six large cross-regional lots across England and Wales. The competition process was "mired in criticism, confusion and delay" (Garside and Silvestri 2012: 12) and in July 2011 the House of Commons Justice Committee noted that:

> The very large and incoherent groupings created for the community payback contracts would not be appropriate vehicles for commissioning other probation initiatives, and would undermine links between probation work and other participants in the criminal justice system.
>
> *(2011)*

The complexity of the commissioning process meant that the original timetable to let al.l six lots during 2011 and 2012 would fall behind schedule, with only the London contract being let to a consortium led by the private contractor, Serco in July 2012. Munro and Harrison in their report on the process commented that complexity and costs involved in the transfer of a relatively small staff group from London Probation Trust to the private provider, Serco, almost destroyed the process (2012).

In March 2012, the Coalition government published a report on the future of probation (Ministry of Justice 2012a). At this point it was still intended that trusts would commission services to meet local need and circumstances, while some services, such as electronic monitoring of curfew requirements, would continue to be commissioned at a national level in order to "get most value for money for the taxpayer" (2012a: 8). The management and supervision of lower risk offenders, alongside other services such as accredited programmes, were to be opened up to competition and incentivised through PbR. It was estimated that these contracts would amount to approximately 60 per cent of the annual £1 billion budget for community offender services (2012a: 14). Probation Trusts could compete for services, but this would require them to become separate entities independent of those probation trusts responsible for the commission of the services.

The replacement of Ken Clarke with Chris Grayling as Justice Secretary marked an intensification of the marketisation of probation services. Whilst at the Ministry for Work and Pensions, Grayling had overseen the implementation of PbR within the Work Programme. One of his first acts was to suspend the community payment-by-results pilots in order to assess the overall strategy but he reiterated that community payment by results "remained a priority" (Ainsworth 2012). By the time that *Transforming Rehabilitation* had been published in May 2013 there was a significant change in direction. The Probation Service was to retain responsibility for high-risk offenders and public protection cases, but the rest of offender services were to be contracted out on a PbR basis. Probation Trusts were to no longer hold a central commissioning role and instead the Coalition government proposed a national commissioning model based on sixteen *contract package areas* (subsequently increased to twenty-one following the consultation process). Under the proposals contained with *Transforming Rehabilitation,* it was not clear as to whether Probation Trusts would be able to bid for the contracts. The Justice Secretary was quoted as saying that he was happy to receive bids that included Probation Trusts but stressed that they must be able to bear the financial risk of contracting on a payments-by-results basis (Webster 2013) – something, of course, Probation Trusts would in reality find difficult to do.

What's all the fuss about: Does it matter who delivers?

This albeit brief overview of the attritional march to segment and privatise the Probation Service reflects the ideological determination of New Labour and the Coalition to deconstruct the public sector. For those defenders of New Labour's record of support for public services, it is worth reminding them that the powers required by the Coalition to largely privatise probation was already on the statute books in the form of the 2007 Offender Management Act. Those who promote and support privatisation usually contend that it does not matter who delivers the service so long as it is delivered to those who need it, in a timely manner and efficiently at a lower cost to the public purse – in other words, it delivers value for money. Muir however has argued that there are services which are generally unsuitable for private sector delivery because there are:

1. Services where the outcomes wanted by or required for the consumer are far too complex to be easily contracted for.
2. Relational services which engage the public very intensively and where the introduction of the profit motive may undermine the trust upon which good quality relationships depend.
3. Services which are there to uphold the law, such as the police and the judiciary, where it is particularly important that private interests are excluded and that there is direct public accountability.
4. Services that are particularly important for the inculcation of values.

(2012: npn)

Clearly, there is a case for contracting a private company to deliver a service where this can add capacity quickly, where the public provider has catastrophically failed or where a private provider can bring innovation and demonstrably improve outcomes. In fact, it could be argued that a false dichotomy has been created between the sectors, largely for political reasons. This is reflected in the language associated with each sector. John Richardson, an expert in critical discourse analysis, has analysed the language used by politicians when discussing privatisation. He argues that private provision is often framed within a positive discourse of *reform, cooperation and partnership*, whereas the public sector is repeatedly co-located with *cost* and *spending*. Indeed, to compound the differences, the private sector is also more likely to be framed in terms of *finance* and *investment* which are clearly more positive terms.

Yet in reality the two sectors are reliant on each other. The public sector has always purchased goods and services from the private sector and most importantly it also provides the infrastructure and investment (education, transport, the rule of law etc) on which the private sector is reliant to sell goods, develop services and make profits. This reliance on the public sector and public finance, is of course, completely overlooked by those amongst the rich and powerful who only see the public sector as a burden and have little or no comprehension of why they should pay their taxes for its upkeep. They therefore enter into a game of tax evasion with both their business interests and their personal wealth.

So does it matter who delivers public services, or is it just a case of ensuring that the relationship between public and private sectors operates in a way which is most conducive to delivering reductions in re-offending while providing value for money? The arguments for what works best are conducted not just in ideological and political terms, but are also expressed in technical industry jargon, with concepts like outcome measures, PbR mechanisms and contractual arrangements. We cover these issues later in the chapter because they are important in determining who should deliver, but there is a fundamental issue about private interests and public accountability (see point three of Muir above) that requires further discussion. Raynor has observed that "offender management needs to be accountable to the community through the courts or through government departments, and decisions need to be made in the public interest, without any conflict of with the interests of shareholders" (2012: 13). It is, therefore, to issues of governance that we now turn to understand the fuller picture of who should deliver.

Governance: Private interests or public good?

> ... the basic pitch is all about efficiency and "modernisation" ... this debate is also about accountability, transparency and the most fundamental aspects of democracy.
>
> *(Harris 2013)*

The withdrawal of public services has inevitably left large gaps in service delivery which private companies are being encouraged to fill and which offer potentially massive shareholder profits. In relation to the Probation Service, as Teague notes, private companies focussed on shareholder-profit are not oblivious to the fact that, in England and Wales, it represents an industry worth some £820 million a year (2013). These rich pickings are within a UK context that now has the most privatised prison system in Europe and although there are not as many private jails as in the United States, the proportion of prisoners in private prisons is actually higher. In a similar vein, with some 105,000 commencements per annum, the electronic monitoring programme in England and Wales is the largest outside of the United States, accounting for approximately 80 per cent of the European market.

Within this context of *big business,* it is somewhat ironic that the government's contention that the old monopolies in the prison and probation system need to be opened up to create a more diverse range of suppliers of criminal justice services, but just three companies – G4S, Serco and Sodexo – dominate the management of private prisons in England and Wales. Clearly this is big and profitable business. G4S for example operates in over 125 countries and employs 657,000 staff. Its turnover in 2011 was £7.5 billion. Rather than increasing competition as intended, economic theory suggests that when production is highly concentrated in very few companies, the market becomes an oligopoly that is inherently less competitive and innovative than a market with more broad-based representation (Culp 2013). Indeed, most of the key companies in the outsourcing game are not in fact specialist providers at all, but conglomerates that have mastered the skill of winning contracts, rather than running services (Milne 2012). The core business of these enterprises is winning government contracts, almost irrespective of the substantive activities involved. These companies secure a dominant position in the market not just by learning how to bid and complete contract forms correctly but by developing close relationships with government officials and politicians at national and local levels (Crouch 2011: 87). Private sector consultants have been influential in shaping government policy under successive governments since the 1990s and the private sector has also extended its influence upon government through powerful lobbying groups such as the Confederation of British Industry (CBI). According to Sim, this has resulted in a *correspondence of interests* between those in dominant positions in society (2010). In turn "the commodification of public services provided a significant financial opportunity for private business whilst enabling government to preach the discourse of modernisation and to claim to be reducing the cost to the public purse" (Bell 2011: 175).

Whilst this does not necessarily suggest that politicians are merely the dupes of private corporations, there has recently been growing concern about the potential threat to democracy arising from connections between parliamentarians and corporations internationally (Wilks-Heeg *et al.* 2012). One study, for example, found that 46 per cent of the top fifty publicly traded firms had a British Member of Parliament as a director or shareholder, the highest of all forty-seven countries studied (Faccio 2006). The UK's corporate-parliamentary connections are of an order which is exceptionally rare among established democracies – running at six times the average for Western Europe and over ten times the average for the Nordic countries (Wilks-Heeg *et al.* 2012). Rules preventing public officials from working as consultants for private firms until a lengthy period had elapsed have been relaxed, precisely in order to facilitate contact between the public sector and private expertise. For example, John Reid, a former Home Secretary with responsibility for security services, subsequently became a consultant to security firms running and bidding for government contracts (Crouch 2011: 93). The Prison Officers Association (POA) launched a judicial review into the G4S consultancy role carried out by Phil Wheatley, when in his former role of Director General of the Prison Service he had overseen the market testing process that allowed private companies to bid for four prison contracts alongside the public sector (Adetunji 2011). Roger Hill, the former National Director of the Probation Service in England and Wales and Andrew Bridges, former HM Chief Inspector of Prisons and Probation, have also taken up roles with, respectively, Sodexo and G4S.

The increasing concentration of market share amongst a small band of private companies means that it becomes evermore difficult for new companies to enter the market. The current proposals envisage the commissioning of probation services on a national basis with delivery being located within twenty-one contract package areas. Because of the scale involved, contracts are likely to be awarded to a small number of multinational companies who will then subcontract service delivery to a complex mix of providers. The Coalition talks a lot about charitable and voluntary sector bodies bidding for the twenty-one contracts but few have the capital reserves or expertise to win the tendering process (Easton 2013). In the case of the forty Work Programme contracts, some 90 per cent were won by large companies including Ingeus, Deloitte, A4e, Serco and G4S (Benjamin 2011) and there are concerns that newcomers undercut existing welfare-to-work providers to win contracts at prices that are too low to get the least job-ready people into work.

If the recent experience of the Department of Work and Pensions is applied to the provision of community sentences, subcontracting to smaller organisations by the *prime provider* is likely to be an important delivery mechanism. Subcontracting models of course pose risks to autonomy and accountability for the smaller voluntary and community organisations. Operating beneath a prime contractor will inevitably mean a change in strategic direction for many organisations, and potentially restrain innovation, given the imperative to demonstrate outcomes in order to receive a financial return (Clinks 2010, Senior 2011). The risk therefore is that marketisation has the paradoxical effect of reducing both the range of providers and their local connectedness, concentrating provision in the hands of a small number of large corporations. Moreover as privatisation "devours core services and displaces public knowledge and capacity, outsourcing becomes more difficult to reverse" (Milne 2012: *npn*).

Of course, our outline of the privatisation of the correctional services pales into insignificance when placed within the overarching context of the much bigger picture of changes to the public sector. In 2011, the value of the outsourced market in the UK had an annual turnover of £80 billion and it is estimated that figure will rise to £140 billion by 2014 (Social Enterprise UK 2012). It has been suggested that what we are witnessing is the emergence of a *shadow state* of extremely powerful private public service companies. Zoe Williams puts it this way:

> What happens when these firms, with their inexorable expansionist logic, bite off more than they can chew? We pay anyway. We paid G4S [for its bungled Olympics security contract] we will pay again when its prisons catch fire. We will pay A4e when it finds no jobs; we will pay Serco when its probation services fail. We will pay because even when they're not delivered by the public sector, these are still public services, and the ones that aren't too big to fail are too important. What any government creates with massive-scale outsourcing is not 'new efficiency', it is a shadow state; we can't pin it down any more than we can vote it out. All we can do is watch.
>
> *(2013: npn)*

This quiet revolution in which large sections of public provision are being transferred to the private sector is taking place with very little public discussion or political dissent, this despite polls showing that over half of those interviewed thought it was unacceptable for private companies to run prisons and two-thirds had never heard of Serco. A larger number had heard of G4S, but only as a result of the adverse publicity resulting from their failure to provide adequate security for the 2012 London Olympics (Social Enterprises UK 2012). It is almost certainly true that the general public are less likely to have heard of the other significant players in this market such as Interserve, Sodexo, Capita and the Compass Group. Of course it could be argued that the public have equally been unaware of the work undertaken by the Probation Service in England and Wales and that this lack of knowledge has made it easier for the government to promote its proposals in *Transforming Rehabilitation* without fully addressing the risks involved. However, a recent report by the Institute for Government by Gash *et al.* found that the public are far less comfortable with private and voluntary sector provision in some public services – such as the prison and probation services – than in others which they associate less closely with the state (2013).

There are also important issues of legitimacy and accountability when statutory responsibilities are given to profit-making organisations or to an organisation whose lines of accountability to the criminal courts and to the public are less clear. In a chain of contracts involving a complex web of providers and service delivery arrangements it becomes more difficult to establish responsibility when things go wrong. Generally speaking, as Crouch argues, "the actions and decision-making processes of public bodies are more transparent than private firms because they cannot use the issue of commercial confidentiality to justify high levels of secrecy in their operations" (2011: 172). So, what happens when things go wrong in the delivery of, for example, rehabilitative services? Geoff Dobson makes the following point:

> If a judge or magistrate has concerns about the supervision of a contracted-out court order, with one or more organisations involved, who do they ask to appear before them?
>
> *(2012: npn)*

If the experience of PbR in other sectors is any kind of guide, there will inevitably be real concerns that require careful scrutiny. The list of work programme prime contractors for example is dominated by private sector companies including G4S, Serco, and A4e who all also have involvement in the criminal justice market. However, all three of these companies have been involved in highly publicised scandals centering on claims that they were manipulating results in order to meet targets for payment (Guardian 2012a and b). The high profile failure of G4S to provide sufficient security for the London 2012 Olympics has also brought into question the assumed efficiency of the private sector (Orr 2012). Yet despite G4S's track record, the company's turnover has almost doubled since 2005, with the percentage of its revenue coming from government contracts rising to 27 per cent in 2011 (Clark 2012: npn). Most recently, both G4S and Serco have been required to pay back millions of pounds resulting from claims for the electronic monitoring of nonexistent offenders. In the House of Commons the Justice Secretary described the behaviour as "wholly indefensible and unacceptable" (Harris 2013). Of course, none of these incidents would necessarily suggest that the private sector shouldn't be involved in the management and delivery of public goods. There are ample examples of scandals and poor practice in the public sector too, and for every Southern Cross care home there is a Mid-Staffordshire NHS Trust. But they do challenge the enduring presumption that the private sector is somehow more efficient and therefore superior to the public sector. One thing though remains clear, the governance of truly public sector organisations, like the Probation Service, has been traditionally embedded in systems of transparent accountability and direct access by the public to their governing bodies. This is an entirely different proposition to the lines of accountability within the private sector that lead back to profit, shareholder interest and wrangles about commercial confidentiality. These are important issues but as Raynor identifies – "The bigger question is, how far the social contract between citizens and the State can be mediated through a private company" (2012: 13).

Efficacy: PbR as a drag on desistance

> Most public services are not about producing microchips, they're about human relationships – care work, parole, job-seeking, even assessing whether or not a disabled person is really disabled; they are about one human being spending time with another. The economist Ha-Joon Chang's famous example of the pitfall of efficiency is that it mainly means making things faster – and yet if you played a minuet at three times the speed, would it improve it?
>
> *(Williams 2013: npn)*

The scale of these developments within the field of corrections is further compromised by the complexity of the change processes involved. As the Probation Chiefs Association has pointed out, the possibility of introducing national commissioning with multiple contracts within a timescale of eighteen months is extremely questionable when the competition for Community Payback in London took over two years and this of course was restricted to a single intervention within a single probation trust (2013). If the Coalition pushes ahead to the current timescales, all the indications are that the contract packages will be over a lengthy period in order to reward private providers for their investment and performance (Webster 2013). This has all the hallmarks of a *scorched earth* policy which a subsequent change of government in 2015 would find difficult to untangle even if it were so inclined.

Many of the key elements of the government's proposals are untested and unproven. The Justice Secretary has been quoted as saying that PbR isn't rocket science and it may not be, but neither is it straightforward. The market and the application of PbR in criminal justice terms is both complex, untested and its implementation raises a number of issues. Firstly, there is likely to be considerable variation across England and Wales in the work that will be required to establish a stable market. In some areas there will be a network of existing organisations, but in others an infrastructure will need to be developed. HMP Peterborough was selected because it had a high proportion of prisoners released to the local area (Disley *et al.* 2011), but this may not be the case in other areas although the Coalition's proposals to turn seventy local prisons into resettlement prisons might go some way to address this. Secondly, PbR raises a fundamental question about the decision making of sentencers, for instance will resources be made available to meet the rehabilitative outcomes of judicial decisions or conversely will the availability of resources ultimately determine the decision making of magistrates and judges?

These changes are being are being introduced at a time of government funding cuts. Whereas under New Labour it was a case of being asked to do more with more public investment, now it is about doing more with less. The government clearly believes that PbR will achieve worthwhile cost savings, but as Fox and Albertson (2011) argue, it does not necessarily follow that reductions in reconvictions will accrue significant savings when the costs of existing services are largely fixed. Evidence from other sectors suggests that whilst PbR enabled potential savings in terms of lower costs in negotiating prices and volumes, these were more than offset by the increased expenditure involved in the recruitment of additional staff, higher costs of data collection, higher monitoring costs and higher enforcement costs. Research by Hudson *et al.* also found little evidence that outcome-based contracting was driving innovation and instead was largely focused on reducing operational costs and achieving performance efficiencies (2010 cited in Roberts 2011). As Barrington-Bush suggests in relation to the Work Programme:

> If your job is on the line over the number of people who have received work-readiness training, you will find a way to make those numbers add up to what they need to. The training might get shortened; one full-day course might become two half-day courses; people might be counted multiple times for what are essentially the same efforts; those who are more difficult to reach will be ignored in favour of the easiest recipients. Whatever the definitions set, you will find ways around them, and so will your organisation
>
> *(2012: npn).*

The government believes that these issues can be resolved through the commissioning process but as Crouch contends, "The problem with the formal contract model is that it cannot cope with the need for frequent adjustment and the implied terms that are intrinsic to any complex task. It is not possible to specify in advance in a contract all the problems and unexpected issues that arise in practice" (2011: 89). The application of PbR in the NHS would suggest that it works best when you have a comparatively straightforward problem that requires a single intervention from a single provider (Roberts 2011: 17). However, many of those individuals subject to community sentences will have complex needs that often require services from multiple providers. Leicestershire and Rutland Probation Trust, for example, found that some individuals were involved with more than twenty different professionals and agencies and that some of the most entrenched offenders fell into families with complex needs (four or more problems excluding offending), including low-income households, mental health issues, unemployment and lack of qualifications (Adetunji 2011). This issue has been recognised by the Justice Affairs Select Committee who commented that having different providers responsible for different elements of a community order could seriously undermine the overall coordination of the sentence (2011). In a national evaluation by the King's Fund into the introduction of PbR into the NHS it was concluded that there were some general lessons to be learnt:

> First, payment systems cannot do everything: they are one of many levers that can be used to achieve change. Second, one size does not fit all. Different services will need different ways of paying providers in order to meet

> different sets of objectives. Related to this is a third point that any payment system needs to be flexible – to deal with unexpected shocks, or unpredicted outcomes. There needs to be flexibility too between national rules and frameworks and local discretion and experimentation.
>
> *(2012)*

It could be argued that the idea of PbR is predicated on a notion of cause and effect that does not fit well with what is known about the nature of desistance. As Andrew Neilson has noted:

> ... for all the labelling in the terminology of 'offender management', we cannot – indeed should not – forget that people going through the criminal justice system are just that: people. People are complicated. Those going through the justice system, often presenting multiple and complex needs, are particularly complicated. The routes to desistance from offending may defy the simple pathways that a payment by results model would seek to impose.
>
> *(2011: npn)*

Although the *Transforming Rehabilitation* strategy paper indicated that payments will be made on both binary (the number of offenders reconvicted within a 12-month period) and frequency (the rate of offences committed by a cohort within a 12-month period), the Ministry of Justice has stated that providers who do not meet the binary target will not receive PbR payment (Webster 2013). It is well documented that the principal measure for PbR, reconviction, is not an adequate measure of desistance. Reconviction, rather than a straightforward measure of behaviour change, is often the result of a series of social interactions and processes in which a range of actors make discretionary judgements about how to react to information, whether in witnessing, reporting, detecting, prosecuting or sentencing a crime. In other words it is a measure of social and professional reactions and these reactions are vulnerable to a wide range of influences. This could lead to rewarding services who cherry-pick low-risk offenders or who process as successes those re-offenders who simply keep their heads down for long enough. By contrast, it risks penalising providers who opt to work with those in the greatest need and at the greatest risk of re-offending, ignoring their possible successes in slowing down or reducing the seriousness of offending while someone makes real but imperfect progress toward desistance. In this respect, it would not appear to matter to the PbR model "if offenders cease to offend, or merely become less easy to catch" (Fox and Albertson 2012: 361).

Delivery: Why pay less?

Few studies have succeeded in producing evidence that private sector provision is more effective than the equivalent public sector service. In fact, according to the latest annual performance ratings, two out of the three worst performing prisons in England and Wales were run by private sector companies (NOMS 2013). Research by Liebling, Crewe and Hulley found that there are major differences between companies – so that (some) values, and performance or quality, may vary more between companies as well as between the public and the private sector. According to the authors, contract prisons have placed more emphasis on *relationship* measures (respect, humanity and trust) whilst public prisons have given greater weight to *regime* measures (fairness, order and safety). Relationships with prisoners were courteous and often friendly in the private sector but this was only one component of respect. Custody officers were less professional and were not always a conduit to meeting prisoners needs – "'Being nice' was not the same as 'getting things done'" (2012: 20). Similarly, Management and Training Corporation (MTC), which is the third largest company providing incarceration in the United States, won a five-year contract to operate the Central North Correctional Centre (CNCC) in Ontario, Canada as part of a pilot project to compare operations of the CNCC facility with a similar publicly-run prison, the Central East Correctional Centre. The Canadian government hired PricewaterhouseCoopers to evaluate the two prisons across a variety of dimensions. The evaluation found that the public prison outperformed the MTC facility overall. While the MTC prison was cheaper to operate and provided a greater variety of programming than the government facility, the public prison rated significantly better on security, recidivism rates, health care and community impact. Ontario decided to turn management of the privatised facility over to the public sector (Culp 2013).

There is some evidence that in England and Wales competition and contracting have delivered broadly comparable levels of performance – albeit with different characteristics – at a significantly lower cost (Sturgess in 2012: 33), but Liebling *et al* also found that there are limits beyond which efficiencies can become counterproductive:

> it seems likely that, even in private prisons with experienced staff, the thin staffing levels that characterise profit-making institutions, and the relatively high turnover among a staff group who are less bonded to their occupation, may limit quality levels in certain areas.
>
> *(2012: 21)*

To the extent that private prison operators do manage to save money, they do so through "reductions in staffing patterns, fringe benefits, and other labor-related costs" (Krugman 2012) and indeed, innovation is often encouraged as a means of cutting costs not enhancing service effectiveness. The most common way for private sector companies to make money from government contracts is by reducing personnel expenses. Because staff cost represents about 80 per cent of the operating cost of a prison, much of the cost savings in private prisons results from paying private correctional officers less than comparable public correctional officers. However, this advantage begins to erode in a market where private companies are dependent upon contract renewals (with more experienced staff) rather than new facilities (with new entry-level staff) (Culp 2013).

Inevitably, once a contract has been awarded to a private concern, control is weakened as private firms can be taken over or bought out. Furthermore, any failings may then be passed on to the state as additional costs. Consider the case of the Education Maintenance Award (EMA) described by Williams:

> when Serco won the probation services contract in London it did so by massively underbidding the public sector with a view to stripping out 100 of the 550 jobs. Not to worry you might think – the others will be covered by TUPE legislation that protects employees when ownership is transferred; pay, terms and conditions will be unaffected. But possibly not – when Liberata won the education maintenance allowance and adult learning grant contract from a number of local authorities in 2007, scores of people were transferred from the public sector. It turned out their pensions weren't always protected. Then the company "restructured", a process that trumps TUPE, and the "scheme leader" tier was simply removed, which meant a pay cut for many of the most qualified staff. Then it turned out that Liberata couldn't handle the contract, but by this time it was so large that the only other company capable of taking it on was Capita. When the present government came in and canned EMA, citing "unaffordability", the galling thing was that private sector bungling had made it quite expensive.
>
> *(2013: npn)*

Whilst it may be viewed by some as a short-term solution (in terms of savings to the public purse) such relationships inevitably tie the state into long-term and costly contracts. Privatisation can serve as a stealth form of government borrowing, in which governments avoid recording upfront expenses (or even raise money by selling existing facilities) while raising their long-run costs in ways taxpayers can't see (Krugman 2012). Private borrowing is more expensive than public borrowing and as Bell points out, "although PFI contracts have encouraged market liberalisation, enabling the private sector to play a significant role in the delivery of public services, they have not delivered value for money or reduced public spending in the long run" (2011: 144). It has been estimated the current PFI schemes could cost up to £25 billion more than if the government had paid for them directly (Milne 2012).

Delivery beyond markets and profit

We are clear that in terms of efficacy and governance, the argument for the wholesale privatisation of correctional services in general and the rehabilitative endeavour in particular cannot be sustained. However, the debate cannot simply be framed in these relatively narrow and technical discourses. If, as Rob Canton has contended, "the value of probation consists in what it represents and embodies about society's duties towards victims and offenders, then its practices are not things to be bought and sold. Security is not a commodity, rehabilitation not a 'product'" (2011: 190).

As we have argued throughout this book, effective supervision is ultimately a moral activity – one that engages the values, outlook, personal strengths and capacities of the individual offender and which should aim to bring citizens together in a greater understanding of their interdependency and mutual interests rather than as a means of separating and further alienating those who offend from the so-called law-abiding majority. This ultimately is the basis of civil society and in the next chapter we turn to wider issues of the engagement between rehabilitative services and the communities within which they are delivered.

References

Adetunji, J. (2011) Extending the reach of community budgets, *The Guardian*, 26 September. http://www.guardian.co.uk (Accessed 7 February 2014).

Ainsworth, D. (2012) Ministry of Justice suspends payment-by-results pilots, *Third Sector*, http://thirdsector.co.uk/Finance/article/1153850 (Accessed 13 February 2014).

Audit Commission (1989) *The Probation Service: Promoting Value for Money*, London: HMSO.

Barrington-Bush, L. (2012) Don't bank on payment by results, *The Guardian*, 22 November. www.theguardian.com/.../22/payment-by-results-voluntary-sector (Accessed 31 March 2014).

Bell, E. (2011) *Criminal Justice and Neoliberalism*, Palgrave Macmillan: London.

Benjamin, A. (2011) Work Programme is a wasted opportunity for charities, *The Guardian*, 21 June. http://www.guardian.co.uk/society (Accessed 29 March 2014).

Bennett, J. (2007) Did things only get better? A decade of prisons under Tony Blair and New Labour, *Prison Service Journal*, 171: 3–12.

Canton, R. (2011) *Probation: Working with Offenders*, Abingdon, Oxon: Routledge.

Carlen, P. (2005) Imprisonment and the Penal Body Politic: The Cancer of Disciplinary Governance in Liebling, A. and Maruna, S. (eds) *The Effects of Imprisonment*, Cullompton: Willan. pp. 421–441.

Carter, P. (2003) *Managing Offenders, Reducing Crime: A New Approach*, London: Home Office.

Clark, N. (2012) G4S's Olympic struggles should derail the drive towards more privatisation, *The Guardian*, 13 July 2012. http://www.guardian.co.uk/commentisfree (Accessed 28 March 2014).

Coalition Agreement (2010) The Coalition: Our programme for government, HM Government: London.

Conservative Party (2008) *Prisons with a purpose: Our sentencing and rehabilitation revolution to break the cycle of crime*, Security Agenda, Policy Green Paper No 4, Millbank: Conservative Party.

Crouch, C. (2011) *The Strange Non-death of Neoliberalism*, Polity Press: Cambridge.

Culp, R. (2013) *The Failed Promise of Prison Privatization*, February 18 Prison Legal News. https://prisonlegalnews.org (Accessed 28 March 2014).

Disley, E., Rubin, J., Scraggs, E., Burrows, N. and Culley, D. (2011) *Lessons learned from the planning and early implementation of the Social Impact Bond at HMP Peterborough*, Research Series 5/11, London: Ministry of Justice.

Dobson, G. (2012) The problem with privatising probation services, *The Guardian*, 22 May 2012. http://www.guardian.co.uk/news (Accessed 27 March 2014).

Drakeford, M. (1988) Privatisation, punishment and the Future for probation, *Probation Journal*, 35.

Easton, M. (2013) Businessmen, lawyers and justice, 9 January 2013. http://www.bbc.co.uk/news/uk (Accessed 26 March 2014).

Faccio, M. (2006) Politically connected firms, *American Economic Review*, 96(1): 369–86.

Fox, C. and Albertson, K. (2011) Payment by Results and social impact bonds in the criminal justice sector: New challenges for the concept of evidence-based policy? *Criminology and Criminal Justice*, 11(5): 395–413.

Garside, R. and Silvestri, A. (2012) *UK Justice Policy Review: Volume* 2, 6 May 2011 to 5 May 2012, Centre for Crime and Justice Studies: London.

Gash, T., Panchamia, N. and Sims, S. (2013) *Making public service markets work: Professionalising government's approach to commissioning and market stewardship*, London: Institute for Government, http://www.instituteforgovernment.org.uk/publications/making-public-service-markets-work (Accessed 1 April 2014).

Gelsthorpe, L. and Hedderman, C. (2012) Providing for women offenders: the risks of adopting a payment by results approach, *Probation Journal*, 2012 (59): 374–390.

Guardian (2012a) DWP 'did not do enough to stop fraud among welfare-to-work companies', *The Guardian*, May 16. www.Guardian.co.uk (Accessed 30 June 2012).

Guardian (2012b) Serco investigated over claims of 'unsafe' out-of-hours GP service, *The Guardian*, May 25. www.Guardian.co.uk (Accessed 30 June 2012).

Harris, J. (2013) Serco: the company that is running Britain, *The Guardian*, 29 July. http://theguardian.com (Accessed 30 June 2012).

Hayes, C. (2010) *Payment by results: What does it mean for voluntary organisations working with offenders?* Clinks. www.clinks.org (Accessed 10 September 2011).

Home Office (1990) *Supervision and Punishment in the Community: A Framework for Action*, London: Home Office.

Home Office (2005) *Restructuring Probation to Reduce Re-offending*, London: Home Office.

Home Office (2006) *Improving Prison and Probation Services: Public Value Partnerships*, London: Home Office.

Home Office (2007) *Offender Management Act 2007*, London: Home Office.

Hough, M. (2006) Introduction in Hough, M., Allen, R. and Padel, U. (eds) *Reshaping Probation and Prisons: The New Offender Management Framework*, Bristol: Policy Press.

Justice Affairs Select Committee (2011) The role of the Probation Service. www.publications.parliament.uk (Accessed 1 September 2011).

Kings Fund (2012) Payments by results: Time for a rethink? Kings Fund, 2 November 2012. http://www.kingsfund.org.uk (Accessed 30 June 2013).

Krugman, P. (2012) Prisons, privatization, patronage, *The New York Times*, June 21, 2012. http://www.nytimes.com/2012/06/22/opinion/krugman-prisons-privatization-patronage.html (Accessed 30 March 2013).

Lilley, J.R. and Knepper, P. (1992) An International Perspective on the Privatisation of Corrections, *The Howard Journal of Criminal Justice*, 31(3): 174–191.

Liebling, A., Crewe, B. and Hulley, S. (2012) Values, practices and outcomes in public and private sector prisons, in Helyar-Cardwell, V. (2012) (ed) *Delivering Justice: The role of the public, private and voluntary sectors in prisons and probation*, Criminal Justice Alliance: London.

Mazzucato, M. (2011) *The entrepreneurial state*, London: DEMOS.

Milne, S. (2012) G4S should make it easier to beat the privatisation racket, *The Guardian*, 17 July. http://guardian.co.uk (Accessed 30 March 2013).

Ministry of Justice (2010) *Breaking the Cycle: Effective Punishment, Rehabilitation and Sentencing of Offenders*, London: Stationary Office.

Ministry of Justice (2011a) *Competition Strategy for Offender Services*, London: Ministry of Justice.

Ministry of Justice (2011b) *2011–2015 Business Pan*, https://www.gov.uk/.../ministry-of-justice-business-plan-2011-15-2 (Accessed 1 April 2014).

Ministry of Justice (2012a) *Punishment and Reform: Effective Probation Services*, London: Stationary Office.

Ministry of Justice (2012b) *Punishment and Reform: Effective Community Sentences*, London: Stationary Office.

Ministry of Justice (2013) *Transforming Justice: A Revolution in the Way We Manage Offenders*, London: Stationary Office.

Munro, H. and Harrison, D. (2012) *The Inaugural Community Payback Competition: The London Story*, London: London Probation Trust.

Muir, R. (2012) After the G4S debacle, it's time to re-think the role of the private sector, *New Statesman*, 17 July. http://newstatesman.com (Accessed 12 August 2012).

Napo (2006a) Contestability prospectus published, *Napo News*, September 2006 No 182, London: Napo.

Napo (2006b) NOMS review, *Napo News*, October 2006 No 183, London: Napo.

Neilson, A. (2011) Justice won't be done with payment by results, 14 March. http://opinion.publicfinance.co.uk (Accessed 15 February 2014).

Neilson, A. (2012) Counterblast: Putting a Price on Rehabilitation: Payment by Results and the March of the Market in Prisons and Probation, *The Howard Journal of Criminal Justice*, 51(4): 419–422.

Nellis, M. (2006) NOMS, contestability and the process of technocorrectional innovation in Hough, M., Allen, R. and Padel, U. (eds), *Reshaping Probation and Prisons: The New Offender Management Framework*, Bristol: Policy Press: 49–68.

NOMS (2013) *Prison annual performance ratings 2012/2013*, London: NOMS.

Raynor, P. (2012) Is probation still possible? *The Howard Journal of Criminal Justice*, 51 (2): 173–189.

Richardson, J. (undated) Under-reporting New Labour's Privatisation Plans. www.sheffield.ac.uk/polopoly (Accessed 10 October 2012).

Ridley, N. (1977) *Nationalised Industries Policy Group Report (PG/10/7738).*

Raynor, P. and Vanstone, M. (2007) Towards a correctional service in Gelsthorpe, L. and Morgan, R. (eds) *Handbook of Probation*, Cullompton: Willan.

Roberts, M. (2011) *By their fruits… Applying payments by results to drugs recovery*, UK Drug Policy commission. www.ukdpc.net/ (Accessed 1 September 2012).

Senior, P. (2011) The voluntary and community sector: The paradox of becoming centre-stage in the big society, *British Journal of Community Justice*, 9 (1/2): 37–54.

Seymour, R. (2012) A short history of privatisation in the UK: 1979–2012, *The Guardian*, 29 March.

Sim, J. (2010) Review symposium: Punishing the Poor – The Neoliberal Government of Insecurity by Loic Wacquant, *British Journal of Criminology*, 50(1): 589–608.

Social Enterprise UK The shadow state: A report about outsourcing of public services. www.socialenterprise.org.uk (Accessed 21 January 2013).

Sturgess, G.L. (2012) The sources of benefit in prison contracting, in Helyar-Cardwell, V. (2012) (ed) *Delivering justice: The role of the public, private and voluntary sectors in prisons and probation*, Criminal Justice Alliance: London.

Teague, M. (2013) The dismantling of probation: Who will profit? http://newleftproject.org (Accessed 3 February 2014).

Travis, A. (2006) Reid wants a bigger role for private sector in probation service, *The Guardian*, 8 November.

Webster, R. (2013) *Is payment by results rocket science?* www.russellwebster.com (Accessed 3 February 2014).

Wilks-Heeg, S., Blick, A. and Crone, S. (2012) How democratic is the UK? The 2012 audit. http://democracy-uk-2012.democraticaudit.com/ (Accessed 3 February 2014).

Williams, Z. (2013) This obsession with outsourcing public services has created a shadow state, *The Guardian*, 7 February. http://www.guardian.co.uk/commentisfree (Accessed 3 February 2014).

Wilson, R. and Bloomfield, J. (2011) *Building the Good Society: A new form of progressive politics*. www.compassonline.org.uk (Accessed 2 February 2014).

6 WIDENING REHABILITATION

Partnership, localism and civil society

> The contradiction at the heart of neo-liberalism was that the retreat of the state from intervention in the capitalist economy in the name of 'free enterprise' had to be matched by a new Leviathan of authoritarianism, to deal with the social tensions inevitably arising from what the great Keynesian JK Galbraith called the counter position of 'private affluence' and 'public squalor'. From Thatcher's determination to destroy the right of miners freely to associate to 'New' Labour's 'ASBOs' to control the young sub-Proletariat, the UK's liberal tradition of civil liberty and tolerance, going back to John Stuart Mill, has been unconscionably discounted.
>
> *(Wilson and Bloomfield 2011: 11)*

Redefining the boundaries of the state

Underpinning the state's move to segment and marketise rehabilitative services, discussed in the previous chapter, we find the government attempting to reposition itself into the role of probation policy-maker, disentangled from the administration and operational delivery of services. In this brave new world, aspirations towards more localised forms of governance that promote notions of community justice, have sat alongside the competing trends of managerialism and marketisation (Bowen and Donoghue 2013: 16). Redefining the boundaries of the state, however, does not simply reflect a desire to alter the techniques and governance of service delivery in line with wider ideological imperatives. As the quote from Wilson and Bloomfield above suggests, it may also require a wider and more diffuse shift in the management and control of individual citizens or groups within their local communities. This is a focus both for this chapter and Chapter Seven, but first of all, some discussion of the details of *widening rehabilitation* is required.

Successive political administrations over the past twenty years have consistently promoted the claims of the voluntary sector as a more innovative and flexible means of service delivery; one closer to the needs of local communities. Public sector agencies on the other hand have been encouraged to regard themselves as purchasers of services provided by private and voluntary sector organisations rather than assuming responsibility for the direct provision themselves. As such, the importance of the voluntary sector has become more than just a means to supplement existing provision. It is now central to the broader project of "post-welfare modernisation" (Corcoran 2011: 34). This, in part, has been a response to the perception that state-provided services were struggling to respond to rising demands and failing to meet the needs of users. Consequently, this has led to the strengthening of partnership work. Adam Crawford comments:

> Networks of interlaced agencies drawing from the public, private and voluntary sectors are heralded as alternatives to a primacy upon bureaucracies and markets as the bedrocks of the new governance.
>
> *(2001: 60)*

A more critical reading of these developments is that "they enhance authoritarian state projects, enrolling state and non-state actors in elitist programmes aimed at the representation of marginalized street populations rather than crimes of the powerful" (Edwards and Hughes 2012: 446). Mary Corcoran argues that whilst these developments are not new, they gained momentum under New Labour because:

> ... the voluntary sector presented a seemingly complementary fit with different strands of crime governance policy including initiatives for fostering community safety partnerships at local levels, the procedural management of offenders under the National Management Service (NOMS), and the stimulation of community-based supports for offenders and victims.
>
> *(2011: 33)*

The Probation Service itself has a history of partnership work, which it has effectively been able to undertake given its "pivotal quality, and long experience, of inhabiting both the criminal justice and the social welfare organisational realms" (Rumgay, J. in Wing Hong Chui and Nellis, M. 2003: 195). The current *Transforming Rehabilitation* agenda fails to acknowledge long-standing relationships between the Probation Service and the voluntary sector. Indeed, the origins of probation can be found in voluntary activity (see Mair and Burke 2012, Chapter One for a discussion of the origins of the Probation Service in England and Wales). Probation has a highly credible record as a founder of local voluntary initiatives to meet the needs of specific groups, such as substance misusers, the homeless and victims of crime. However, as Judith Rumgay points out "often these initiatives derive from the practical efforts of committed individuals within the Service at least as much as from organisational planning and expenditure" (2003: 203). She identifies four discernible contemporary policy strands which have affected the Probation Service's role in partnership work - contracting for supervision services; community crime prevention; targeting of special groups; and coordinated social planning and provision. These themes have been worked out in terms of its participation in interagency developments such Drug Action Teams, Youth Offending Teams, Multi-Agency Public Protection Panels and *Supported People* Consortia for Social Housing.

The contemporary appeal of partnership work would seem to lie in its promise to fulfil a number of policy goals for the resolution of social and crime problems, combined with the rationalisation of resources and expenditure. At its most basic level, partnership entails "cooperative relationships between two or more organisations to achieve a common goal" (Liddle *et al.* 1994), however, how these common goals are agreed upon and put into practice is another matter. Robinson (2011) states that the proliferation of partnership work can be understood on three levels:

1. As a mechanism for distributing responsibility for crime and criminal justice from statutory criminal justice agencies towards a greater constituency of organisations and communities.
2. As an attempt to harness a greater variety of skills and resources to address complex situations.
3. As an attempt to integrate fragmented systems and service delivery.

Within this formulation, it is clear that levels one and three may well stand in opposition when the desire to distribute responsibility could actually exacerbate the fragmentation of service delivery across agencies and accountabilities. For the Probation Service, as Judith Rumgay argues:

> … this complex partnership enterprise has entailed forging a range of inter-agency relationships that serve different policy purposes: contractual arrangements for service delivery by non-statutory agencies; community-wide strategies for risk reduction and support of vulnerable people; and targeting of specific groups of individuals for multi-agency monitoring and intervention.
>
> *(2003: 199)*

These sometimes conflicting drivers reflect an ambiguity as to what partnerships entail and their purpose, inclusiveness, responsibilities, working relations and lines of accountability. It is not just the modus operandi of service delivery and target populations that presents such challenges however, but less tangible forces and factors. Adam Crawford puts it this way:

> The discussion tends to treat partnerships as if the public sector, voluntary organisations, private businesses, communities and groups are undifferentiated clusters of organisations, as if they present the same issues and opportunities as well as difficulties. There is little sense of the diverse priorities and forces as well the plural traditions, cultures and practices which differentiate such clusters of interests. Little concern is given to the problematic task of managing such networks, particularly in light of the reality that conflicts are overlain by very different power relations and access to resources (both human and material).
>
> *(2001: 60)*

The proliferation of these disparate policy meanings, accountabilities and operational outcomes in modern day partnership arrangements has been accompanied by a shift toward emphasising the importance of particular contributors and introducing new actors into what was once perceived as the responsibility of the public realm. This has resulted in both fragmentation and a dispersal of control which has been "encouraged by the introduction of privatisation and quasi-markets through purchaser/provider splits, where services could not easily be privatised" (Crawford 2001: 61).

Formalising partnership arrangements: Integrating or fragmenting relationships?

Whilst the primacy of the market in the great neoliberal enterprise of the past four decades continues to gather momentum and shape, focussing on distribution of the spoils at the policy level, within the criminal justice system the emphasis has been more on *joined-up* working. Formal working partnerships with other statutory agencies such as the police and prisons as part of the Multi-Agency Public Protection Arrangements (MAPPA) and with local authorities in Crime and Disorder Reduction Partnerships (CDRPs) and Integrated Offender Management (IOM) have taken on a greater importance in the fabric of design and delivery at the local level. These initiatives have been mainly driven by a wider management of risk agenda and in this respect it could be argued that they are "characterised by a strategic and pragmatic rejection of rehabilitative ideals in favour of controlling crime rates" (Reeves 2013: 41). As such they bear the hallmarks of a *community protection* approach characterised by "compulsory conditions, surveillance and monitoring, enforcement, compulsory engagement in treatment and an emphasis on victim and community rights over those of offenders" (Weaver 2014: 16). They also reflect the recognition that the management of problematic and high-risk individuals requires a coordinated response that draws on the knowledge, skills and resources of a range of agencies. This has forged and developed a working alliance between the police and probation, bringing about significant cultural changes in the working practices of the two agencies. Traditionally, certain organisations were seen to be in opposing camps, although in reality it was always much more complicated and nuanced. This has led some commentators to warn of the *polification* of probation work (Nash 2008) resulting in a more controlling approach and loss of the distinctive identity and culture that has marked the Probation Service. However, research by Mawby and Worrall (2012) found that closer working between probation and police had in fact enhanced the work of both agencies in the management of high-risk offenders, especially when the respective skills of each of the organisations were acknowledged. Ironically though, the authors found a worsening of relations between probation and the Prison Service. This, despite attempts by the Labour government (outlined in Chapter Three) to integrate the two services, culminating in the creation of the National Offender Management Service (NOMS). According to Mawby and Worrall this was because the consultation paper *Joining Forces to Protect the Public: Prisons-Probation* (Home Office 1998) needed proper reference and the *Carter Report* (2003) that paved the way for NOMS failed to understand that the probation landscape was changing and it was the police rather than the prison service who were now its *natural partners* (2012: 85). As we have argued elsewhere,

> Rather than being obsessed about integration and common ways of doing and thinking which reflects the current tensions within NOMS about how to bring Prisons and Probation together, the best partnerships between Police and Probation have delivered precisely because the two agencies are culturally and operationally different and therefore have different skills, approaches and capabilities to bring to joint ventures.
>
> *(Burke and Collett 2010: 13)*

Reeves (2013) found that relationships between agencies not only reflect different cultural traditions, but are also shaped by the allocation of statutory responsibilities. In her study of the dynamics of Multi-Agency Risk Assessment Conferences (MARAC), the author found that probation and police representatives tended to take on the role of *expert* because of their *responsible authority* status. The relationship between statutory criminal justice agencies and other agencies that had *a duty to cooperate* was weaker and more fragmented. For some organisations from the voluntary sector, working with serious sexual and violent offenders was not a service priority and thus their involvement in the decision-making process was often irregular and had to be balanced against competing demands for time and resources. This led the author to conclude that "MARACs are not homogenous bodies operating on an egalitarian democratic basis but rather there is a structural inequality evident in the holders and keepers of knowledge, who have power to direct the MARAC" (2013: 53).

Notwithstanding the internecine positions of the various agencies, it can also be argued that rather than positively mobilising communities and reviving community values, the community protection model can itself be viewed as more of "a set of defensive and largely exclusionary reactions to the deep sense of insecurity and uncertainty produced by 'late modernity' and its associated phenomena of globalisation and social fragmentation" (Kemshall and Maguire 2002: 12). Rather than *widening rehabilitation,* this has restricted partnership work to local state agencies, resulting in a closed professional expert system of risk management. These authors further argue that MAPPAs are only inclusionary in the sense of attempting to place individuals in local communities, but do little to help them integrate within those communities or engage with community life (2002: 23). Canton, likewise, has questioned the ethical basis of these schemes and how they can potentially exacerbate the level of social exclusion experienced by individual offenders:

> Access to rehabilitative services is a component of these schemes. But social inclusion ought to mean that people have access to the services as a right as citizens or members of the community; it should not be contingent on their inclusion in a crime reduction project. Nor, while effective inter-agency work is to be welcomed, should all agencies be encouraged to see their role as in the service of crime reduction. Unintended consequences must also be considered; perhaps some interventions can make things worse; for instance by aggravating social exclusion through stigmatisation, disrupting spontaneous developments towards desistance or by undermining legitimacy with service users' ... Schemes of this type should also have regard to proportionality and to the rights of offenders.
>
> *(2011: 142)*

Integrated Offender Management (IOM) schemes emerged from existing arrangements and built upon other initiatives such as the Prolific and other Priority Offenders (PPO) programme and the Drug Intervention Programme (DIP). Unlike the Intensive Alternative to Custody (AIC) pilots which were created at the same time and had a specific purpose of attempting to divert offenders from short-term custodial sentences, IOM has been less clearly defined and according to Wong it is unclear as to whether such schemes are, firstly, a strategic process for bringing together agencies to tackle offenders in their localities, secondly, an extension of existing offender management processes, or thirdly, a way of bringing more coherence to the management of repeat offenders. Or indeed, perhaps all three (2013a: 62)?

There are approximately 67 IOM schemes across England and Wales for whom strategic responsibility is shared between the 322 community safety partnerships and 41 Local Criminal Justice Boards (Wong 2013a). According to one study, the role of the voluntary sector within the IOM arrangements produced a somewhat mixed picture of voluntary sector efficacy and variations across the schemes, particularly amongst small voluntary organisations who had a limited track record in working with offenders (Wong *et al.* 2012). Although measuring the impact and financial benefits of these schemes has been a challenge for government, a recent evaluation by Sheffield Hallam University of the Sussex IOM scheme, found that for each £1 spent, there is a potential benefit to society of £1.78 from the estimated reduction in crime by those on the scheme (2012).

These arrangements rely on a level of trust and cooperation involving pooled resources and shared information at the local level which can take considerable time to develop and could well be undermined by the introduction of competition into the system as the Coalition's *Transforming Rehabilitation* envisages. The safeguarding and sharing of personal information presents a particular challenge in an environment where personal information about individual offender identities, if lost or leaked, could result in major public safety incidents. Cultures conducive to managing collaborative partnerships and constructive networks, maintaining control and confidentiality over sensitive information and protecting staff are often rooted more in the identification of shared values, mutual trust and the respect of common principles and diverse contributions than in competitive market mentalities or managerial performance comparison (Crawford 2001: 71). There is a danger that opening up the criminal justice market will in reality lead to "competition at the expense of partnership" (Fletcher 2005) as providers jostle for position in this new correctional landscape. A preoccupation with securing a market share of the rehabilitative endeavour could undermine professional relationships as quasi-markets and competition produces new sites of inter-agency conflict, discourages interdependence and leaves inter-organisational networks unstable. As such, competition can serve to undermine both reciprocity and trust. Mills *et al.*, for example, found that as voluntary sector providers were encouraged to take on some of the responsibilities traditionally associated with probation, the threat posed by commissioning had strained relationships and partnership working on the ground (2012).

It is ironic that the proposals contained within *Transforming Rehabilitation* will almost inevitably weaken probation's links with the local community and replace political accountability at the local level with systems of contractual accountability located at regional or national level. *The arrangements for statutory partnerships with Transforming Rehabilitation* (Ministry of Justice 2013) envisages key public protection mechanisms such as MAPPA and the Victim Contact Scheme remaining within the National Probation Service. In the case of the former, the newly formed CRCs will not be *responsible authorities* but will have *a duty to cooperate*. This could clearly lead to a confused governance model resulting in conflicts of interest in terms of providers' accountability to the courts and to the national or regional purchaser. The success of schemes such as the Manchester Intensive Alternative to Custody (IAC) project would appear to be based on the fact that they are locally designed and owned whilst working within national parameters (Taylor *et al.* 2014). A key element of this has been their ability to successfully market their schemes to the local courts. In this way the scheme avoided the problems associated with loss of accountability and loss of the *local* identified above. Nevertheless, the inevitable fragmentation that will be created by the *Transforming Rehabilitation* initiative will generate an even greater demand for coordination to draw together fragmented services in these new *tangled webs* (Crawford 2001: 61).

Although police and crime commissioners who were appointed in November 2012 have a key role in commissioning some services at the local level, commissioning of offender-management services will be retained centrally by NOMS. This clearly has the potential for making it increasingly difficult for commissioners of services to ascertain effectiveness in this increasingly complex and fragmented landscape. In essence, the government has devolved responsibility for identifying what works to the individual providers and the Ministry of Justice has recently written up a *Justice Data Lab* pilot which gives organisations the opportunity to measure how effective their work is at reducing re-offending. To use the service, organisations provide details of the individuals with whom they have worked and information about the services they provide. The Lab then supplies aggregate one-year proven re-offending rates for that group with a matched control group of similar offenders. Despite some methodological controversy – statistics are based on administrative datasets provided by the organisation and so may not contain all the information required for *matching* purposes – during the initial six months covered by the scheme, only just over a third (13 out of 36) of the reports provided sufficient evidence of impact (or lack of) on re-offending (Webster 2013). This would seem to add weight to Wong's assertion that "innovation driven by practice entrepreneurship does not lend itself to the experimental paradigm for generating evidence of effectiveness" (2013). Furthermore, as Faulkner and Burnett argue, the effectiveness of such schemes should be judged not on reductions in re-offending alone but should also include *softer* measures in terms of "social integration or changes in offenders or their families' attitudes or outlook ..." (2012: 81).

From *respect* to the *Big Society*

Whilst our analysis, so far, has focused largely on the relationship between the state, the voluntary sector and the market, there is another sphere of activity that is represented by what is often referred to as *civil society*. We understand this term to mean more than the formal relationships between the state, service providers and consumers – it is a nuanced and less clearly defined notion of how people live together and conduct their daily lives – "It defines all those extensions of the scope of human action beyond the private that lack recourse to the primary contemporary means of exercising power: the state and the firm" (Crouch 2011: 153). David Faulkner and Ros Burnett reflect that successive governments, regardless of their political persuasion, have been attracted to strengthening civil society for a variety of reasons:

> ... a general view that a strong civil society is a mark of a strong and healthy society more generally; a belief that it will exercise social control and

> encourage compliant behaviour; a hope that civil society will work in support of government and help it achieve its political objectives; or an attempt to save public expenditure.
>
> *(2012: 73)*

The Labour government's *Civil Renewal Strategy* advanced civil society as a means of "regenerating communities, fighting social exclusion and bringing forth a new kind of social citizenship" (Hodgson 2004: 139). Its urgency and focus reflected the belief that Thatcherism had created a permanent *underclass* of people, jobless and often homeless, cut off from mainstream society; a belief that was informed the party's social policy when it came to power in 1997. A Social Exclusion Unit (SEU) was set up within weeks of New Labour taking office and although it was initially located in the Cabinet Office and then under the control of the Deputy Prime Minister, it was cross-departmental. To this end, in order to *Bring Britain Together* (Blair, 1997), the government envisaged a more coherent, integrated way, across departmental boundaries and with all the agencies – public, private and voluntary – to tackle social exclusion and promote social capital. Subsequent legislation and policy documents such as the *Framework for Neighbourhood Renewal* (Social Exclusion Unit 2000) emphasised the role of social capital and community processes in reducing crime. Voluntary activity was seen as the means through which "skills are acquired and developed, personal self-confidence enhanced and training for work provided" (Hodgson 2004: 139) and for citizens this was to be achieved through involvement in volunteering, mentoring and the governance of community sentences. Directed at offenders, it involved the imposition of unpaid and reparative work and involvement in restorative justice schemes. In what can be seen as an extension of the idea of the *active citizen* which was introduced under previous Conservative administrations, it was hoped that through these mechanisms, communities would take responsibility for offenders and "the support required for an offender to make the leap from offender to law-abiding citizen" (Home Office 2005: 6).

The importance of *community* took a different turn during the spring and early summer of 2001 when a number of disturbances broke out in towns and cities in England involving significant numbers of people from different cultural backgrounds. Lack of *community cohesion* rapidly became not just an explanation for the disturbances but the dominant principle for government's approach to issues surrounding multiculturalism, racial equality, integration and national identity (Home Office 2005). The government set up a *Ministerial Group on Public Order and Community Cohesion* (Denham 2001) to examine and consider how national policies might be used to promote better community cohesion, based upon shared values and a celebration of diversity. At the same time, a *Review Team*, led by Ted Cantle, was established to seek the views of citizens, in particular residents and community leaders in affected towns.

The subsequent report produced by the Review Team presented the disturbances as symptomatic of deeper-lying problems within *multicultural* towns and cities (Cantle 2001). It argued that policies aimed at improving race relations had encouraged separate *ethnic* identities, focussing on notions of *equality* for different ethnic/religious groups whilst profoundly neglecting the need to promote respect and *good relations* between those different groups.

> Whilst the physical segregation of housing estates and inner city areas came as no surprise, the team was particularly struck by the depth of polarisation of our towns and cities. The extent to which these physical divisions were compounded by so many other aspects of our daily lives, was very evident. Separate educational arrangements, community and voluntary bodies, employment, places of worship, language, social and cultural networks, means that many communities operate on the basis of a series of parallel lives. These lives often do not seem to touch at any point, let al.one overlap and promote any meaningful interchanges.
>
> *(Cantle 2001: 9)*

According to John Lea, the riots were understood not "as a sign of social and economic marginalisation but rather as *self-exclusion* ultimately due to the pathology and lack of motivation of the poor white and Asian communities themselves" (2011). Rather than acknowledging the detrimental impact of global competition in the textile industries on which many of these communities relied for employment, "the terminology of job creation was used but it had metamorphosed from Keynesianism to neoliberal free market inspired injunctions to poor communities to stop fighting each other and adopt the right attitudes and motivations so as to attract footloose global investment into these once thriving but now economic backwaters" (Lea 2011). One measure proposed in the subsequent report of the Review Team was that a commitment to community cohesion should be a precondition of support from central government and other agencies (Cantle 2001: 21). This was advanced through measures such as advising local authorities and public bodies as to how they should promote and measure *Community Cohesion* (Local Government Association 2002). In addition, under the 2006 Education and Inspections Act, schools were called upon to *promote cohesion*. Local authorities were expected to prepare a *Community Plan* to advance community cohesion. However as Thomas points out, despite the emphasis on community cohesion, there has been very little empirical evidence of how this is understood and practised by people at the grassroots of social policy operation (undated). Other critics have been focussing on the apparent sidelining of structural racism as an explanation (Kundnani 2001), the downplaying of the role of far-right racist groups in causing the riots (Bagguley and Hussian 2003) and the questionable notion of *segregation* itself (Kalra 2002, Robinson 2005). Nevertheless, according to Robinson the emergence of the community cohesion framework was politically expedient for New Labour as it diverted attention "away from more intractable problems ... and directed towards virgin political territory that the government could colonise with its own priorities and preoccupations" (2008, cited in Bannister and O'Sullivan 2013: 92).

Influenced by the communitarian ideas of Amitai Etzioni (1955) and the notion that the decline in community life had led to a corresponding decline in public morality, the cooperation of local communities was also increasingly viewed in policy terms as being a vital ingredient in tackling crime and antisocial behaviour. In fact, soon after coming into power, Labour steered its crime, antisocial behaviour and crime reduction intentions through parliament and on 31 July 1998, its landmark Crime and Disorder Act received royal ascent. Section five required local authorities and local police services to act as *responsible authorities* for the formulation and implementation of crime reduction strategies. Both also had a duty to engage with probation, who were given a *responsibility to cooperate, as were* other local agencies. Ultimately, before New Labour lost power, their Policing and Crime Act 2009 required local authorities to give consideration to reduce re-offending in the exercise of all their duties and probation was made a *responsible authority* of the rebadged community safety partnerships (CSPs), discussed in more detail in Chapter Three. Crime reduction ultimately morphed into a strategy for reducing re-offending although New Labour did develop a *National Community Safety Plan* 2008–2011, essentially a *top-down* attempt to align nationally prescribed indicators with local issues (Faulkner and Burnett 2012: 71).

New Labour persevered with its notions of civil renewal, respect, engagement and partnership throughout its time in power. In *Active Citizens, Strong Communities: Progressing Civil Renewal*, the Home Secretary stated that "Justice is not something far removed from ordinary people, the individuals and communities affected by crime" (Home Office 2003: 40). Building public confidence and crime prevention needed to be undertaken from the ground up, which required full engagement at the local level. This involved the creation of a myriad set of arrangements involving CDRPs, Local Criminal Justice Boards, Local Strategic Partnerships (LSPs) and Local Authority Area Agreements (LAAs) that relied on coordinated local action and partnership (see Chapter Three for details of criminal justice partnership arrangements).

The moral crusade behind communitarianism as a building block to construct a civil society resulted in conflict with the managerialist focus on administrative efficiencies and cost effectiveness which were at the heart of the New Labour agenda. It is worth remembering that within the *velvet glove* of localism and partnership, there was always an iron fist of comprehensive target regimes linked to financial incentives, rewards and centrally driven initiatives. Crawford, for example, argues that the managerialist reforms actively pursued by New Labour perversely served to increase the isolation and introspection of many criminal justice agencies and other public sector organisations drawn into the web of partnership work (2001). Managerialist reforms by definition tend to focus upon efficiency, economy and value for money, on hierarchical control and on clear distribution of authority and responsibility and as such were primarily concerned with internal reorganisation rather than the more complex process of negotiating shared purposes, particularly where there was no hierarchy of control. Similarly, a focus on outputs and performance measurement can make agencies concentrate their energies upon their core tasks and activities at the expense of peripheral ones (Crawford 2001, Rumgay 2003 cited in Robinson 2011). In the case of the Probation Service, a preoccupation with responding to the demands of an increasingly performance-led culture that prioritised risk management and enforcement ironically resulted in an insularity that was something of an anathema to effective partnership working at the local level. A surfeit of initiatives and short-term funding of *signature* projects undermined continuity and suffocated creative local solutions to local problems. Rumgay also argued that the emphasis on delivering *What Works* was for the Probation Service at the expense of its traditional concerns with social justice and inclusion and partnership activity that focussed on broader social problems (2004).

The approach by New Labour could also be seen as an attempt to manufacture a particular model of civil society based upon a highly moralistic agenda. Through mechanisms such as contracting and funding streams, centrally-imposed initiatives and performance targets, a form of control emerges "through the setting of norms and the correction of deviations from them" (Crawford, 2001: 63). Similarly Janet Newman has argued that

> ... manufactured civil society can be viewed as a means of controlling what happens within the community and civil society more broadly. Rather than a redistribution of power and influence, what we may be witnessing is the extension of state power via a range of social actors. At the very least, civil society can be said to be caught in the middle of contradictory influences between the centralising and decentralising tendencies of government policy.
> *(2001 cited in Hodgson 2004: 157).*

It has also been observed that "New Labour's enthusiasm for the activated citizen essentially drew on not only social democratic and communitarian conceptions of the citizen but also neo-liberal concerns to "'liberate' the citizen from the state" (Clarke 2005: 448). In New Labour's worldview the ideal citizen was presented as a moralised, choice-making, self-directing subject who was the bearer of responsibilities as well as rights. However, by New Labour's third term in office, the balance had very much shifted toward responsibilities as encapsulated in its *Respect Action Plan* (2006), which sought to advance a model of social democratic citizenship. The new cross-departmental *Respect Task Force* was headed up by Louise Casey, who was renowned for her uncompromising attitude toward law and order issues. Central to this new agenda was the belief that a rampant individualism was undermining civic virtues such as good manners and respect for others and their property. In this way, both the community cohesion and antisocial behaviour policy discourses were "infused with the rhetoric of civility" (Bannister and O'Sullivan 2013: 92). Focussing on the poorest in society and those whose behaviour was seen as problematic in an attempt to encourage them to adopt the values of mainstream society was less of a challenge and therefore more politically expedient than tackling structural factors involving the redistribution of wealth and increasing social mobility (Morgan 2012: 6). This was evident in the perceived *antisocial behaviour* of young people, which during New Labour's three terms of office was reconceptualised from being a *cause* of crime to *the* crime, requiring a punitive response (Gaskell 2008: 224), thereby enabling New Labour to present itself as being on the side of hard pressed communities (Bowen and Donoghue 2013: 11). However, the dominant definition of *community* that is invoked in such discourses is one of homogeneity and shared interests (Kelly *et al.* 2005). In reality, as Crawford notes "Public definitions of disorder and community safety are in reality inconsistent. Different audiences define the same behaviour differently. Furthermore, many of the neighbourhoods with high levels of crime and incivilities are inscribed with a general lack of consensus about such issues" (2001: 69). Moreover, whilst communities can positively promote *social capital* they can also be sites of exclusion. Within this context then, New Labour's approach became somewhat Janus-like in that the *social exclusion* and *respect* agendas covered much of the same territory, albeit from a very different starting point. This was compounded by internal battles over funding which led to claims the vulnerable were losing out to Whitehall *turf wars* (Wheeler 2006).

Faulkner and Burnett contend that ascertaining the success of New Labour social policy is difficult to judge as new initiatives were often introduced without due regard to what had gone before and existing schemes were constantly vulnerable to changing priorities and demands. As a result "The search for 'quick wins', for immediately visible results and short-term political advantage diverted attention from long-term sustainable change" (2012: 72). Ultimately, according to Hutton, New Labour's approach was essentially one of defensiveness in that "It bought into the doctrine that there was no alternative to the existing system, so all it could do was tinker at the margins, do its best to mitigate inequality and invest in public services. It could not challenge the political economy of today's capitalism because it had to remain business friendly at all costs" (2010: 60). Although over its three terms, New Labour increased investment in public services and developed some positive and discrete social policies such as Sure Start, the introduction of a minimum working wage and Health Action Zones, these were not enough to form a durable record of moral reform. As a result, Hutton argues that New Labour in "its technocratic universe of targets clothed in the uninspiring, morally neutral language of helping the many rather than the few while differentiating between the deserving and the undeserving poor created an enormous window of opportunity for the Conservatives to regain power" (2010: 280). New Labour's obsession with delivery of local services *controlled* from the centre gave the political opposition an easy target.

Shifting power and responsibility to local communities was offered as a counterbalance to this top-down approach to policy and micro-management of services.

As a response to this big statism the *Big Society* initiative was introduced by David Cameron in 2009 as a way of engaging individuals to take care of themselves and their neighbourhoods, rather than relying on the state to do it for them. If New Labour had reduced society's ills to a single cause – lack of respect – then the Coalition government led by Cameron put them down to a decline in personal and social responsibility (Atkins 2013). In the Hugo Young Memorial Lecture, David Cameron claimed that the state had failed because it took away from people more and more things that they should and could be doing for themselves, their families and their neighbours (cited in Defty 2014: 14). Alongside this general ideological stance, the increasingly influential right-wing think tank, the Centre for Social Justice, were producing reports that not only highlighted traditional Conservative concerns such as family breakdown and welfare dependency but linked them to concerns about the social impact of issues such as addiction and the rise of personal debt (Defty 2014: 13). The way in which welfare reforms have been developed and delivered in the form of vicious attacks on some of the poorest and most vulnerable through the bedroom tax, fit-to-work assessments and disability-benefits reform seems strangely at odds with the mundane and prosaic notions contained within Cameron's *Big Society*. The Cabinet Office published *Building the Big Society* (2010) in which it cites the five key elements:

1. Giving communities more powers. This includes a commitment to recruit and train up to 5,000 community organisers. It will also give local areas greater say in local planning decisions. Finally, it also includes a commitment to allow local organisations to take over and deliver certain public services.
2. Encouragement for citizens to become involved in their communities. This includes support to engage in volunteering and a national 'Big Society Day'. Young people will have the opportunity to take up a National Citizen Service. There will be initiatives to increase charitable giving and philanthropic activity.
3. Transfer of power from central to local government. This includes providing local government with greater financial autonomy as well as a 'power of competence'. This basically means that local authorities could undertake any lawful activities which promoted and responded to the best interests of local residents. They wouldn't be constrained by only being able to act if there was specific statutory authority to do so.
4. Support for mutuals, co-ops, charities, and social enterprises. These non-profit organisations will be supported and encouraged to take over the running of public services. Public sector workers themselves will be helped to form employee-owned charities and be able to more independently deliver services. New funding for increasing capacity in the voluntary sector will come from dormant bank accounts – a Big Society Bank.

5. Publish government data. This involves giving the public access to government 'data-sets', including information about crime at the local level in order that the police can be held accountable for their delivery (Thomson 2010b: 3).

To facilitate this, the idea of an active but lighthanded state was advanced in order to support community level action (Power 2012), but these ideas also conveniently chimed with traditional Conservative values aiming to reduce public funding and find cheaper alternatives. As Ryan has argued:

> One way of making sense of what is going on here is to interpret this narrative as a non-too subtle attempt by the Coalition to put a *progressive* gloss on a policy that is primarily about driving down costs in an expensive area of public policy at a time when the state is going through one of its periodic attempts to balance the books. The Coalition is encouraged to do this, in spite of its obvious contradictions, because it wants to sell the Big Society as a good in itself, as *progressive*, a bold vision of people empowerment.
>
> *(2012: 23)*

The Localism Act of 2011 introduced provisions for volunteers to take over community assets, while the Police Reform and Social Responsibility Act of the same year replaced police authorities with directly elected Police and Crime Commissioners on a turnout of just 14.9 per cent. Initiatives such as the Manchester *Transforming Justice* initiative have, it could be argued, stimulated greater creativity amongst criminal justice agencies at the local level, through the removal of ring-fenced budgets. However, as Bowen and Donoghue argue, the Coalition's interest in local justice has not been matched by a commitment to community justice (2013). In October 2013, the government announced its decision to close the North Liverpool Community Justice Centre, largely on grounds of cost. This initiative was set up by the previous Labour government and combined the Magistrates and Crown Court, to be presided over by a single judge. Complementary services were located within the court buildings in order to better serve the local community while providing easy access for offenders. Subsequent evaluations suggested that although there had been some improvements in the administration of justice, this was not matched in terms of engagement with the local community (Booth *et al.* 2012).

Some commentators (Kisby 2010, Defty 2014) contend that the *Big Society* draws heavily on notions of *active citizenship,* developed by previous Conservative ministers such as Douglas Hurd and John Patten during the 1980s, not only as a way of compensating for the rolling back of the state under Thatcher, but also as a means of building social capital. In creating its vision of a *Big Society,* government promoted the idea of intermediate institutions as enablers that brought the state and society together, allowing individuals to help themselves (Hutton 2010). This approach reinforced the delivery of public services from the central to the local state and from public bodies to the private and voluntary sectors. Indeed a key component of the Coalition's *Rehabilitation Revolution* was to give these sectors a greater role in the delivery of probation services on the grounds that it would "produce more efficient services with better outcomes for the public" (Dominey 2012). As Kevin Wong notes, the government's approach to the voluntary sector would appear to reinforce three competing narratives about the sectors and the delivery of public services:

> First, that the VCS can deliver services as effectively, if not better than public and private sector agencies. Second, that 'we're only a charity' and therefore the VCS cannot deliver as well as or as effectively as private and public sector agencies, unless assisted to do so, through capacity building initiatives; and third, the 'Heineken effect' i.e. that the VCS can deliver niche services to individuals in ways that neither the public nor private sector can.
>
> *(2013b: 278)*

To some extent this casts the role of the voluntary sector as being *inherently good* and in this respect "If anything the Cameron vision of a Big Society appears to have privileged the VCS in a way that neither the public or private sector could ever hope to experience" (Wong 2013b: 291).

From the *Big Society* to *Big Business*

The *Big Society* initiative can be seen as suffering from the same definitional issues as previous attempts to strengthen civil society in that it is simply aspirational, providing little concrete commitment to social justice or reducing inequality. Hancock *et al.* argue that rather than signalling a reduction in state activity, the *Big Society* has in reality masked "more authoritarian, punitive and harsher interventions into the lives of the poor and those within the benefit system" (2012: 356). From this perspective, it is ultimately divisive as it is used to "define and frame both the broken, irresponsible, welfare dependent society and the big, caring, mutual and self-reliant society to secure its intensification" (Hancock *et al.* 2012: 347). Unprecedented cuts in benefits, the compulsory elements of schemes such as the *Work Programme*, and an increasingly hostile punishment rhetoric within criminal justice have been disproportionately aimed at poor, disadvantaged communities who have felt the brunt of government austerity measures.

Another criticism of the *Big Society* initiative is that it is merely a means of delivering services on the cheap and exploiting volunteers and low paid workers. As Edwards and Hughes contend "the context of austere public finances places an even greater onus on leveraging inward corporate investment to localities with a concomitant increase in the structural power of business to set local policy agendas"(2012: 450). At the same time the voluntary sector is being promoted in government policy and its qualities eulogised, its funds are being cut. In 2012, half of the local authorities in England and Wales made disproportionate cuts in funding to voluntary organisations (Singleton 2013). As a result, larger voluntary sector organisations are required to aggressively bid for smaller contracts, sometimes diverting into new areas of work and thereby displacing smaller local organisations who are "often less familiar with the technicalities of the bidding to meet precise specifications for service delivery, and unable to call upon the same degree of expertise and resources" (Maguire 2012: 487). For example, Clinks, an organisation formed to support the voluntary sector working with offenders has claimed that

> The experience of working within the regional commissioning structure of the National Offender Management Service (NOMS) has been mixed for our part of the Sector, and it has been acknowledged that these arrangements have disadvantaged small local organisations.
>
> *(Thomson 2010a: 7)*

There are also concerns that the larger voluntary sector organisations, which are unrepresentative of the sector, are beginning to *ape* the private sector in taking on the language and practices of the marketplace in an attempt to become more *professionalised* and *managerial* in their approach, chasing ever reducing public funding (Silvestri 2009). This has led to the formation of working alliances between private companies and charitable organisations, as very few of the latter have the capacity to successfully bid on their own for large nationally, or regionally commissioned projects. As Clinks notes, "Notwithstanding the extraordinary growth in the VCS over the past twelve years, it still comprises only 2.4% of the total UK workforce. There will be a big challenge to transfer the delivery of public services to the VCS at the speed and the quantity that is implied in government statements" (Thomson 2010: 7). The size of individual voluntary sector organisations also needs to be placed within this wider picture. It has been the estimated that the annual income of just over 60 per cent of organisations who work with offenders and their families is less than £100 thousand (Gojkovic *et al.* 2011). This problem of being realistically able to engage in the brave new world will be further compounded by the introduction of commissioning mechanism based on *Payment by Results* (PbR), as many of these organisations will be unable to finance a proportion of the delivery costs upfront and underwrite the risk of non-payment if desired outcomes are not achieved. In the Work Programme, the majority of voluntary sector organisations' involvement is on a *sub-contractor* level to the *prime contractor*, in some cases delivering interventions designed and specified by others (see Chapter Five). This may well compromise the relative independence of the sector and make it more difficult for them to adopt a critical stance against the dominant governmental discourse. As more organisations gain access to the policy-making process, they also face difficult decisions in terms of maintaining their independence and autonomy against the opportunity to gain influence.

There is, for us, another fundamental concern about the independence and autonomy of voluntary sector agencies undertaking responsibilities that were previously those of the state alone. In a study into voluntary and community involvement conducted in the Yorkshire and Humberside regions (Sheffield Hallam University 2005), researchers identified tension between the statutory responsibilities of enforcement and compliance for organisations that had developed within a framework of voluntarism and consensual engagement. This example highlights the risk to the culture and values that drive voluntary organisations and make them different, diverse and innovative. If voluntary organisations decide not to jeopardise their unique approach to service delivery, it could signal a struggle to survive and on a wider level lead to "the dystopian vision of a 'penal market' dominated by a small number of powerful private companies and corporate style TSOs (Third Sector Organisations), from which principled and innovative third sector providers have been largely squeezed out" (Maguire 2012).

Is *Big Society* merely a front for replacing state activity with the *Big Market*, as Rod Morgan (2012) warns? For example, the bulk of NOMS' s own outsourcing was absorbed by spending on services supplied by private providers (Corcoran 2011: 38). All the indications are that, rather than promoting the voluntary sector, *Transforming Rehabilitation* is likely to see the voluntary sector subordinated to a small number of multinational private providers. Thus *Big Society* can be viewed as merely a repackaging of the role of the voluntary sector to fill the gaps in communities resulting from a withdrawal of public resources. Liverpool City Council, which had been designated one of the four *Big Society* pilot areas, withdrew its support for the scheme in 2011 claiming that it was unsustainable in the light of savage cuts in public funding. According to Hancock *et al.* this highlights "the gap between what community can achieve as a policy instrument without structural support" (2012: 357). The contradiction at the heart of the Coalition government's approach is that it seeks to reenergise public morality whilst at the same time deregulating the markets and commodifying public goods, ultimately leading to greater economic inequality. In the last twenty years Britain has moved from being one of the most equal societies in Europe to one of the most unequal, largely as a result of tax and benefit changes (Hutton 2010). Public spending cuts have also fallen disproportionately on the most disadvantaged communities. Food banks (the use of which has risen from 41,000 to 500,000 under the Coalition government) have become a poignant symbol of the *Big Society*.

Rather than distancing economic relations from social relations in any meaningful analytical sense and conceiving of civil society almost in opposition to the role of the state, it is much more accurate and compelling to understand strong civil society as constructed from many alliances and interests, existing hand in hand with a strong state. In the *Good Society,* Robin Wilson and Jon Bloomfield encapsulate this view in the following way:

> The richness of 'civil society', therefore – not private wealth, still less its flaunting before a dissatisfied public – is what makes a society 'good'. So in

> the 'good society' it is civil society which is the dominant sphere, not the economy nor the state. On the contrary, the economy must be socially – and environmentally – steered. And the state should not be an oppressive force but should offer support to civil society activity through legislative, administrative and funding frameworks conducive to the production of public goods.
>
> *(2011: 22)*

Big Society proposals emphasised strengthening communities through volunteering, but as Somerville points out, there is little evidence that a community-based policy agenda has delivered active citizenship (2011 cited in Hancock *et al.* 2012), nor has the *Big Society* ideal itself garnered much public support (Defty 2014). Societies like Sweden, which have a much stronger network of third-sector organisations – including social enterprises – than the UK, are characterised by a supportive, not a shrinking state. Crucially, they have strongly regulated and well-funded welfare systems. Volunteering is seen as a duty of citizenship rather than merely unpaid employment or a replacement for a public sector worker. Around half the Swedish population between 16 and 74 years of age are engaged in some form of voluntary activity and, of those, seven out of ten are also members of the organisation concerned (Wilson and Bloomfield 2011: 35). Indeed, one of the main reasons attributed to the *out of the ordinary* fall in the use of imprisonment in Sweden has been the role of the 4,500 lay supervisors (roughly the same number as those imprisoned in that country) drawn from the general public who volunteer to befriend and assist offenders under supervision (James 2013). This suggests that a fundamental cultural shift is required that entails more than experiments with public sector mutuals, sporadic embraces of localism, and the introduction of outcome-based commissioning mechanisms. Notions of a *Big Society* are ultimately meaningless to those who are disenfranchised, marginalised and unable to exercise the levers of choice assumed in a consumerist policy-based framework.

So where does that leave offenders and the rehabilitative endeavour in this discussion of the *Big Society?* Faulkner and Burnett contend that a *good society* rather than a *Big Society* would be a more suitable aspiration for contemporary society. According to the authors, such a society

> … should be founded on a set of social values that sees those who are vulnerable, disadvantaged or troublesome, or who have committed offences or are at risk of committing offences, as members of society and not as excluded from it.
>
> *(2012: 85)*

There is a real danger that rather than encouraging self reliance, the government's approach to public services and welfare may instead unleash further pent-up frustrations for those who continue to find themselves excluded from the mainstream. We turn our attentions to this in the next chapter.

References

Atkins, J. (2013) *Mending "Broken Britain": From the Respect Agenda to the Big Society*, Blogs.lse.ac.uk. London: LSE. (Accessed 6 February 2014).

Bagguley, P. and Hussain, Y. (2003) *The Bradford 'Riot' of 2001: A Preliminary Analysis*, Paper presented to the Ninth Alternative Futures and Popular Protest Conference, Manchester Metropolitan University, 22–24 April 2003.

Bannister, J. and O'Sullivan, A. (2013) Civility, Community Cohesion and Antisocial Behaviour: Policy and Social Harmony, *Journal of Social Policy*, 42(1): 91–110.

Blair, T. (1997) *Bringing Britain together*. www.britishpoliticalspeeches.com (Accessed 8 February 2014).

Booth, L., Altoft, A., Dubourg, M.G. and Mirlees-Black, C. (2012) *North Liverpool Community Justice Centre: Analysis of re-offending rates and efficiency of court processes*, Ministry of Justice Research Series 10/12, July 2012, London: Ministry of Justice.

Bowen, P. and Donoghue, J. (2013) Digging up the grassroots? The impact of marketization and managerialism on local justice, 1997 to 2013. *British Journal of Community Justice*, 11: 9–21. No 2/3/ Winter 2013, Sheffield: Sheffield Hallam University.

Burke, L. and Collett, S. (2010) People are not things: What New Labour has done to probation, *Probation Journal*, 57(3): 232–249.

Cabinet Office (2010) *Building the Big Society*, 18 May, London: Cabinet office.

Cantle, T. (2001) *Community Cohesion: A Report of the Independent Review Team*, London: Home Office.

Canton, R. (2011) *Probation: Working with offenders*, Abingdon, Oxon: Routledge.

Carter, P. (2003) *Managing Offenders, Reducing Crime: A New Approach*, London: Home Office.

Clarke, J. (2005) New Labour's citizens: activated, empowered, responsibilized, abandoned? *Critical Social Policy*, 25(4): 447–463.

Corcoran, M. (2011) Dilemmas of institutionalization in the penal voluntary sector, *Critical Social Policy*, 31(1): 30–52.

Crawford, A. (2001) Joined-up but fragmented: contradiction, ambiguity and ambivalence at the heart of New Labour's 'Third Way' In Matthews, R. and Pitts, J. (2001) *Crime Disorder and Community Safety*, London: Routledge.

Crouch, C. (2011) *The Strange Non-death of Neoliberalism*, Cambridge: Polity Press.

Darke, S. (2011) The enforcement approach to crime prevention, *Critical Social Policy*, 31(3): 410–430.

Defty, A. (2014) Can you tell what it is yet? Public attitudes towards 'the Big Society, *Social Policy and Society,* 13 (1): 13–24. Cambridge: Cambridge University Press.

Denham, J. (2001) *Building Coherent Communities, Report of the Ministerial Group on Public Order and Community Cohesion*, London: Home Office.

Dominey, J. (2012) A mixed market for probation services: Can lessons from the recent past help shape the near future? *Probation Journal*, 59(4): 339–354.

Edwards, A. and Hughes, G. (2012) Public safety regimes: Negotiated orders and political analysis, *Criminology and Criminal Justice*, 12(4): 433–458.

Etzioni, A (1955) *The Spirit of Community*, London: Fontana.

Faulkner, D. and Burnett, R. (2012) *Where Next for Criminal Justice?* Bristol: The Policy Press.

Fitzgibbon, W. (2013) Risk and Privatisation, *British Journal of Community Justice*, 11(2): 87–90.

Fletcher, H. (2005) *NOMS risk exposed, Napo news*, 169: May, London: Napo.

Gaskell, C. (2008) But they just don't respect us: young people's experiences of (dis) respected citizenship and the New Labour Respect Agenda, *Children's Geographies*, 6(3): 223–238.

Gojkovic, D., Mills, A. and Meek, R. (2011) *Scoping the involvement of third sector organisations in the seven resettlement pathways for offenders*, Working Paper 57, Third Sector Research Centre, Southampton: University of Southampton.

Green, S. (2002) Ideology and community – The communitarian hi-jacking of community justice, *British Journal of Community Justice*, 1(2): 49–62.

Hancock, L., Mooney, G. and Neal, S. (2012) Crisis, social policy and the resilience of the concept of community, *Critical Social Policy*, 32(3): 343–364.

Hodgson, L. (2004) Manufactured civil society: Counting the cost, *Critical Social Policy*, 24(2): 139–164.

Home Office (1998) *Joining Forces to Protect the Public: Prisons-Probation, A Consultation Document*, London: Home Office.

Home Office (2005) *Managing Offenders, Reducing Crime: The Role of the Voluntary and Community Sector in the National Offender Management Service*, London: Home Office.

Home Office (2006) *Respect Action Plan*, London: Home Office.

Hutton, W. (2010) *Them and us – Changing Britain: Why we need a fair society*, London: Hachette Digital.

James, I. (2013) Why is Sweden closing its prisons?, *The Guardian*, 1 December 2013. http://www.theguardian.com/society/2013/dec/01/why-sweden-closing-prisons (Accessed 1 December 2013).

Kalra, V.S. (2002) Extended View: Riots, Race and Reports – Denham, Cantle, Oldham and Burnley Inquiries, *Sage Race Relations Abstracts,* 27(4): 20–30.

Kelly, K.D., Caputo, T., and Jamieson, W. (2005) Reconsidering sustainability: Some implications for community-based crime prevention, *Critical Social Policy*, 25(3): 306–324.

Kemshall, H. and Maguire, M. (2002) Community Justice, Risk Management and the Role of Multi-Agency Public Protection Panels, *British Journal of Community Justice*, 1(1): 11–25.

Kisby, B. (2010) The big society: power to the people, *Political Quarterly*, 81(4): 486–491.

Kundnani, A. (2001) From Oldham to Bradford: the violence of the violated in *The Three faces of British Racism*, London: Institute of Race Relations.

Lea, J. (2011) Riots and the crisis of neoliberalism. http://www.bunker8.pwp.blueyonder.co.uk/misc/riots2011.html (Accessed 16 January 2014).

Liddle, A.M., and Gelsthorpe, L., (1994) *Inter-agency crime prevention–organising local delivery*, London: Home Office Crime Prevention Unit.

Local Government Association (2002) *Guidance on Community Cohesion*, London: Local Government Association.

Maguire, M. (2012) Response 1: Big Society, the voluntary sector and marketization of criminal justice, *Criminology and Criminal Justice,* 12(5): 483–494.

Mair, G. and Burke, L. (2012) *Redemption, Rehabilitation and Risk Management*, London: Routledge.

Mawby, R.C. and Worrall, A. (2012) They were very threatening about do-gooding bastards – Probation's changing relationships with the police and prison services in England and Wales, *European Journal of Probation*, Bucharest: University of Bucharest.

Mills, A., Meek, R. and Gojkovic, D. (2012) Partners, guests or competitors – Relationships between criminal justice and third sector staff in prisons, *Probation Journal*, 59(4): 391–405.

Ministry of Justice (2013) *The arrangements for statutory partnerships in Transforming Rehabilitation*. www.justice.gov.uk (Accessed 9 February 2014).

Morgan, R. (2012) Crime and Justice in the 'Big Society', *Criminology and Criminal Justice*, 12(5): 463–481.

Mythen, G., Walklate, S, and Kemshall, H. (2013) Decentralizing risk: The role of the voluntary and community sector in the management of offenders, *Criminology and Criminal Justice*, 13(4): 363–379.

Nash, M. (2008) Exit the 'polibation' officer? De-coupling police and probation, *International Journal of Police Science & Management*, 10(3): 302–312.

Newman, J. (2001) *Modernising Governance: New Labour, Policy and Society*, London: Sage.

Power, A. (2012) *The state has a key role in providing the framework for action and policies to ensure fairness on behalf of all its citizens*, 8 October 2012. http://blogs.lse.ac.uk/politicsandpolicy/archives/27427 (Accessed 9 February 2014).

Reeves, C. (2013) How multi-agency are Multi-Agency Risk Assessment Committees?, *Probation Journal*, 60(1): 40–55.

Robinson, A. (2011) *Foundation for Offender Management: Theory, Law and Policy for Contemporary Practice*, Bristol: The Policy Press.

Robinson, D. (2005) The search for Community Cohesion: key themes and dominant concepts of the public policy agenda, *Urban Studies*, 42(8): 1411–1427.

Robinson, D. (2008) Community cohesion and the politics of communitarianism in Flint, J. and Robinson, D. (eds) *Community Cohesion in Crisis? New Dimensions of Diversity and Difference*, Bristol: Policy Press.

Rumgay, J. (2003) Partnerships in the Probation Service in Chui, W.H. and Nellis, M. (eds) (2003) *Moving Probation Forward: Evidence, Arguments and Practice*, Essex: Pearson Education Limited.

Rumgay, J. (2004) The barking dog? Partnership and effective practice in Mair, G. (ed) (2004) *What Matters in Probation*, Cullompton: Willan Publishing.

Rummery, K. (2006) Partnerships and Collaborative Governance in Welfare: The Citizenship Challenge, *Social Policy and Society*, 5(2): 293–303.

Ryan, M. (2011) Counterblast: Understanding Penal Change: Towards the Big Society? *The Howard Journal of Criminal Justice*, 50(5): 516–520.

Ryan, M. (2012) Delivering pain in the Big Society, *Criminal Justice Matters*, 89(1): 22–23.

Silvestri, A. (2009) *Partners or Prisoners? Voluntary sector independence in the world of commissioning and contestability*, London: Centre for Crime and Justice Studies.

Singleton, R. (2013) Voluntary sector independence 'under direct challenge' *The Guardian*, 22 January 2013. http://www.theguardian.com/voluntary-sector-network/2013/jan/22/voluntary-independence-direct-challenge (Accessed 1 February 2014).

Social Exclusion Unit (2000) *National strategy for Neighbourhood Renewal: A framework for consultation*, London: Cabinet Office.

Somerville, P. (2011) *Understanding Community*, Bristol: Policy Press.

Sheffield Hallam University (2005) *Research carried out by Sheffield University examining the current relationship between correctional services and the voluntary sector in Yorkshire and Humberside*, Sheffield: Sheffield Hallam University.

Sheffield Hallam University (2012) *IOM Sussex Evaluation*, www.sussexcriminaljusticeboard.org.uk (Accessed 1 February 2013).

Taylor, E., Clarke, R. and McArt, D. (2014) The Intensive Alternative to Custody–'Selling' sentences and satisfying judicial concerns, *Probation Journal*, 61(1): 44–59.

Thomas, P. (undated) The 2001 riots and the emergence of 'Community Cohesion'. http://academic.shu.ac.uk/aces/franco-british-riots/attachments/paul%20thomas%20birmingham%20paper%20summary.doc (Accessed 25 March 2014).

Thomson, M. (2010a) *Criminal justice outsourcing: What is the potential role of the Voluntary Community Sector*, London: Clinks.

Thomson, M. (2010b) *The big society: Constraints and potentials*, Clinks.org (Accessed 7 February 2014).

Weaver, B. (2014) Control or change? Developing dialogues between desistance research and public protection practices, *Probation Journal*, 61(1): 8–26.

Webster, R. (2013) *Reoffending rates*. www.russellwebster.com (Accessed 10 February 2014).

Wheeler, B. (2006) *The politics of exclusion*. http://news.bbc.co.uk/1/hi/uk_politics/4746592.stm 24 February 2006. (Accessed 8 February 2014).

Wilson, R. and Bloomfield, J. (2011) *Building the Good Society: A new form of progressive politics*. www.compassonline.org.uk (Accessed 2 February 2014).

Wong, K. (2013a) Integrated offender management: Assessing the impact and benefits – holy grail or fool's errand?, *British Journal of Community Justice*, 11(2/3): 59–83.

Wong, K. (2013b) The Emperor's new clothes: Can Big Society deliver criminal justice? in Cowburn, M., Duggan, M., Robinson, A. and Senior, P. (eds) *Values in Criminology and Community Justice*, Bristol: Policy Press: 277–293.

Wong, K., O'Keefe, C., Meadows, L., Davidson, J., Bird, H., Wilkinson, K. and Senior, P. (2012) *Increasing the voluntary and community sector's involvement in Integrated Offender Management*, London: Home Office.

7

BLAMING REHABILITATION

Citizenship, exclusion and the state[1]

Whatever you may think of the value of IQ tests, it is surely relevant to a conversation about equality that as many as 16 per cent of our species have an IQ below 85, while about 2 per cent have an IQ above 130. The harder you shake the pack, the easier it will be for some cornflakes to get to the top.

And for one reason or another – boardroom greed or, as I am assured, the natural and God-given talent of boardroom inhabitants – the income gap between the top cornflakes and the bottom cornflakes is getting wider than ever. I stress: I don't believe that economic equality is possible; indeed, some measure of inequality is essential for the spirit of envy and keeping up with the Joneses that is, like greed, a valuable spur to economic activity.

It seems to me therefore that though it would be wrong to persecute the rich, and madness to try and stifle wealth creation, and futile to try to stamp out inequality, that we should only tolerate this wealth gap on two conditions: one, that we help those who genuinely cannot compete; and, two, that we provide opportunity for those who can.

(Boris Johnson 2013)

The poor in particular are now subject to a widespread prejudice whereby, it is nastily and quietly said, they must have something wrong with them if they are not able to work their way out of poverty. In the end the rich have to believe there is something wrong with other people in order for them to believe it is fair to leave so much of their money to their own children rather than do something more useful with it.

(Danny Dorling 2013: 28)

Citizens or objects?

In the preceding chapters, we have sought to place our analysis of *delivering rehabilitation* within the context of a neoliberal ideology and its requirements for particular types of economic transactions and mechanisms for the delivery of public services. To begin this chapter, we chose the two quotes above because they demonstrate for us the distance between those who embrace neoliberalism and the economic utility of inequality and those who identify its malign influence on our understanding of those who fail. Indeed, the notion of blame, implicit in these quotes will be a central theme of the chapter. Whilst we are certain that the refinement of Thatcherite economics has been the goal of all political administrations since 1997, we have also been at pains to highlight the positive if faltering approach toward and contradictions within various attempts to overhaul the criminal justice system and offender rehabilitation. As such, the process has not been inexorable and deterministic to the point where social and criminal justice policy has not offered some sense of a humanitarian and positive way forward. Reviewing the period before the election of the Coalition government in 2010, we have argued elsewhere (Burke and Collett 2010) that whilst New Labour and its creation, NOMS, had done the Probation Service few favours, there was some ground for optimism in terms of a growing awareness and commitment to a number of practice and organisational approaches that would support local Probation Services in rehabilitating offenders.

There was also a political commitment under New Labour to a *localism* that might support the freeing up of Probation Areas to work with local partners to deliver effective and imaginative approaches to reducing re-offending and preventing crime. Nevertheless, in overall terms, the past fifteen years represent an unprecedented attack on the Probation Service and its future existence as a public sector agency, publicly funded and accountable to local communities. We have argued in chapters three and four that the strong value base of probation linked to its professional occupational culture has made it a target for political administrations that see such strength as inimical to the market and the prescriptions of *New Public Management*. Furthermore, ideas of partnership, localism and civil society, like motherhood and apple pie, make effective sound bites but reveal the distance between political aspirations for local democratic accountability and the desire for control from the political and bureaucratic centre.

This attack then is a reflection of the ideological drive, begun under New Labour and accelerated under the current Coalition arrangements, to segment and privatise correctional services. Implicit, of course, within this endeavour has been a necessary and mutually reinforcing redefinition of, or at least an intensification of, reactionary notions of the causes of contemporary social problems, including crime. We are particularly concerned about the technocratic and authoritarian way in which offenders have been increasingly depicted and official responses tailored accordingly – a theme caught perfectly in David Ramsbotham's phrase, he used it in a Lords' debate on the future of Probation Services – *People are not things*. He forcefully argued that these words should be "emblazoned on the hearts and desks of every minister and official with any responsibility for probation" (Ramsbotham 2010: 1144).

So who shall we blame?

This heightened authoritarian and technocratic approach to the *responsibilisation* of offenders, which ignores or at best attenuates wider social and economic determinants of crime, is now being applied to groups within our communities who are deemed to behave in antisocial and lawless ways. This in turn begs questions about the efficacy of the state itself, and specifically, the rehabilitative capacity of the Probation Service. This is not a technical debate about reconviction rates per se, rather an attempt to make probation and the local state in part *responsible* for significant social breakdown including, as we will argue, the English riots of 2011. Furthermore, the wider political, social and economic context within which neoliberal hegemony both defines social problems and the state's response to them has been further refined following the Western banking crisis. Whilst the fallout from this crisis has led to a renewed analysis and questioning of the values, dominance and efficacy of neoliberalism from a wide range of perspectives (Dorling 2013, Klein 2007, Standing 2011), there has, nevertheless, been a continuing significant shift toward creating markets for the delivery of social, health and educational services. In turn, this attack on the size and nature of the public sector has been both justified by, and obscured under, the supposed *reasonableness* of the need for austerity.

The post-war consensus, based on Keynesian economic strategic planning and the supportive pillars of the welfare state, assumed the need to provide material and personal support to individuals and families who suffer the consequences of dynamic change within a capitalist economy. Official discourse around the causes of crime has never encompassed a critical understanding of the relationship between class and inequality in defining criminal acts as well as the underlying causes of most crime; nevertheless, to varying degrees over the post-war period, there has been recognition of the poor material circumstances in which offenders find themselves and from which they find it difficult escape. Under New Labour, this material and economic inequality found expression in the analysis of the revolving door of short-term prisoners' lives (SEU 2002), but more recently and particularly under the Coalition and the work of the Centre for Social Justice, the old chestnuts of family breakdown, inadequate parents and welfare dependency have come to be relied upon to obscure a wider analysis of the social, political and economic factors that shape contemporary social problems. So it was, during and in the wake of the August 2011 riots, when analysis was at its weakest, the fear of the mob was tangible and the existence of a *feckless subclass* – a modern day *lumpen proletariat* – was paraded in the media and by the political elites as a social fact. Then shortly after the riots, in December 2011, the Prime Minister announced that a *Troubled Families*

Team led by Louise Casey would be targeting some 120,000 families who were seen to be undermining the fabric of society as well as wasting the resources of the state.

The mindset of neoliberalism, with its belief in the efficacy of the unbridled market and the necessity of inequality as a driver for economic prosperity, brooks no understanding of crime other than as a reflection of the malfunction of individuals and the families to whom they belong and who are unable to contribute to the overall good of society. Identified as blameworthy for significant social breakdown such as the 2011 riots are individuals already confirmed in a criminal and lawless lifestyle. Furthermore, dysfunctional families that comprise the new poor, a group who are unable to exploit the many opportunities laid at their feet for social and economic advancement, are also to blame for the failures of their offspring. We can add to this list, as we will argue, a correctional system that is apparently not fit for purpose.

Beyond social class: Blaming the poor

We turn our attention in this chapter, then, to an analysis of the English riots of 2011 and to a consideration of what meritocracy, social mobility and opportunity mean for the lives of many of the poorest people in our communities. In a world apparently driven remorselessly forward by the innovation, energy and ability of a burgeoning meritocratic majority, some discussion of social class is required as a context for understanding both the rehabilitative endeavour of probation and the behaviour of those who offend. We are not attempting to offer a political or economic analysis of class, or indeed, to theorise it in the context of probation work (see Walker and Beaumont 1981 and 1985, McWilliams 1987). Rather, our consideration is of class as a contemporary social phenomenon and the implications of its apparent redefinition in sub-cultural terms for the policy and practice of rehabilitation.

Within the bureaucratic context of probation, social class has proved to be a difficult concept to articulate and official discourse has been framed in terms of subtexts of, for example, vulnerability, disadvantage, marginalisation, exclusion and poverty. Absent from the conversation is any attempt at anchoring these social and economic features in the overarching collective experience of local communities. The notion of *inequality* is almost completely absent from official discourse as it has become more and more difficult to acknowledge the cultural strengths and diversity of working-class life, as well as the problems and challenges faced by ordinary individuals and families. Paradoxically and more insidious though, is a more recent phenomenon – the *disappearance or invisibility* of social class itself. This is the result, so the argument goes, of a prolonged period of meritocratic access to the opportunities for social, educational and economic advancement and success.

In his book, *Chavs: The Demonization of the Working Class* (2011), Owen Jones argues that the working class is increasingly understood in terms of ethnicity rather than social and economic difference and subsequently caricatured as feckless, feral, bigoted, racist and undeserving.

> By defining the white working class in terms of ethnicity rather than social class, liberal chav-haters ascribe their problems to cultural rather than economic factors. It is the way they live that is the problem, not the unjust way society is structured. If white working-class people are oppressed it is the result of their own fecklessness. While a liberal chav-hater will accept that massive discrimination against minority groups explains issues like unemployment and poverty and even violence, they do not believe white working-class people have such excuses.
>
> *(2011: 16–17)*

Jones argues that the attack on working-class institutions, organisations and communities initiated by the Thatcher government, an assault that has continued under subsequent administrations has effectively led to the apparent disappearance of class. Likewise, Polly Toynbee, writing in *The Guardian*, points to the invisibility of class across a wide spectrum.

> ... Working-class people have completely ceased to exist as far as the media, popular culture and politicians are concerned ... all that exists are nice middle-class people who own their own home, who the Daily Mail like. Then there are very bad people. You don't get much popular imagery of ordinary people of a neutral, let alone a positive kind.
>
> *(quoted in Jones 2011: 28–9)*

This disappearance of class serves a particular purpose and Jones's critical argument is that without an understanding of class differences, the supposed development of a modern meritocratic society espousing equality of opportunity simply blames those who do not avail themselves of the abundant opportunities available. Chavs, the residual working class, the underclass, the poor – however they may be described – increasingly attract little empathy or understanding within mainstream society. As another social commentator, Suzanne Moore puts it in terms of poverty:

> Poverty is not a sign of collective failure, but individual immorality. The psychic coup of the neo-liberal thinking is just this: instead of being disgusted by poverty, we are disgusted by poor people themselves. This disgust is a growth industry. We lay this moral bankruptcy at the feet of the poor as we tell ourselves we are better than that.
>
> *(Moore 2012a: 5)*

The historian, David Starkey's contribution to a Newsnight debate of 13 August 2011 on the riots provides ample testimony to this. He described the riots as completely superficial – *it's shopping with violence* – but his main point was that they signified a profound cultural change in society. Facing Owen Jones in the studio he said,

> What has happened is that the substantial section of the chavs that you wrote about have become black. The whites have become black. A particular sort of violent, destructive, nihilistic gangster culture has become the fashion and black and white, boy and girl operate in this language together, which is wholly false, which is this Jamaican patois that has intruded in England. This is why so many of us have this sense of literally a foreign country.
>
> *(Starkey 2011)*

Showing little understanding of Jones's position about class, he continued to argue that culture, rather than skin colour, explained the rioting and toward the end of the debate, whilst he accepted that rioters were often drawn from the ranks of the poor and marginalised, he continued to maintain that a key problem was that minority culture militates against educational success. Clearly, so exercised by his dislike of the poor, he couldn't see the irony of his position – providing evidence for Jones's assertions about the description of the white working class in terms of ethnicity rather than their social and economic status. Additionally, Starkey weaves within his overall argument the notion that people like him have become strangers in their own land. This judgement of foreignness, as the late Geoff Pearson reflected "is very much part of the dead-end discourse against troublesome youth" (2012: 61).

The 2011 riots

Such notions of class as cultural separation from the mainstream of society rather than economic exclusion and inequality are important in neoliberal thinking because they locate blame for and understanding of social problems within the individual, their family and their communities rather than in the structures of disadvantage within the economy and its supporting institutions. These notions were eagerly evoked in the response to the occurrences over a five-day period in August 2011, collectively referred to as *the riots,* when local people lost their businesses and livelihoods and five people lost their lives. We do not underestimate the carnage, but our interest in exploring descriptions of and explanations for the riots stems from a desire to link notions of class and inequality and specifically perceptions of *the working class* with neoliberal approaches to dealing with social problems, crime and re-offending.

The August 2011 riots were and continue to be referred to by the media, politicians and social commentators as the *worst disturbances of a generation.* Arguably, however, the public has found explanations and understanding for the behaviour and motivation of the rioters more difficult to fathom than for previous disturbances over the past 30 years. As Lea and Hallsworth have commented:

> if previous riots had a specific target or grievance – stop and search, competition for jobs, last summer's riots were a diffuse and generalised rage of a dispossessed population angry at a system that has failed them but with no vision of an alternative. This is why they are more serious than any that have gone before.
>
> *(2012: 31)*

Unfortunately, the seriousness of these riots and any analysis of what they might reflect on a broader level was quickly abandoned in terms of the immediate management and manipulation of public opinion. This, for example, was the Prime Minister's first response:

> For me, the root cause of this mindless selfishness is the same thing I have spoken about for years. It is a complete lack of responsibility in parts of our society, people allowed to feel the world owes them something that their rights outweigh their responsibilities and their actions do not have consequences. Well, they do have consequences. We need to have a clearer code of standards and values that we expect people to live by and stronger penalties if they cross the line. Restoring a stronger sense of responsibility across our society in every town, in every street, in every estate is something I am determined to do.
>
> *(Quoted in New Statesman 2011)*

Meanwhile the Home Secretary, Theresa May, described the rioters as an unruly mob who were *thieving, pure and simple.* Writing in the *Mail on Sunday*, May said the riots were not about "protest, unemployment or cuts. They weren't about the future, about tomorrow and a person's place in the world. They were about today, about now. They were about instant gratification" (quoted in *The Guardian* 2011a). Amongst the right-wing commentators, Melanie Phillips was clear about the causes. In an attack on Britain's liberal intelligentsia, she stated:

> What has been fuelling all this is not poverty, as has been so predictably claimed, but moral collapse ... There has been much bewildered talk about 'feral' children, and desperate calls upon their parents to keep them in at night and to ask them about any stolen goods they are bringing home. As if there were responsible parents in such homes! We are not merely up against feral children, but feral parents. Of course these parents know their children are out on the streets. Of course they see them staggering back with whatever they have looted. But they are too drunk or drugged or otherwise out of it.
>
> *(2011)*

These early utterances didn't seem to entirely convince everybody and our sense of the public mood from listening to interviews of local residents caught up in the riots was that however abhorrent the actions of the rioters were, blaming mothers or absent fathers or children themselves didn't wash. The film, *Riot From Wrong*, produced by a group of young people from across London both during and in the aftermath of the riots, gives a fascinating account of the action from both participants and victims. Their accounts contradict many of the misrepresentations generated from national and local media (Fully Focussed 2013). Likewise David Lammy, the local Tottenham MP who grew up in the riot area, whilst condemning the actions of the rioters nevertheless warned that there was a grave danger that language that uses words like *underclass* "perpetuates the problem that it refers to, ghettoising a group of people by ignoring the relationship between them and the rest" (2011: 57).

In the wake of the riots, two pieces of work were set in motion which yielded some very interesting evidence. Probably the best known and most widely-discussed evidence about the riots has emanated from the research initiated by *The Guardian* newspaper in conjunction with the London School of Economics (*The Guardian*/LSE 2011). Whilst *The Guardian*/LSE review was right to point out that "there was to be no Scarman-style inquiry into the causes" (2011: 1), the riots have, in fact, generated a significant number of reviews. Some of these examined very specific aspects of the riots (House of Commons Home Affairs Committee 2011; HM Inspectorate of Constabulary 2011) and others have been locally commissioned in areas affected by riots (for example, Ealing Council Scrutiny Panel and the Tottenham Community Panel and Tottenham Citizens Inquiry). A number of these local reports eventually fed into the work of the Riots, Communities and Victims Panel (RCVP 2012). This was the panel, chaired by Darra Singh and established by the Prime Minister, Deputy Prime Minister and the leader of the opposition, to "investigate the causes of the riots and to consider what more could be done to build greater social and economic resilience in communities" (RCVP 2012: 3).

Both *The Guardian*/LSE and the RCVP reports offer an illuminating focus on the actual riots, while offering useful profiles of those actively engaged on the streets of their local communities. Both reports accepted that there was significant variation in the exact nature of rioting across the specific locations. Following the shooting of Mark Duggan by a police officer on Thursday, 4 August in Tottenham Hale, a peaceful protest was organised, but later during the evening violence broke out. By the Sunday the riots had spread to twelve areas within London and by the time the riots petered out, some sixty-six areas across the country had experienced rioting. Interestingly, according to the RCVP report, local public services in many areas felt that disturbances would have spread if the riots had continued for much longer (2012: 22), and few ruled out the prospect of future riots (2012: 23). As one commentator put it: "The most surprising thing about this summer's riots was the surprise that greeted them" (Jefferson 2011: 8). The RCVP report estimated that somewhere between 13,000 and 15,000 people were actively involved in the riots which cost the lives of five people and probably cost the country some half a billion pounds (2012: 16). This level of involvement was supported by *The Guardian*/LSE research, which estimated that some 2,000 people were arrested for riot-related offending (2011: 1).

Whilst the RCVP report can be criticised for its perpetuation of notions of the *deserving* and *undeserving* poor (see Bridges 2012) and its prescriptions regarding *character* and *resilience* (Fitzgibbon *et al.* 2013: 454), it nevertheless offered some uneasy messages for the Prime Minister and Home Secretary about deprivation, wealth inequality, branding and corporate social responsibility and the failure of punishment alone. In terms of a basic profile of the rioters, the report's findings can be summarised as follows:

- The age profile was, as would be expected, predominantly young people. Some 26 per cent were 10–17 years old and a further 47 per cent were between 18 and 24 years old.
- Of those 10- to 17-year-olds brought before the courts, compared with the general population, they were four times more likely to be living in poverty, three times more likely to have special educational needs and four times more likely to be persistently absent from school.

The analysis, in part, relied on relating those individuals who had been arrested and appeared before the courts to their place of residence and indices of multiple deprivation. Consequently, the report was able to state the following:

> There appears to be a link between deprivation and rioting. Our unique analysis shows that 70 per cent of those brought before the courts were living in the 30 per cent most deprived post codes in the country. Although many deprived areas did not riot, of the 66 areas that experienced riots, 30 were in the top 25 per cent most deprived areas in England.
>
> *(RCVP 2012: 18)*

Reflecting a different database of information on the rioters, the conclusion of *The Guardian*/LSE research was similar in that it estimated that some 59 per cent of rioters came from the most deprived 20 per cent of areas in the United Kingdom (2011: 14). As Tim Newburn, who led *The Guardian*/LSE research later reflected – all the available evidence from three different government departments, research and government reviews is consistent – "The picture painted by all of them makes it quite clear that those involved in the riots came disproportionately from our poorest urban communities and, to use the justice secretary's phrase, felt themselves to be 'cut-off from the mainstream'" (2012: 334).

Race and police activity were also identified as important background factors to the riots. Stop and search was cited as a major source of discontent particularly by young black men living in London (RCVP 2012: 24). *The Guardian*/LSE research reported that only 7 per cent of rioters felt that the police did a good or excellent job compared with 56 per cent of the population, according to the latest British crime survey figures (2011: 20). The report went on to summarise the highly-negative attitude to the police:

> Nowhere was the singling out of black people more apparent in the minds of rioters than when the police use stop and search. Overall 73% of the people interviewed in the study had been stopped and searched at least once in the past year. In our research, the frequent complaint of a sense of harassment … was made in every city the research took place and by interviewees from different racial groups and ages.
>
> *(2011:19)*

The official review of recorded crimes and arrests resulting from the riots showed that just over three-quarters (78 per cent) of rioters had a previous caution or conviction, including a significant proportion (41 per cent) with more than five previous convictions. However, while those taking part in the disorder were much more likely than the general population to have previous convictions, they had slightly less extensive criminal histories than the population of matched offenders sentenced for offences in 2010–2011 (Ministry of Justice 2012: 16). Whilst the nature and accuracy of these official statistics can be challenged in that they reflect the outcome of very specific approaches of the respective police services to the outbreak of localised rioting, it is nevertheless the case that the sentencing of those who pleaded or were found guilty before the courts was draconian. For those sentenced in the magistrates' court, the rate of immediate imprisonment, at 36 per cent, was three times as high as for offenders sentenced for similar offences in England and Wales in 2010, and in terms of sentence length across all courts,

> Of those sentenced, 1405 (66 per cent) have been sentenced to immediate custody with an average custodial sentence length (ACSL) of 17.1 months. This compares to an ACSL of 3.7 months for those convicted at magistrates' courts, but sentenced at any court for similar offences in England and Wales in 2010.
>
> *(Ministry of Justice 2012: 4)*

The same source was also able to report the ethnic makeup of those appearing before the courts as 35 per cent white, 13 per cent not stated and the remaining 52 per cent from a minority ethnic background. One in ten of those brought before the courts was female (Ministry of Justice 2012: 6).

Beyond the basics: Searching for explanations

About 50 per cent of *The Guardian*/LSE *Reading the Riots* interviewees were unemployed, and the overwhelming tenor of their views reflected a sense of marginalisation, invisibility, exclusion from work and training, poverty of lifestyle, with the term *justice* cropping up regularly in the course of interviews. The RCVP report also acknowledged that it wasn't always the *usual suspects* that rioted and opportunism played a part – a third of under-18s had no previous convictions – the authors added that

> the fact that many people abused society's moral and legal codes when the opportunity arose paints a disturbing picture. The Panel was disturbed by the feelings expressed by some rioters that they had no hope and nothing to lose.
>
> *(2012: 24)*

It is difficult to summarise, perhaps other than in Tottenham, exactly why the riots happened when they did and in the particular locations they did. Nevertheless, the general context, as Tim Newburn has reflected (2012) was one of poor, unemployed young men and women living in some of the poorest parts of Britain; not only are they and their families poor, but they tend to live in the poorest parts of those poor local communities. They consider themselves to have been harassed by officialdom, with race an issue never far below the surface in terms of their perceived treatment by the police. These characteristics have been identified from previous analyses of the inner-city riots of the 1980s (see Waddington and King 2009). Additionally, individuals did not consider poor parenting to have been a factor in their engagement in rioting (Guardian 2011b: 9) and gangs, despite the panic whipped up by the media, were not instrumental in the organisation of the disorder. *The Guardian*/LSE report quoted the view of a 22-year-old unemployed man, who was present at the Manchester and Salford riots as indicative of a more widely-held attitude.

> I became involved in Salford because it was a chance to tell the police, tell the government and tell everyone for that matter that we get fucking hacked off around here and we won't stand for it.
>
> *(2011: 20)*

Some academics have argued that the participants in the 2011 riots, unlike previous disturbances, were unable to articulate any specific reasons for their actions beyond the desire to loot. Treadwell *et al.*, for example, argue that the forces of neoliberalism have disintegrated modernity's solidarity and consequently, "... subjects are forced to stew over the bleak reality of their material conditions and their durable but objectless sense of exploitation, irrelevance and anxiety in isolation. Unable to divest themselves of torment and nagging doubt, perpetually marginalised youth populations have become moody and vaguely 'pissed off' without ever fully understanding why" (2013: 3). In fact, the authors argue that these young people have nowhere to take their anger and resentment but to the shops. They are not convinced by the initial empirical accounts of rioters' motivations that centralise dissatisfaction with unequal opportunities, the erosion of welfare or antagonism toward the police, and so go on to argue:

> Very little outrage seemed to be articulated and aimed at contemporary Britain's widening social inequality and injustice, or the systematic degradation of democracy and the anti-social behaviour of our economic elites. Instead, the rioters appeared not to oppose, but to be animated by the ruling ideology: grab what you can, look out for 'number one' and transform the self into a winner in advanced capitalism's interminable competition over the ability to acquire and display symbolically charged consumer goods. In keeping with the times, the rioters were energetic pragmatists and opportunists rather that idealists, and possessed no discernable political orientation.
>
> *(2013: 14)*

This analysis seems to reinvent Marcuse's *One Dimensional Man* (1964) for the post-modern consumerist age, but whilst there may not be the motivational clarity behind the actions of the 2011 rioters, one-size-fits-all explanations do not necessarily work. Platts-Fowler argues that the empirical evidence available from *The Guardian*/LSE database suggests that looting was not as prevalent as many accounts suggest (2013). Furthermore, drawing on the work of Mac Ginty, she cautions that whilst looting is a term "used by the powerful, usually to imply acts of criminal acquisition motivated by greed" (2013: 22), the term itself "conflates a wide range of activities that can differ greatly in terms of organisation, scale and the object of looting" (2013: 23). Her position is that

> There is evidence that some people took part in the 2011 disturbances for personal and material gain. However, the number of riot events that did not involve looting directly undermines the argument that criminal acquisition was the primary driver of unrest. Capitalist and consumerist ideologies undoubtedly influence many aspects of our behaviour, but clearly other factors were at play.
>
> *(2013: 28)*

In fact, according to the Home Office's own overview of recorded crimes and arrests resulting from the riots, it was only in the London Metropolitan Area where acquisitive crime accounted for more than half of all the recorded crimes. Nationally, acquisitive crime represented 50 per cent of all crime with criminal damage being the second largest category at 36 per cent (Home Office 2011: 13).

Other more human and idiosyncratic factors are movingly captured by Rebecca Clarke's portrayal of probation clients caught up in the riots. Her case studies from

Greater Manchester describe individuals already existing on the margins of society who were dragged into the action because the looting and criminal damage occurred within the social and physical spaces occupied on a daily basis by these individuals. In particular, the case of Lucy and "her struggle with daily life on the margins of society, drinking on the streets and coping with a history of abuse, makes the riots a somewhat unremarkable event. For Lucy the riots came and went, and her circumstances generally remain unchanged" (Clarke 2012: 298). As Clarke herself reflects, the history and circumstances of Lucy will be well known to any probation practitioner who has worked with petty offenders who are regularly spun through the revolving door of inadequate social provision and imprisonment. For Lucy, the price of handling a few cigarettes and bottles of spirits was a remand in custody followed by a suspended prison sentence of forty weeks, which unsurprisingly was activated following further petty offending (2012: 292).

Blaming families

Contemplating the causes of the riots is important and it is almost certainly true that explanations that do not acknowledge a process "from protest to provocation to plunder" (Briggs 2012b: 37) will be lacking in some vital ingredients. However, whilst the outcomes of theorising or explaining the riots will undoubtedly remain tentative and subject to further conjecture, we remain concerned that the general contexts – social, economic, personal, criminal – are given adequate expression in terms of the realities of the lives of offenders and their families. Many of the rioters were well known to probation and as the vignette of Lucy so clearly demonstrates, individuals caught up in the riots cannot be simply defined by their actions during a week in September 2011.

As the sentencing of convicted rioters concluded, the RCVP set about its work. The Panel's final report can be criticised for its failure to analyse the marginalisation and exclusion of individuals, families and communities within any structural notions of inequality, particularly when it resorted to quoting the headmaster (sic) of Eton College on the importance of building character and resilience (RCVP 2012: 50). Nevertheless, it attempted to convey some sense of reality about the lives of poor families in poor areas. From a criminal justice perspective, whilst acknowledging the role of punishment, the report argued from the first-hand experience of its members that the public wanted something more than simple punishment for offenders (2012: 31).

This type of approach was never going to satisfy a Coalition administration and its leading spokespeople who had made it clear that the riots were simply an outbreak of criminality – *pure and simple*. Nevertheless the authors of the RCVP report must have been somewhat disappointed, when the Coalition's formal response was published by the Department for Communities and Local Government (DCLG) in July 2013 (DCLGa 2013). This response, surprisingly thin given the significant occurrences in the summer of 2011 as well as the detailed attention given by the

RCPV report, was largely a rehash of what the government already had in place. It was acontextual in the sense that there was no mention of the austerity programme of public spending cuts that were biting into services such as Sure Start – ironically an initiative that was praised in the government response itself and is generally well regarded by families who are consumers of the services on offer.

It was also published some sixteen months after the Coalition's overarching strategy, *Social Justice: Transforming Lives* which was published by The Department for Work and Pensions (DWP). This document offered the following analysis of poverty:

> Frequently, very low income is a symptom of deeper problems, whether that is family breakdown, educational failure, welfare dependency, debt, drug dependency, or some other relevant factor. Many people are beset by a combination of these factors, interlinking with one another and driving a cycle of deprivation.
>
> *(2012: 10)*

The government's response to the RCVP report unsurprisingly echoes this view by reiterating that

> Previous approaches to tackling poverty have focussed on increasing income levels to bring people above the poverty line. The Social Justice Strategy goes much further, exploring how tackling the root causes of problems can make real and sustained changes to the lives of those facing multiple disadvantage.
>
> *(DCLGa 2013: 15)*

Rather than seeing the myriad of personal and social problems emanating from economic inequality, it reverses this view and blames the individual and the malfunctioning family. Notions of family inadequacy and fecklessness are, of course, recurrent themes in British social policy and surface in concepts like the *cycle of poverty* and *transmitted deprivation* used by Keith Joseph in his famous 1972 speech to the Pre-Schools Playgroup Association (see Jordon 1974: 1–15). What seems to be different now is the intensity with which such notions are used as an inclusive explanation for society's woes, including crime and disorder.

The identification of the problem is one of family dysfunction and breakdown inter-generationally transmitted and the remedy is one of prevention and early intervention in order to maximise the participation of the individual in work and society and in their overall social mobility. The much trumpeted *Troubled Families* initiative is at the centre of this approach with its *Family Intervention* modus operandi targeted on some 120,000 families who, the government continually emphasises, cost the taxpayer annually some £9 billion (DCLGb 2013: 9). The initiative defines a qualifying family as one meeting three of the four criteria: involved in youth crime or anti-social behaviour, children regularly truanting, has an adult on out-of-work benefits and causes high costs to the taxpayer (DCLG 2112: 9).

Whilst some of the interventions outlined are laudable in themselves, there is little discussion of wealth, income and inequality and, as Suzanne Moore has commented, the range of speeches on social mobility are "utterly disconnected from economic reality" (2012b: 5). A research report produced for Action on Children, the children's society and the NSPCC concluded that the Troubled Families budget of £448 million would just offset the losses "which vulnerable families are suffering from the rest of the fiscal package" (Reed 2012: 72). Within this context, it is prescient to consider former Sure Start senior civil servant, Naomi Eisenstadt's, description of the Coalition's approach of switching from income support to behavioural intervention as disrespectful – "in the absence of any talk about paying the bills, this focus is disrespectful because it assumes that these are the problems that poor people have and does not recognise that the main problem poor people have is not having enough money" (quoted in Gentleman 2011: 36).

Whilst conceding that that there is little evidence of an overlap between those families subject to Troubled Families intervention and the rioters' families, the RCVP report nevertheless went on to argue that a further 500,000 families can be identified who

> ... bump along the bottom' with their children. These children are often absent, excluded or performing poorly at school and often known to the police – characteristics of the core group of rioters – and are destined for similar outcomes as their parents.
>
> *(2011: 38)*

As Alan Pratt has critically observed, from a neoliberal perspective, poverty is "... culturally determined by the values, attitudes, mores and lack of aspirations transmitted across generations. Therefore, if the policy objective is to improve the conditions of the poor, then the behaviour of the poor themselves must be changed" (2006: 21). The stereotyping is therefore more than disrespectful – it is ideological. It is repeated ad nauseam by the political elite and accentuated within the media, despite being most effectively dealt with in *The lies we tell ourselves: ending comfortable myths about poverty* (Baptist Union *et al.* 2013), a series of essays reminding the reader that earned poverty is now more common than poverty due to unemployment.

Blaming Probation

When faced with disturbances across Britain in 1981, the government response was what could be described as a broadly interventionist one to an essentially neo-Keynesian analysis offered by Lord Scarman. He concluded that the rioters, though wrong, had found a very effective form of protest and that social stability within Britain's inner cities required significant investment in jobs, educational, recreational and leisure opportunities (1981). As Lea has commented, Scarman in the current climate would be simply shouted down (2011a, 2011b: 17) and we will return to the themes highlighted in the preceding section to consider this failure to acknowledge the needs of the poor and marginalised and its impact on probation practice. Initially, however, as Fitzgibbon *et al.* point out, a feature of Scarman "... was a refusal to blame the communities from which the rioters came. Absent is any discourse of failed parenting and dysfunctional families" (2013: 447–448). Indeed, the overall tenor of the Scarman Report gave probation and the local state services much to think about in terms of responding more appropriately to the needs of the community and the resources and services they required (Fitzgibbon *et al.* 2013: 448).

In Liverpool, the disturbances occurred at the beginning of July 1981 and centred on the Toxteth area of the city. The historical legacy of slavery in terms of the depth of disadvantage and discrimination in housing, health, employment, education and training coupled with outright racist policing of Liverpool's black population was such that an agency like probation, of itself, could not tackle, let al. one solve, these institutionalised disadvantages. However, the Service was, in a number of important respects, geared up to make an important impact – it was community-based in the sense that it was not only used to operating in the homes and neighbourhoods of offenders, but it was intertwined with local partner agencies outside as well as within the criminal justice system. Probation had begun to develop community-based or *detached* services which were co-located with other agencies in, for example, tenement flats (see Simpson and Crawley 1985, Broad 1991). Ironically probation's relationship with the police was virtually non-existent but in the aftermath of disturbances, the Service's credibility within the local community was such that it was able to operate as an *honest broker* between community representatives and local agencies including the police. As the 1988 Gifford Inquiry outlined the situation:

> ... the service sponsored an employment scheme under the government's community Programme. The scheme brought in a number of Black employees to probation offices in Liverpool 8. It provided job opportunities, as well as learning experience for the probation office staff. Black workers became involved in the probation service, victim support, youth work and voluntary agencies and some were recruited into the probation service as a career.
>
> *(Gifford et al. 1989: 203)*

The response to inner-city dereliction was completely inadequate, but the point was that probation as a community-based service with a vision wider than a narrowly correctional one was able to effectively use what few resources were made available for the longer-term benefit of the local community. It was also able to influence future patterns of service delivery. However, probation's response was not without its problems. Author Bob Broad studied the Services' work in the 1981 post-riot areas (Handsworth, Bristol, Toxteth, Brixton and Tottenham), which aimed to make probation more relevant to poor, alienated black and white communities. The initiatives struggled in the face of organisational control and centralised objectives (1991: 123). Wider issues of changes to practice also tended to be subsumed under the daily pressures of frontline work, but in Broad's view there was some move toward a focus on prevention of crime (1991: 183). To some extent, the disturbances of the 1980s acted as a wake-up call to probation areas to engage more fully and in more relevant ways with the communities they served.

Identifying where the causes of criminal behaviour lie has a long and enduring history in criminology and probation literature, but part of neoliberal ideology requires a very determined focus on the offender and on whole sections of society whose cultural norms are seen to create, support and inter-generationally transmit crime and disorder. However, blaming "a feral underclass, cut off from the mainstream in everything but its materialism" as the then Justice Secretary described the rioters (Clarke 2011) didn't seem to go far enough. Indeed, there was also a concerted effort to blame, in part, the correctional services, for the August 2011 riots.

This is not fanciful thinking, for unlike previous disturbances, where the operation of the police and local authorities came under scrutiny and criticism, a very clear link was now being made between the rioters themselves and the ineffectiveness of rehabilitation measures. Kenneth Clarke, who was considered a social liberal within the Conservative Party despite his role in undermining key provisions of the 1991 Criminal Justice Act, forcefully made the link between the offending dealt with by Probation on a day-to-day basis and the criminality subsumed within the riots. Whilst accepting that reform could not stop at the penal system alone, the Justice Secretary wrote in *The Guardian* in September 2011, shortly after the riots:

> It's not yet been widely recognised, but the hard core of the rioters were, in fact, known criminals. Close to three-quarters of those aged 18 and over charged with riot offences already had a prior conviction. That is the legacy of a broken penal system – one whose record in preventing re-offending has been straightforwardly dreadful. In my view, the riots can be seen in part as an outburst of outrageous criminal behaviour by the criminal classes – individuals and families familiar with the justice system who haven't been changed by their past punishments.
>
> *(Clarke 2011: 34)*

Clarke's views reinforces the sense of individuals and families as objects of criminal justice policies and lays responsibility in a way that makes the agencies of the state and specifically probation accountable for the riots. This was not only a clever political move but timely in providing, de facto, evidence of the need for the Coalition's much-vaunted *Rehabilitation Revolution*. Indeed the move from contestability under New Labour to full blown privatisation under the Coalition's *Transforming Rehabilitation* has gone on apace, as has the inexorable rise in the prison population, perverse but all-embracing performance frameworks linked to budgets and over-emphasis on public protection and offender risk. The irony of such criticism of probation lies in the fact that according to official measures of success, the service nationally and locally has delivered all that has been asked of it (see Chapter Three) even when delivering on targets that were identified by probation staff as counter-productive in reducing re-offending.

Although New Labour's *localism* offered some cause for optimism in terms of local services being in a position to build on the success of, for example, multi-agency public protection arrangements (MAPPA) and prolific and priority offender (PPO) schemes, the overarching correctional focus has come with a significant cost in terms of the Service's withdrawal from the offender's family, their communities and some of our traditional partners outside the criminal justice system (Burke and Collett 2008: 9). As Fitzgibbon has observed, the retreat to risk assessment and box ticking is "… an easy exit from the complexities of working in such an environment and one in which the front line practitioner frequently has little choice" (2011: 69). Additionally, a palpable lack of political support for probation in terms of its delivery of both community sentences and public protection has served to shape a stretched and defensive service that retreated into its newly-acquired correctional shell. The irony is that those features of probation practice that were seen as positive in the aftermath of the 1981 disturbances have been displaced by approaches characterised by protection of the public, risk assessment, offender cognitive deficits and individual responsibility and parallel "rather precisely the emphasis on individual resilience and 'character' within the RCVP report" (Fitzgibbon *et al.* 2013: 454).

Exclusion, citizenship and the holy grail of social mobility

It would be easy, therefore, to see the development of probation as a case example in how not to manage a public service and many of us who have worked throughout the period from the creation of the National Service in 2001 to its gradual erosion post-Carter (2003) could see it as a process of continual tinkering to get the system right to deliver rehabilitation. However, seen through the prism of macro politics and economics, the so-called modernisation of public services, including probation, makes sense in terms of the demanding hegemony of neoliberalism. Our argument is that in making the economic aspects of class invisible and defining failure in a meritocratic society as cultural rather than structural, certain kinds of interventions become the norm. As a corollary, social mobility, rather than measures to redress social and economic exclusion fit perfectly with the requirements of neoliberalism to maintain its vigour and structure. Nearly two decades ago, the American academic, Christopher Lasch in his brilliant analysis of contemporary politics and business, saw no contradiction in the pursuit of social mobility by the elites in society. He argued that:

> High rates of mobility are by no means inconsistent with a system of stratification that concentrates power and privileges in a ruling elite. Indeed, the circulation of elites strengthens the principle of hierarchy, furnishing elites with fresh talent and legitimising their ascendancy as a function of merit rather than birth.
>
> *(1995: 77)*

Class disappears, socio-economic inequality becomes increasingly irrelevant and social mobility becomes the endgame of increasingly targeted and specialised responses to perceived social and personal problems. Take, for example, two recent reports produced by the Coalition, one signed off by the Deputy Prime Minister, Nick Clegg – *Opening Doors, Breaking Barriers* (Cabinet Office 2011) and the other championed by Iain Duncan Smith – *Social Justice: Transforming Lives* (DWP 2012). The two reports are seen as complementary, with *Opening Doors* covering the general challenges of widening social mobility whereas the social justice report bears down very much on those families who are deemed to be dysfunctional. It makes the link to the 120,000 families who come within the remit of the Troubled Families Initiative announced by the Prime Minister in December 2011, with Duncan Smith commenting that their "… lives are so chaotic they cost the Government some £9 Billion in the last year alone" (DWP 2012: 1).

The apparent concern that the poor and excluded should be given every opportunity to thrive in and contribute to the economy masks some coercive social policies geared to punishing those deemed capable of work or those in social housing with a spare bedroom. Likewise, the upbeat language of the *Rehabilitation Revolution* and its latest iteration, *Transforming Rehabilitation* is laced with expressive notions of punishment. The penal arms race continues apace and the question now becomes one of who is to deliver? David Faulkner, in a letter to *The Guardian* in 2012 urged the government to provide "a clear principled sense of direction based on prevention, rehabilitation, problem solving and restoration ..." which would be consistent with the older traditions of the Conservative Party, but he brilliantly captured our current state when he concluded that the debate on criminal justice had already relapsed into "*the dreary language of punishment and competition*" (Faulkner 2012: 31, italics added).

The search for the rehabilitative ideal so brilliantly illuminated in a set of readings assembled and edited by Priestley and Vanstone (2010) show that whilst there is little completely new in the world of punishment and rehabilitation, the ebb and flow of official responses to crime and punishment reflects the prevailing social, economic and political environment. However, what we are suggesting is that the ideological ascendency of neoliberalism and its claim to meritocracy and equality of opportunity has returned civil society to a harsher view of those who are seen to fail. The ideology that drives social and criminal justice policy has become invisible through its appeal to strong action, condemnation and supposed common sense and in the absence of any dissenting socio-economic analysis, wider social problems can be laid at the door of those who are seen to fail within the modern meritocratic state – particular families become the problem and must, therefore, be targeted by the state and coerced to change.

In the absence of analysis and action about the links between marginalisation, inequality and poverty and an emphasis on policing and repression, Gary Younge has argued that welfare and housing agencies will be brought into an extended police family "... with threats of benefit reduction and termination of housing tenancies against families with members convicted of rioting seems aimed at achieving what the military call 'full force dominance'" (2011: 31). Whilst this may sound somewhat exaggerated, documents obtained by *The Guardian* in 2012 suggested that police services were already increasing their expenditure on what are now referred to as *attenuating energy projectiles* (rubber bullets). The Home Office was looking for ideas to increase the range of hardware that could be deployed in riots and "No idea's too stupid or off the wall" according to an internal briefing note (Guardian 2012: 8). There is now an active debate within police and political circles about the procurement and deployment of water cannons for the first time on mainland Britain (Harris 2014).

Under the Coalition's wider plans, it is clear, then, that the state intends to bear down on those whom it considers waste public money through their dysfunctional, antisocial and criminal behaviour. The neoliberal state's conception of the problem, though, feeds into the insecurity that its citizens already have about crime and antisocial behaviour. Through its symbolism, technology, language and actions, the state effectively separates and further alienates those who offend from the so-called law-abiding majority, in the process reducing the possibility for creating a greater understanding of inter-dependency and mutual interests within local communities.

Picking up on the trends becoming increasingly evident in New Labour's approach to criminal justice, Hindpal Singh Bhui argued that respect for individual rights and needs inherent in humanitarian approaches to probation work were at the root of anti-racism and anti-discriminatory probation practice. Reflecting that the whole concept of values and their importance to practice seemed too complex to be seriously incorporated into official discourse, he argued that managerial certainty and control were a myth in an environment of time-consuming complexity "if criminal justice agencies are to engage with real lives" (2006: 181). Under the Coalition, neoliberal thinking has moved the debate on from managerial control to one which ultimately reduces the art of rehabilitation to anything that the market accepts as profitable. It sees the social world as a simple one in which the price mechanism, shareholder profits and the imposition of a good dose of public school values (see RCVP 2012) will deliver what the public sector has failed to do.

Unlike the post-riots environment of the early 1980s, where there was some investment in the things that mattered to local communities, particularly in relation to access to employment, education and social services, state intervention is increasingly seen as a residual activity using prescribed, targeted and selective measures to secure compliant behaviour. Probation will, therefore, be faced with seeking to rehabilitate offenders who already consider themselves the subject of coercive state intervention in an environment of ever-limiting material opportunities – an environment where levels of deprivation have been described by one of the most comprehensive recent studies of poverty as returning to levels found thirty years ago (see PSE 2013). This is within an overall context in the UK where in 2010, while the top 10 per cent received 31 per cent of all income, the bottom 10 per cent received just 1 per cent. In terms of wealth, in 2010 45 per cent of all wealth in the UK was held by the richest 10 per cent. The poorest 10 per cent held only 1 per cent (The Equality Trust 2014). It is also within an environment that belies the Coalition's triumphal messages about reducing unemployment, that there are more people living in poverty in working families than workless ones (MacInnes *et al.* 2013: 3).

However, it is not just the general levels of poverty that are deeply concerning but the attack on those services that often provide a lifeline for those supervised by probation. Crisis, the homeless charity, report increasing trends in both visible (rough sleeping) and hidden (sharing and overcrowded households) homelessness, with the number of statutory homeless acceptances having risen by 34 per cent over the 2010–2013 period. Rising numbers of people are being made homeless by loss of private sector tenancies (Fitzpatrick *et al.* 2013) as the increasingly evident *Rachmanism* of private sector landlords returns as housing need grows (Toynbee 2014: 31). Furthermore, the Crisis report offers little optimism for the immediate future:

> Most key informants interviewed in 2013 expect a new surge in homelessness associated with the ramping up of welfare reform, particularly the social sector bedroom limits and the introduction of Universal Credit. At the same time, housing market pressures seem unlikely to ease, particularly in London and the South. A range of specialist homelessness funding programmes intended to ameliorate the impact of these negative structural trends on particularly vulnerable groups are also due to end in 2014.
>
> *(Fitzpatrick et al 2013: 9)*

Other ameliorative services benefitting those under probation are being withdrawn under the Coalition's austerity measures. For example, the Department of Work and Pensions intends to scrap a £180 million hardship fund which provides emergency help for low-income families who suffer sudden financial crisis as a result of domestic violence, ill-health or natural disasters (Butler 2014: 8). This is occurring at the same time that the Family Rights Group report a massive increase in domestic violence problems amongst families, the majority of whom live in poverty and have few financial alternatives (Ashley and Kanow 2014). The personal, social and economic circumstances of offenders are well known (SEU 2002) and yet the austerity programme chips away at those services that often provide a lifeline to individual offenders and their families. In many respects, a substantial number of probation's clientele are drawn from the sharp end of an ever increasing *precariat* – an emergent class within neoliberal states which Guy Standing has persuasively argued experience anger, anomie anxiety and alienation.

> The precariat feels frustrated not only because a lifetime of flexi-jobs beckons, with all the insecurities that come with them, but also because those jobs involve no construction of trusting relationships built upon meaningful structure or networks. The precariat also has no ladder of mobility to climb, leaving people hovering between deeper self-exploitation and disengagement.
>
> *(2011: 19–20)*

Within this analysis then, the psycho-social security and outlook of individuals is more concretely grounded within the class system or at the very least within a system of real, grinding day-in, day-out social and economic uncertainty. Isn't this, after all the reality for most individuals who appear before the criminal courts? (see Collett 2013: 181). So, rather than inadequacy, fecklessness and sheer wanton criminality to which the correctional services make misguided and ineffective responses, the analysis can be turned on its head and the legitimacy of the state itself – the extent to which citizens accept the authority of the government – can be questioned. In a fascinating attempt to link legitimacy to social unrest, Taylor-Gooby set out to test the assertion that whilst a generous and inclusive welfare state bolsters the legitimacy of government in unequal but democratic capitalist societies, the current welfare cuts and restructuring of work may work in the opposite direction. On his own admission, the analysis is exploratory and the data has its limitations, but he is able to make two important points:

- The increase in poverty, resulting from the combination of benefit cuts disproportionately affecting those on the lowest incomes and the public sector cutbacks which increase unemployment, is likely to have a real effect in generating social disorder;
- The policies which expand the role of the private sector are also likely to contribute in undermining legitimacy and social stability. The cutbacks themselves have a weaker, but still real, influence. It is the way they are channelled to bear on those already on low incomes that is of more importance.

(2013: 12)

These findings do not augur well for either the future stability of communities or the capacity of the very poorest in our communities to lead crime-free and trouble-free lives. Those who represent us within the political process and form our opinions through the news media have become increasingly removed from the reality of everyday life for sizeable sections of our communities.

They are able to further disengage from our public services as they use their economic power to buy privatised health, education and social care. Unfettered by any contact with social and economic realities, they are free to pontificate about the lives of the poor whilst congratulating themselves for their success and wealth. A social reality of class differences reflecting income and resource inequality is displaced by the myth of an open, meritocratic society where individuals – feckless, inadequate or simply criminal – are taken away from welfare dependency and *helped* on their meritocratic way by increasingly coercive and repressive state approaches – whether that be the withdrawal or reduction of benefits and services to the poor or the technology of water cannons for future would be rioters.

Increasing differences in wealth and income between the rich and the poor supported by an entrenched neoliberal momentum ultimately make the rehabilitation of offenders more and more difficult by widening the distance between those who consider themselves law abiding and those who appear before the courts. As Danny Dorling comments in *Injustice: Why social inequality persists:*

> ... the rich talk of the laziness, laxness, fecklessness and general uselessness of the poor in contrast to their perceptions of themselves as great risk takers and great labourers, as highly efficient, intelligent and sensitive people. What they really have is a very highly developed sense of personal self worth. It is difficult not to think like this if you are affluent, and it is how most affluent people think; if you are rich and admit to being only human too, well, how do you excuse your riches?
>
> (2013: 220)

In similar vein, Lasch commented nearly twenty years ago, "When money talks, everybody is condemned to listen" (1995: 22) and twenty years before that Bob Dylan sang in *It's Alright, Ma (I'm only bleeding)* "... money doesn't talk, it swears". These notions are not new but the increasing gulf in material and economic circumstances and social distance between individuals and communities within neoliberal Britain create a pressing need for understanding rather than antagonism. Writing in the *Observer*, Will Hutton commented that "The sheer unfairness of the wealth divide is a challenge to all of us as moral human beings" (2014: 37). That same challenge is one that applies to all of us in relation to defining, explaining and responding to crime and to the rehabilitation of offenders.

References

Ashley, C. and Kanow, C. (2014) *Desperate for Help: Report analysing calls to Family Rights Group's advice service from families of children in need or at risk*, Family Rights Group, January.

Baptist Union of Great Britain, The Methodist Church, the Church of Scotland and the United Reform Church (2013) *The lies we tell ourselves: Ending comfortable myths about poverty*, Methodist Publishing.

Bhui, H.S. (2006) Anti-racist practice in NOMS: Reconciling managerialist and professional realities, *The Howard Journal of Criminal Justice*, 45(2): 171–190.

Bridges, L. (2012) Four days in August: the UK riots, *Race and Class*, 54(1): 1–12.

Briggs, D. (ed) (2012a) *The English Riots of 2011: A Summer of Discontent*, Hampshire: Waterside Press.

Briggs, D. (2012b) Frustrations, Urban Relations and Temptations: Contextualising the English Riots in Briggs, D (ed) (2012) *The English Riots of 2011: A Summer of Discontent*, Hampshire: Waterside Press.

Broad, B. (1991) *Punishment under Pressure: The Probation Service in the Inner City*, London: Kingsley.

Burke, L. and Collett, S. (2008) Doing with or doing to: What now for the probation service? *Criminal Justice Matters*, 72: 9–11.

Burke, L. and Collett, S. (2010) People are not things: What New Labour has done to probation, *Probation Journal*, 57(3): 232–249.

Butler, P. (2014) Emergency fund for low-income families to be scrapped, *The Guardian*, 4 January.

Cabinet Office (2011) *Opening Doors, Breaking Barriers: A Strategy for Social Mobility*, London: Cabinet Office.

Carter, P. (2003) *Managing Offenders, Reducing Crime: A New Approach*, London: Home Office.

Clarke, K. (2011) Punish the feral rioters, but address our social deficit too, *The Guardian*, 6 September: 34.

Clarke, R. (2012) Profiling The 'Rioters': Findings From Manchester in Briggs, D. (ed) (2012) *The English Riots of 2011: A Summer of Discontent*, Hampshire: Waterside Press.

Collett, S. (2013) Riots, revolution and rehabilitation: The future of probation, *The Howard Journal of Criminal Justice*, 52(2): 163–188.

Department For Communities & Local Government (2012) *Working with Troubled Families: A guide to the evidence and good practice*, London: DCLG.

Department For Communities & Local Government (2013a) *Government Response to the Riots, Communities and Victims Panel's Final Report*, London: DCLG.

Department For Communities & Local Government (2013b) *The Fiscal Case for Working with Troubled Families: Analysis and Evidence on the Costs of Troubled Families to Government*, London: DCLG (February).

Department For Work and Pensions (2012) *Social Justice: Transforming Lives*, London: DWP.

Dorling, D. (2013) *Injustice: Why Social Inequality Persists*, Bristol: Policy Press.

Faulkner, D. (2012) Harsh lessons for the coalition (Letters Page), *The Guardian*, 8 May: 31.

Fitzgibbon, W. (2011) *Probation and Social Work on Trial: Violent Offenders and Child Abusers*, London: Palgrave Macmillan.

Fitzgibbon, W., Curry, D. and Lea, J. (2013) Supervising rioters: The role of probation, *The Howard Journal of Criminal Justice*, 52(5): 445–461.

Fitzpatrick, S., Pawson, H., Bramley, G., Wilcox, S. and Watts, B. (2013) *The Homelessness Monitor: England 2013 Executive Summary*, Crisis, December 2013.

Fully Focussed Productions (2013) *Riots From Wrong Video*, available from http:/www.fullyfocussedproductions.com.

Gentleman, A. (2011) Parenting classes don't pay the gas bill, *Society Guardian*, 23 November.

Gifford, L., Brown, W. and Bundey, R. (2009) *Loosen The Shackles: First Report of the Liverpool 8 Inquiry into Race Relations in Liverpool*, London: Karia Press.

Guardian (2011a) Rioters were "unruly mob" seeking instant gratification, claims May, *The Guardian*, 19 December.

Guardian (2011b) Reading the riots – don't blame our parents – we got involved despite them, say rioters, *The Guardian*, 7 December.

Guardian (2012) CS gas, pepper spray, skunk oil: the new range of weapons coming to the riot police, *The Guardian*, 10 April: 8.

Guardian/LSE (2011) *Reading the Riots: Investigating England's Summer of Disorder*, London: *Guardian*/LSE.

HM Inspectorate of Constabulary (2011) *The Rules of Engagement: A Review of the August 2011 Disorders*, London: HM Inspectorate of Constabulary.

Home Office (2011) *An Overview of Recorded Crimes and Arrests Resulting from Disorder Events in August 2011*, London: Home Office.

House of Commons Home Affairs Committee (2011) *Policing Large Scale Disorder: Lessons from the Disturbances of August 2011, Sixteenth Report of Session 2010–12*, London: TSO.

Hutton, W. (2014) We are scared to face the real issue – It's all about inequality, *Observer*, 19 January.

Jefferson, T. (2011) Policing the riots: from Bristol and Brixton to Tottenham, via Toxteth, Handsworth etc, *Criminal Justice Matters*, 87 (March): 8–9.

Johnson, B. (2013) *Extracts from the third Margaret Thatcher Lecture delivered on 27 November*, http://www.cps.org.uk/files/factsheets/original/131128144200-Thatcherlecturev2.pdf (Accessed on 17 December 2013).

Jones, O. (2011) *Chavs: The Demonization of the Working Class*, London: Verso.

Jordon, B. (1974) *Poor Parents: Social Policy and the Cycle of Deprivation*, London: Routledge and Kegan Paul.

Klein, N. (2007) *The Shock Doctrine*, London: Penguin.

Lammy, D. (2011) *Out of the Ashes: Britain after the Riots*, London: Guardian Books.

Lasch, C. (1995) *The Revolt of the Elites and the Betrayal of Democracy*, New York: WW Norton.

Lea, J. (2011a) *Riots and the Crisis of Neoliberalism*, http://bunker8.pwp.blueyonder.co.uk/misc/riots2011.html (Accessed 16 January 2014).

Lea, J. (2011b) Shock Horror: Rioters Cause Riots! Criminals Cause Crime, *British Society of Criminology Newsletter*, 69 (Winter): 17–19.

Lea, J. and Hallsworth, S. (2012) Understanding the riots, *Criminal Justice Matters*, 87: 30–31.

Mac Ginty, R. (2004) Looting in the context of violent conflict: A conceptualisation and typology, *Third World Quarterly*, 24(5): 857–870.

MacInnes, T., Aldridge, H., Bushe, S., Kenway, P. and Tinson, A. (2013) *Monitoring Poverty and Social Exclusion 2103*, Joseph Rountree foundation (December) www.jrf.org.uk (Accessed 14 February 2014).

Marcuse, H. (1964) *One Dimensional Man*, London: Abacus.

McWilliams, W. (1987) Probation, pragmatism and policy, *The Howard Journal of Criminal Justice*, 26: 97–121.

Ministry of Justice (2012) *Statistical Bulletin on the Public Disorder of 6 to 9 August 2011 – September 2012 Update*, London: Ministry of Justice Statistical Bulletin.

Moore, S. (2012a) Now instead of being disgusted by poverty, we are disgusted by poor people themselves, *The Guardian 2*, 16 February.

Moore, S. (2012b) It's time we faced up to it: A few people might have made the leap 40 years ago, but social mobility no longer exists, *The Guardian 2*, 24 May.

New Statesman (2011) Cameron searches for the "root cause" of the riots, *New Statesman*, 10 August.

Newburn, T. (2012) Counterblast: Young People and the August 2011 riots, *The Howard Journal of Criminal Justice*, 51(3): 331–335.

Pearson, G. (2012) Everything Changes, Nothing moves: The Longue Duree of Social Anxieties About Youth Crime in Briggs, D. (ed) (2012) *The English Riots of 2011: A Summer of Discontent*, Hampshire: Waterside Press.

Phillips, M. (2011) Britain's liberal intelligentsia has smashed virtually every social value, *Daily Mail*, 11 August.

Platts-Fowler, D. (2013) *Beyond the loot: Social disorder and urban unrest*, Papers from the British Criminology Conference volume 13.

Pratt, A. (2006) Neo-liberalism and social policy in Lavalette, M. and Pratt, M. (eds) *Social Policy: Theories, Concepts and Issues*, London: Sage.

Priestley, P. and Vanstone, M. (2010) *Offenders or Citizen: Readings in Rehabilitation*, Cullompton: Willan.

PSE (2013) *The Impoverishment of the UK: PSE UK First Results: Living Standards*, ESRC.

Ramsbotham, Lord D. (2010) House of Lords Debate on the Probation Service, *Hansard*, volume 716, cols 1144–80, 21 January.

Reed, H. (2012) *In the Eye of the Storm: Britain's Forgotten Children and Families: A Research Report for Action on Children*, The Children's Society.

Riots, Communities and Victims Panel (2012) *After the Riots: The Final Report of the Riots, Victims Panel*, London: Riots, Communities and Victims Panel.

Scarman, L. (1981) *The Scarman Report: The Brixton Disorders 10–12 April 1981*, Harmondsworth: Penguin.

Simpson, P. and Crawley, P. (1985) Myrtle gardens: moving into the inner city in D. Scott, D., Stone, N., Simpson, P. and Falkingham, P. (eds) *Going Local in Probation? Case Studies in Community Practice*, Norwich/Manchester: University of East Anglia Social Work Programme/University of Manchester Department of Social Administration.

Social Exclusion Unit (2000) *National Strategy for Neighbourhood Renewal: A Framework for Consultation*, London: Cabinet Office.

Standing, G. (2011) *The Precariat: The New Dangerous Class*, London: Bloomsbury

Starkey, D. (2011) The whites have become black, http://www.bbc.co.uk/news/uk-14513517 (Accessed 20th August 2011).

Taylor-Gooby, P. (2013) Riots, Demonstrations, Strikes and the Coalition Programme, *Social Policy and Society*, 12: 1–15.

The Equality Trust (2014) *About Inequality: Scale and Trends*, www.equalitytrust.org.uk/about-inequality/scale-and-trends (Accessed 29 January.2014).

Toynbee, P. (2014) Rachmanism is back. But where is Labour's outrage? *The Guardian*, 14 January.

Treadwell, J., Briggs, D,. Winlow, S. and Hall, S. (2013) Shopocalypse Now: Consumer Culture and the English Riots of 2011, *British Journal of Criminology*, 53: 1–17.

Waddington, D. and King, M. (2009) Identifying common causes of UK and French riots occurring since the 1980s, *The Howard Journal of Criminal Justice* 48: 245–59.

Walker, H. and Beaumont, B. (1981) *Probation Work: Critical Theory and Socialist Practice*, Oxford: Blackwell.

Walker, H. and Beaumont, B. (1985) *Working with Offenders*, London: Macmillan.

Younge, G. (2011) Indifferent elites, economic hardship and police brutality: All reasons to riot, *The Guardian*, 5 December.

Note

1 Part of this chapter draws significantly on Steve Collett's 2012 McWilliams Lecture – *Riots, Revolution and Rehabilitation: The Future of Probation* – which was published by John Wiley & Sons Ltd. in the *The Howard Journal of Criminal Justice*, (2013) 52(2): 163–189.

8
CONCLUSION
Reimagining rehabilitation

> Acts of violence and property destruction are wilful crimes deserving punishment commensurate with their seriousness. It is inconceivable that unemployment is such a mitigating circumstance that the offender should be regarded as absolutely blameless and without responsibility. But a demand for justice must go beyond retribution for the offence and reparation for the victim, it has to include a demand for *understanding* the offender. It needs this not in the hope that the offender will then be excused, condoned or justified. Nor does understanding the offender necessarily shift the blame to the victims. The demand for understanding is necessary because *although people choose to act, sometimes criminally, they do not do so under conditions of their own choosing.* Their choice makes them responsible, but the conditions make the choice comprehensible. These conditions, social and economic, contribute to crime because they constrain, limit or narrow the choices available. Many of us, in similar circumstances, might choose the same course of action. Furthermore, if we understand the intimate relationship between economic and social circumstances and criminal behaviour, then we might be in a better position to intervene effectively and humanely to reduce the incidence of crime.
>
> *(Steven Box 1987: 29 original italics)*

Why do governments so quickly turn to penal solutions to deal with the behaviour of marginal populations rather than attempt to address the social and economic sources of their marginalization? Because they have few political opponents, comparatively low costs, and they accord with common sense ideas about the sources of social disorder and the proper allocation of blame.

> Because they rely upon existing systems of regulation, and leave the fundamental social and economic arrangements untouched. Above all, because they allow controls and condemnation to be focussed on low-status outcast groups, leaving the behaviour of markets, corporations and the more affluent social classes relatively free of regulation and censure.
>
> *(David Garland 2001: 200)*

> If there was a prize for 21st century organisational meddling and ineptitude, despite a strong field, the Home Office and then Ministry of Justice would certainly make the short list for their treatment of the Probation Service.
>
> *(Rob Allen 2013: 12)*

Solidarity lost

We have considered carefully the quotes which begin this chapter and therefore end the book. For us, the late Steven Box encapsulated in one tightly written paragraph, the dimensions of the rehabilitative endeavour and in his plea for understanding, balances the needs of victims with those of offenders and the retention of personal culpability with the conditions that a modern social democratic society should respond to. It is a view that encourages humility and reduces the distance between *them* and *us*. David Garland, however, provides a dystopian reminder that *understanding* may have little relevance to the macro-economic interests of a globalised neoliberal economic strategy and that the penal separation of increasing numbers may be the price worth paying for the maintenance of profit and inequality. Finally, Rob Allen's recent take on the operation of central government departments draws attention to the bureaucratic consequences of delivering ideological and macro-political change; repercussions that play out daily to the bemusement, frustration and on occasion to the disbelief of those who work with troubled and troublesome people.

These three quotes also help to remind us that our aim in writing this book was to capture the middle ground between ideological abstraction, political and theoretical contexts for contemporary rehabilitative endeavour and the more painstaking and necessarily detailed analysis of the bureaucratic, administrative and policy frameworks within which correctional services ply their trade. We have drawn on many sources which display, on one hand, significantly greater theoretical sophistication, and on the other, more detailed analytical insights. We will have missed much and underplayed specific issues in our attempt to make sense of ideology, mezzo politics, personalities and events of the past fifteen years or more. What our approach does illuminate though, is that in all the posturing and personal vanity of key players and the attendant ignorance and confused politicisation of probation's role in delivering rehabilitation, offenders, their families and communities have been poorly served. Just as importantly, the victims of crime and those whose personal and social conditions make them particularly susceptible to victimisation have also been ill-served (and on occasions put at further risk) by politicians whose grandstanding for short-term political gain has avoided consideration of progressive changes to a criminal justice system that largely separates victims from offenders, pitting the interests of one against the other. The tax payer too has been short-changed as initiatives and developments in the delivery of rehabilitation have been subject to a continuing *cultural revolution of perpetual change* which has thwarted effectiveness in outcomes and efficiency in the use of scarce public resources. Not only has the search for the perfect structure seen vast sums of public money entirely wasted but the attritional effect has been to denigrate, downgrade and ultimately destroy an integrated public service – probation – which has served English and Welsh communities with distinction for over a 100 years.

It has been outside both the scope and perhaps more accurately the time period for this text to develop a critique of probation in the period when it was more autonomous and in control of its own affairs (see Mair and Burke 2011). In the post war period up until the late 1970s and beyond, a range of criticisms could be laid at probation's door, both in terms of indulgent professional stances within its internal world and its ambivalent relationships with the wider criminal justice system. Nevertheless, it seems to us that in its own modest way, it contributed to the delivery of a vision, supported by the political process and accepted by wider society that required offenders to be supported, reintegrated and ultimately rehabilitated. In wider terms, Garland captured it thus:

> In the middle decades of the last century, the criminal justice system formed part of a broader solidarity project. Its programmatic response to crime was part of the welfare state's programmatic response to poverty and destitution. Criminal justice was shaped by the politics of social democracy, and its ideals were the re-integrative ideals of an inclusive welfare state society. And if its actual practices fell far short of these ideals, as they typically did, they could at least be criticised by reference to these ideals, and reformed in ways that lessened the gap. Today, welfare state institutions still play a supporting role in economic and social life, just as penal-welfare institutions still underpin criminal justice. But that solidarity project no longer dominates the rhetoric of policy or the logic of decision-making. The high ideals of solidarity have been eclipsed by the more basic imperatives of security, economy and control.
>
> *(2001: 199)*

In Chapter Two, we briefly referenced Garland's twelve indices – *currents of change occurring over the last thirty years* of the century – reflecting that most workers in the arenas of community justice and community safety would, we believe, attest to their continuing authenticity, some attenuated and others more exaggerated than at the turn of the century. Of course, Garland's *currents* were not simply descriptions, they reflect his analysis of a period when the certainties of post-war economies and their welfare states were changing as were the old solidarities and certainties for their populations – "over time, our practices of controlling crime and doing justice have had to adapt to an increasingly insecure economy that marginalises substantial sections of the population" (2001: 194). In truth, the pattern and nature of crime had also been changing for the worse, particularly following the impact of heroin on working-class communities from the early 1980s (Parker *et al.* 1988). However, a long-term and enduring trend in falling levels of crime since the early 1990s seems to have gone on almost unheeded by the political elite except when the quarterly publication of the official figures allows some media showboating. Likewise, the disjunction between this trend and a continuously rising prison population over recent years, standing on the 4 April 2014 at 85,285, remains largely undebated within the political realm. The abduction of James Bulger, caught on CCTV, and the subsequent arrest, trial and imprisonment of his killers in 1993 provided the public moment to turn the screw as never before. The nexus of reality and rhetoric provided the ideal opportunity to move beyond reason and understanding (see Collett 1993) and define crime and criminality in ways that suited the social conservatism of the political elite and played on the fears and uncertainties of the wider public. It also fed, with increasing vigour, the ideological requirements of neoliberalism whether managed by the Tories or the future administrations of New Labour and the Coalition government.

Ideology reinvigorated

The exact relationship between social control, punitiveness, and general criminal justice reactions to crime in late modernity and the imperatives of neoliberalism are complex, confusing and contested. In the *Culture of Control,* Garland argues that crime control strategies are an adaptation to late modernity – "to the specific problems of social order produced by late modern social organisation" (2001: 210), whilst Wacquant is more deterministic, arguing that rather than a reaction to uncertainty around crime, the state's actions are a ruling class response as part of a mission aimed to "establish a new economic regime based on capital hypermobility and labour flexibility and to curb the social turmoil generated at the foot of the urban order by public policies of market deregulation and social welfare retrenchment that are the core building blocks of neoliberalism" (2007: 303). In her introductory chapter to *Criminal Justice and Neoliberalism,* Emma Bell provides a very accessible account of the various theoretical and ideological positions within this overall debate (2011: 1–11), and whilst positioning herself within the broad sweep of those frameworks, she nevertheless argues that punitiveness is not necessarily intrinsic to neoliberalism and that notwithstanding its ideological intent, neoliberalism does not automatically reduce the role of the state:

> In many ways the welfare state in Britain has actually been extended with the development of an ever-wider range of social programmes, although this does not necessarily mean that it does not become more punitive in this sphere.
>
> *(Bell 2011: 4)*

We are drawn to Bell's position for a number of reasons. It is surely the case that alongside the privatisation of public assets and services, the state has been busy organising the conditions for and the control of the marketisation process. It has also committed and directed its ideological efforts to designing services that have become more selective and conditional and less universal, more controlling and punitive and more directed at the behaviour and thinking of the recipients and less about their material circumstances.

Whether intrinsic or not, punitiveness has been the name of the game within the English and Welsh criminal justice system and its treatment of individual offenders for the past twenty years. However, from a perspective that looks upward, attempting to reflect day-to-day practice with offenders, local management of resources and the leadership of Probation Areas, the organisational meddling and ineptitude that Allen refers to in one of our opening quotes reflects more than simply the grinding logic of the grand neoliberal project. Alongside the poor stewardship of public resources, we have seen examples of excellent initiatives in practice, policy and organisational focus when a talented civil service has been allowed to develop work with local agencies free from day-to-day political interference. The development of multi-agency approaches to the management of dangerous offenders and the protection of victims, alongside the transformation of working relations with the Police Service, have served communities well. The original strategic guidance for the development of the local Prolific and Priority Offender schemes requiring governance and operational responsibility to be shared across the police, probation and relevant local authorities, provided the opportunity for the new local criminal justice boards (LCJBs) to use co-terminosity to embed reducing re-offending (as opposed to reducing crime and antisocial behaviour) in the mindset of the local state. Furthermore, these multi-agency approaches, reinforcing the contribution of the non-criminal justice agencies to the challenges set out within the report of the Social Exclusion Unit (2002), fitted well with the *localism* approach of New Labour in the early years of this century. There was also significant support in the early days of the National Probation Service for the *Effective Practice* or *What Works* initiative pushed hard by HMI Probation. It is worth reminding ourselves that in the foreword to Strategies for Effective Offender (Underdown 1998) the then Chief Inspector of Probation, Graham Smith, began with these words:

> This is the most important foreword I have ever written. The evidence drawn on in this report, states at its simplest that certain community programmes involving the same population significantly outperform custodial sentences

> in reducing offending. Further, we now know or at least have a beginning understanding of what makes those programmes so successful.
>
> *(Underdown 1998: III)*

Graham Smith, himself a former chief probation officer, and Cedric Fullwood, Greater Manchester's Chief Probation Officer, led the push toward a revitalised approach that offered optimism not only for the outcome of interventions with individuals, but for the Probation Service itself. Indeed, there was much to commend in that report and Underdown outlined a service design which encompassed the requirements for deploying basic community services and resources, as well as the more clinical and targeted interventions to tackle the specific problems of individual offenders (1998: 57). However, the political process needed certainty and could not tolerate or deal with the nuances and caution about understanding exactly what works. The environment, shaped by the needs of the Treasury, became programme and target completion driven even when the targets were wrongly calculated or indeed made no sense whatsoever. Cognitive behavioural therapy became the order of the day and the bureaucratic control of both performance and delivery made it difficult for probation areas to deliver a balanced multi-agency approach to reducing re-offending. In essence, as *What Works* became bureaucratised within a system of offender assessment and case management, the resultant correction drift

> … reinforced an increasing distance and separation between the day to day work and operation of probation within its local communities and our understanding of the nature of crime, the offender and the concerns of the community. A correctional framework driven by the unerring requirements of public service modernisation encourages technicist and rigid responses to situations rather than real engagement with individual offenders, their families and their community networks. Whether its command and control or the mechanisms of commissioning and contestability, a magic bullet for solving crime does not exist.
>
> *(Burke and Collett 2008: 10)*

What of course is so deeply ironic, as we argue in Chapter Three, is that as New Labour and then the Coalition administrations set more and more targets, probation rose to the challenge despite deep reservations about the overall direction of the correctional services. Yet in the end, probation was singled out for failure to reduce re-offending sufficiently, even with individuals for whom it had no responsibility (prisoners serving less than twelve months). In fact, part of the political deceit of the Coalition government has been linking the failure of short-sentence prisoner rehabilitation with the failure of the Probation Service in general.

Probation has been ill served on many fronts – the posturing and deceit of political leaders, often to gain short-term political advantage even if that meant wrecking the careers of exemplary probation leaders, bureaucratic dysfunction and infighting as the Prison Service mentality came to dominate both central control and local direction. Above all, probation has not had over the recent past the level and type of support required to develop an approach to effective offender supervision that the public would support. We do not adhere to the view that there was a golden age for probation and it is fair to say that probation needed to change significantly to meet the political and public requirements of a rapidly changing society. However, once it lost its shelter and support within the consensus of post-war social democracy, it has been too politically weak to rebuff the nonsense of the past fifteen years, and in trying to respond to the successive demands made upon it, probation has slowly written its own death note.

Whilst we have sought to highlight the impact of personalities and events, such considerations have to be put within the overall context of a grinding ideological momentum and a state whose imperatives to downsize government and find market solutions for the cheaper delivery of more effective rehabilitation. This in effect sums up *Transforming Rehabilitation* on the immediate level of government business and completes a process begun almost as soon as the National Probation Service came into existence in 2001. Alongside this marketisation process has been the concomitant removal of local governance arrangements in the form of the Probation Boards that replaced Probation Committees in 2001. Under *Transforming Rehabilitation,* both Probation Trusts and their boards have disappeared and so too will accountability to local communities. This process, of course, began with the removal of sentencers from the trust boards soon after they were introduced in 2010. From our personal experience, one of the ironies in this overall war of attrition on local accountability was that those board members specifically recruited because of their private sector experience were the ones most critical of creeping privatisation and the bureaucracy that inevitable accompanied it.

Behind the drive to privatisation lurks the leviathan of neoliberal economic and social imperatives that shapes an increasingly precarious population. We have argued in Chapter Seven that the social and personal consequences of the new economic order and indeed the impact on *community* has required an ideological response to the diminution of previously state-sponsored solidarity and inclusion. However, we were careful to distinguish between the delivery mechanisms and partnership arrangements of *post-welfare modernism* and a broader ideological adjustment to the conditions created by neoliberal economic policies. In relation to the former, we have detailed a myriad of arrangements operating at the local level which often constituted mechanisms for more effective service delivery. However, in relation to the broader ideological adjustments, our concern was to trace commitments by all recent governments to strengthen civil society. Although committed to the continuation of Thatcher's neoliberal project, New Labour was nevertheless obliged to deal with her legacy – an army of the new poor seen to be cut off from the mainstream. The work of the Social Exclusion Unit and the development of a civil renewal strategy reflected this analysis and as Bell argues, New Labour became highly interventionist in a failed attempt to manage the social consequences of what she refers to as *phase one roll back neoliberalism* (2011: 205). Whilst it could be argued that New Labour's overall approach initially was to ameliorate the worst effects of a changing and increasingly global economy, the *Respect Agenda* hardened political attitudes toward the poor, and by the time New Labour lost power, criminal justice and wider social policy was largely interested in crime and those who committed it, as opposed to its wider causes. Bell perfectly summarises New Labour's overall political position and its failure to

> ... foster a culture of responsibility or to successfully legitimise its own power. It has instead fostered a culture of irresponsibility towards others by fostering a form of exclusive, egotistical individualism.
>
> *(2011: 207)*

When the Tory-led Coalition came to power in 2010 with David Cameron championing his notion of the *Big Society*, it was clear that there would be an acceleration in deregulation and specifically in a criminal justice context, transfer of probation to the private sector. The key questions were more about *how and when* rather that *why and if*. What was also evident before the election and thereafter was that welfare reform would be a key area of state policy that would work with the grain of increasing inequality, labour uncertainty and precarious existences for an ever-widening number of individuals. When the riots of 2011 occurred, it therefore gave the forces of reaction both within and outside parliament an ideal opportunity to come down with venom on those considered inferior and incapable of leading useful lives. As we charted the reaction to the riots in Chapter Seven, we also argued that notions of equality of opportunity and meritocracy, when devoid of any structural analysis of socio-economic disadvantage, are used by the rich and powerful elites to criticise not simply the poor and marginalised for their own failures but the state sector itself.

Just when the personal and community requirements for measures of social integration and solidarity are increased, the logic of neoliberalism dictates that support is withdrawn for those most vulnerable. More accurately, income support and unconditional resources are reduced or withdrawn in favour of targeted and conditional interventions that effectively blame those who are at most peril from a dynamically changing free market. Certain institutions then are held up as paragons of virtue, for the state sector and the poor to take note of, particularly when they exemplify the production of personal qualities of character and reliance. Compared to the vituperative language of Tory politicians and *Daily Mail* columnists, the RCVP report represented a moderate voice in response to the 2011 riots, but having chronicled the extraordinary levels of deprivation associated with the rioters and the riot areas, the authors were still able, seemingly without embarrassment, to quote the headmaster (sic) of Eton College:

> By the time he leaves school, we want each boy to have that true sense of self-worth which will enable him to stand up for himself and for a purpose greater than himself, and, in doing so, be of value to society.
>
> *(RCVP 2012: 50)*

Whilst many of us might be happy to endorse such outcomes for our children from the education system, it is the very lack of context that makes such utterances not only absurd and meaningless but ideologically loaded in two different directions. Firstly, it asserts that, provided institutions deliver excellence, meritocracy will automatically ensue; secondly, it assumes that personal characteristics and strengths are the key to a successful life. In all this, the objective environmental and material conditions of existence and the precariousness of work, income, personal security and accommodation become only marginally relevant.

The process of responsibilisation, as we have argued in Chapter Seven has moved from the individual to whole groups of people who are held to have common characteristics which require increasingly targeted levels of control, punishment and intervention. Individual agencies such as probation (and indeed the local state) have been made responsible for the offending behaviour of problem populations, thus justifying the withdrawal of the state in favour of the private sector, and shutting down any debate about the social and economic dimension to criminal behaviour. Service delivery mechanisms, though, are only part of the story and alongside free and deregulated markets and a diminishing role for the state in service provision, neoliberalism also promotes a profound sense of social conservatism. In order to do this in a manner which attracts public and political legitimacy, neoliberalism continually reiterates social mobility, equality of opportunity and meritocracy as its battle cry. Both the public and private sectors are charged with giving every single person the opportunity to become a *master of the universe* in order to maintain capitalism's buoyancy and dynamism. Given this moral imperative and commitment, however illusionary, concepts of personal and economic equality are beyond the lexicon of modern political thought and discourse. If this be the case then, failure is a personal tragedy and individuals have only themselves to blame. The poor, then, are largely to blame for their own situation, for their failure to take advantage of the same meritocratic world that others succeed in – they must therefore be saved from welfare dependency, access to financial benefits and spare bedrooms subsidy, and ultimately they must be morally rejuvenated to operate within contemporary social and economic conditions. It is within this overall context then that the rehabilitative endeavour is practised, and the nuanced and contested arguments about the relationship between punishment and social control in the neoliberal age, whilst critically important to our understanding of neoliberal hegemony, seems a world away from the reality of remaining crime-free in such an unequal and unremittingly hard environment for many individuals on Probation Service caseloads. An environment, we would add, where the political and media messages along with the punitive narratives that support the delivery of welfare continually tell individuals that they are worthless.

What we know about rehabilitation

We provided in Chapter One an overview of the issues germane to the rehabilitative endeavour, and in Chapter Four we considered the professional underpinnings to probation work. For us, a number of key issues emerge supporting our contention that the technicism of late modern rehabilitative approaches is counterproductive and ultimately ineffective. Much more positively, rehabilitation has been reconceptualised as a process or journey in which individuals move from partial exclusion to full citizenship. Techniques of intervention and assessments of risk and dangerousness and responsivity still have currency, but once the notion of strengths rather than deficits becomes a focus for the rehabilitative endeavour, then the role of rehabilitative services becomes one of supporting the process of desistance rather than merely delivering packages of treatment. It remains a skilled professional activity that requires workers who can place the lives and struggles of individuals within a wider context of the social and personal resources that will make a difference to the individual's life. Furthermore, probation isn't just about reducing re-offending but rather delivering justice (Canton 2013, McNeill 2011) and in this respect it is also a moral enterprise because it is about how we (on behalf of society in general and more particularly, local communities and victims) should respond to those who commit crime and how individuals who commit criminal acts should reciprocate. Rob Canton captures this in his assertion that "Desistance is not something that can be pursued as a direct objective, but something that is accomplished in the course of living a life of a certain kind. A good life is not a goal to be scored or a target to be hit, but an on-going accomplishment" (2013: 589).

We also know that delivering effective rehabilitative services requires the integration and cooperation of criminal and non-criminal justice agencies, acknowledging that cultural differences between agencies are strengths when properly valued. Developments such as Integrated Offender Management (IOM) schemes appear to be very successful and may embody "localism at its very best" (Gould 2013: 210), but they also take years to develop a modus operandi based on common understanding, trust and integrity. Such schemes need the commitment and support from non-criminal justice agencies that have the power to allocate social resources to reducing re-offending. Critically, it requires the engagement of local communities. This is because the expression of a humanitarian response to crime and to those who commit it is incomplete without such engagement – an engagement that can demonstrate reciprocal rights and responsibilities as well as offering help to and acknowledging the contrition of individuals who offend.

Community engagement though is not the end of the story. In terms of engaging victims directly within the operation of the criminal justice system, the case for restorative justice (RJ) has been strongly demonstrated in that it has the potential to lead to greater victim empowerment and satisfaction. RJ initiatives have also demonstrated cost effectiveness and a positive impact on the perpetrator of the crime. Estimates from National Victim Support and also the Restorative Justice Council suggest that using pre-sentence restorative justice, with 70,000 adult offenders convicted of burglary, robbery and violence, would produce cost savings to the criminal justice system of £185 million from reductions in re-offending alone (Prison Reform Trust 2012). As Gavrielides notes, "restorative justice finds its strengths in communities and is most effective at a local level. It is driven by its passionate practitioners and it works well when it is initiated by victims and the parties involved" (2012: npn).

We mentioned above that probation is about delivering justice as well as rehabilitation and notwithstanding the diminution in the formal links between probation and sentencers and the degrading of the role of probation worker as *an officer of the court,* rehabilitative work begins at the point of sentence and is prescribed within a formal sentencing framework. We do not accept the premise that the type of *just deserts* approach incorporated within the 1991 Criminal Justice Act inevitably leads to a punitive approach to offending and the enhanced use of imprisonment, although this has clearly happened since the slow demise of the Act's sentencing framework, that began in the mid-1990s. Criminal Justice Acts may reflect political intent but they do not have a life of their own and in the 1991 Act, there was the possibility for a rational and purposeful approach to sentencing that could have balanced the need for punishment with rehabilitative intent on behalf of a public who understood the damaging and self-defeating nature of imprisonment. It is indeed deeply ironic that the developing body of evidence about what helps individuals to make the journey from offender to citizen – the process of desistance – could have been applied within a framework that would have supported long-term individual journeys to redemption and rehabilitation. Instead, the last two decades have seen the proliferation of what is deemed a criminal offence, the widening of the criminal justice net through the increasing use of civil orders that ultimately have a criminal justice sting in their tails, along with increasingly complex and prescribed sentencing rules overseeing new and draconian sentences of the court. The notions of *restriction on liberty* and *suitability* contained within the 1991 Act could have supported the desistance approach – whatever else punishment achieves, it does not aid rehabilitation.

Why *Transforming Rehabilitation* will fail

Within our generally pessimistic and critical review of recent probation developments, we have acknowledged a range of innovations and initiatives that work with the grain of desistance approaches. There has been some recognition of the specific problems faced by some individuals who offend and of the inadequacy of the criminal justice response. Baroness Jean Corston's ground-breaking report calling for a *distinct, radically different, visibly-led, strategic, proportionate, holistic, woman-centred, integrated approach* (2007) caught the imagination and political commitment of both New Labour and the current Coalition government to move away from imprisonment and develop responses to women offenders based on principles of service normalisation and integration rather than exclusion. Though a welcome development, formal discourse is still bounded by the rhetoric of tough community-based punishments directed at women whose personal problems are atomised into a mist of misunderstanding about the poverty, inequality and lack of options that underpin many personal problems and individual lives (Ministry of Justice 2013, Ministry of Justice 2014). What is equally depressing is the government's strategic reliance on *Transforming Rehabilitaion* as a tool for rehabilitating female offenders (Ministry of Justice 2014).

We have rehearsed the arguments for why *Transforming Rehabilitation* is doomed to failure in the body of the book, but wish to stress the following points: Firstly, we can see little hope that it will lead to improved rehabilitative outcomes. We are certain that the notion of a service designed and delivered locally by agencies that are fully integrated, publicly accountable and responsive to local needs, is the most effective means of delivering rehabilitation. The alternative vision of national commissioning and an outcome-based PbR system that ultimately benefits the shareholders of large (most probably multinational) corporations rather than the individuals subject to community supervision or the communities in which they reside is simply not plausible. During the period covered by this book, billions of pounds of public assets have been transferred to the private sector without any corresponding evidence that it has brought about improved efficiency. The main beneficiaries of this funding shift appear to be those who run these corporations and private firms – headed by individuals who, it has been calculated, are paid as much as fifty times their public sector equivalents (Dudman 2014: npn). Rather than strengthening local delivery through engaging civil society (see Chapter Six), *Transforming Rehabilitation* will, it's our contention, lead to the concentration of a small number of powerful providers with all the issues of governance and transparency that we highlighted in Chapter Five. The role of the voluntary sector, on the other hand, will be further distorted as its historic role in campaigning (often to change or to improve government policy) and in service innovation will be subsumed into the mainstream delivery of what was the work of the state. As a report by *The Baring Foundation Independence Panel* has recently warned, "If the voice of the sector falls silent and charities look to their contract terms rather than their mission when vulnerable people turn up on their door step for support, our democracy is damaged, our society is less compassionate" (cited in Marples 2013: 27).

Secondly, there is no existing evidence that PbR as a mechanism for commissioning scarce resources is or is likely to be effective. The *binary* outcome measures are useful but only to a limited extent. Desistance is a process that may take time and include many players linked through kinship, family and informal ties rather than employment contracts. How, therefore do you determine who has been successful at what and reward them appropriately? Many of the government's claims for expanding PbR across the majority of rehabilitative services appear to be based on preliminary findings from the HMP Peterborough pilot, but if *What Works* has taught us anything, it is that showcase pilots are often unreliable indicators of effectiveness when implemented on a larger scale. As Carol Hedderman – an acknowledged expert in such evaluations – has pointed out, there have been "some rather large claims about success from a weakly designed reconviction analysis in which a sample of prisoners serving sentences of at least one year at one prison, who received additional support in relation to some resettlement needs, was compared with a poorly matched national sample" (2013: 44). The Justice Secretary's retort to this observation was that "… you just have to sit in Peterborough Prison with the offenders who are going through this programme to know that this is what needs to happen" (BBC File on 4). Grayling's response reflects the scant evidence on which the current policies are founded. It also suggests a depressing future of obfuscation by both government and the large corporations about their success or failure in delivering rehabilitation. If *Transforming Rehabilitation* fails to deliver on the ground as we predict, it will certainly not be allowed to fail in the current political arena or indeed in the revenue streams to multinational corporations.

Our third concern is not just that the delivery mechanisms for rehabilitation will fail to deliver in terms of apparent efficiency or effectiveness, but more importantly, they will impact deleteriously on those aspects of partnership and integrated delivery that support desistance. As Mawby and Worrall point out, "Probation workers in recent decades have been especially adept at working collaboratively, including with organisations like police services which have hitherto been regarded with suspicion and distrust. As such, probation workers have become accustomed to 'holding the ring', facilitating the operation of criminal justice processes by their ability to combine with partners and promote effective inter-agency working" (2013: 117). Our belief is that delivering rehabilitation is most effectively achieved in the long-run through strengthening professional commitment and values and building on existing relationships, rather than through performance targets, financial incentives and stringent managerial controls.

Fourthly, within *Transforming Rehabilitation* the notion of a complex moral endeavour by skilled workers engaging troubled and troublesome individuals, on behalf of and accountable to the public, is being lost. We have argued throughout this book that the concept of rehabilitation is ultimately a moral one because it is about what society ought to do to rehabilitate and reintegrate offenders. In destroying the ethos of probation and the occupational strengths of its workers through fragmentation and privatisation, this moral narrative and purpose will be undermined. Other things will be lost in the process. Private sector corporations will look to strip out costs which will effectively mean driving down wages, extending casual working practices and using less qualified staff. As Berry and Winterburn contend, "we need to have an approach that enables staff to improve services, rather than outcome-based management that drives dysfunctional behaviour, fosters cheating and hides failure" (2014: npn).

Finally, we are concerned that the organisation of delivery under *Transforming Rehabilitation* and indeed the privatisation of rehabilitation itself will undermine any sense of public responsibility for reintegrating offenders into the communities within which they live and where they offend. This is not just about the diminution of the concept of the state's social contract with its citizens but also about unintended and perverse outcomes that markets can deliver. As the political philosopher Michael Sandel has argued, we need to think carefully about how markets operate, what the limits of the market are, and the need to ensure that whilst the increasing penetration of public services by the private sector persists, issues of legitimacy and public interest are at the forefront of political and public discussions. In arguing that we have drifted from having a market economy to being a market society, Sandel describes the former as a tool for organizing productive activity whereas the latter becomes a way of life in which market values encroach into every aspect of public life (2012: 10). Sandel questions the morality of market economies that reduce public goods to mere commodities that can be bought and sold to the highest bidder. He warns that such a situation not only widens inequalities but ultimately corrupts the values of society because "markets don't only allocate goods; they also express and promote certain attitudes towards the good being exchanged" (2012: 8).

Rehabilitation re-imagined?

> ... supervision is not about **correcting offenders** so that we can reinsert them into **solid society** but rather supporting service users and communities in working out how to travel together towards better lives.
>
> *(McNeill 2012: 98* emphasis in original*)*

We have sought to place our analysis of *delivering rehabilitation* within a critique of successive government's ideological commitment to an economic neoliberalism and accompanying social conservatism which helps to make sense of the shambles that correctional policy has come to represent. Having worked within the Probation Service for many years, we are not unaware of the entrenched problems that individual offenders bring to the criminal justice system – some are deeply troubled individuals and others are highly troublesome and even dangerous, but for many, their circumstances make their actions intelligible, as Steven Box's quote suggests. In essence, probation has always drawn on the notion that offending can only be understood within its social context, but probation workers, close to the impact of crime on victims, have also stressed that the offender has a personal responsibility to tackle problems within their own personal reach.

However, the stretch required by individuals seems to us to be more and more challenging. *Transforming Rehabilitation* is being implemented within the context of an increasingly unequal society where the Coalition government has unleashed a strategy of welfare reform which the writer, John Le Carre has described as being tantamount to "planned penury" (cited in Keegan 2014). The very material and community resources that could make an individual's desistance journey become a reality are already difficult to access and will become more so. This, we fear, will make the ability to desist from crime a lottery, as those individuals who are able to access, develop and utilise social and personal capital on their desistance journey will be adjudged successes, but those who can't will be written off as failures. In effect, we may see the establishment of an *offender meritocracy* whereby those who fail will be subject to further incarceration and singling out for coercive treatment. This is, though, not just a matter of how individual offenders respond. As the case study of the riots suggests, criminal behaviour, whilst continuing to reflect entrenched problems of racism, inequality, economic exclusion and community deprivation, also reveals a response to the nil hours, low pay culture and degraded workplace relationships of much work that is available. Add to that an ongoing nihilistic and vitriolic attack waged by the political elite and their media friends on the poor and it's clear that neoliberal hegemonic thinking requires the historically practised vilification and castigation of individuals to be conferred on ever larger groups of people, even whole communities.

Even though we have embedded our analysis of probation within wider political and ideological environments than many texts on rehabilitation do, we could nevertheless be accused of too narrowly identifying crime and offending as that defined by criminal statute and criminology itself. We are drawn to the approach that places criminal activity within a framework of the social harm it generates because this seems to us to offer the possibility of exposing the real villains who never have direct contact with their victims, but nevertheless take decisions that impact deleteriously on many and sometimes whole communities. Much of the crime that requires the individual perpetrator to be rehabilitated relates to specific acts against identified individuals or property, but as Danny Dorling *et al.* remind us:

> Yet the greater moral culpability that is attached both legally and popularly to acts of intention can also allow those implicated in corporate crimes to rationalise away the consequences of their actions.
>
> *(2005: 11)*

Any rational approach to the definition and control of crime must surely take harm into account and it seems absurd to us that, for example, women are still sent to prison for fine default resulting from non-payment of a television licence whilst deaths through corporate violation of health and safety legislation go largely unpunished. Our focus, however, has been on the examination of the rehabilitative endeavour in the space where ideology connects with day-to-day practice and we draw on Bill McWilliams' notion of personalism within probation practice to justify why the probation worker has to operate as the world is, not how we would like it to be. He wrote that "in the last analysis personalists, as probation officers, see their central task as the enhancement of the offender as a person within society as it exists" (1987: 114). We are convinced that the values, commitment and professional expertise that probation staff will carry into the new *Transforming Rehabilitation* arrangements will continue to benefit individual offenders, but their task will be made significantly more difficult, frustrating and bureaucratically complex.

The destruction of probation as an accountable local service has been as unedifying as it has been drawn out. Probation has been the fall guy over the last decade for a number of critical incidents within the criminal justice system, but rather than try and learn from the mistakes, senior politicians have used them to attack probation and what it stands for. In *The Shock Doctrine*, Naomi Klein calls the orchestrated raids on the public sphere in the wake of catastrophic events, combined with the treatment of disasters as exciting market opportunities, "disaster capitalism" (2007: 6). Her field of vision was major international events but over the recent past, we could be forgiven for thinking that the assault on probation has been a form of minor, bureaucratically-induced disaster capitalism, or an example of what David Beetham, professor emeritus at Leeds university, calls "the distortion and subversion of the public realm in the services of private interests" (2013: 4).

From the perspective of *delivering rehabilitation*, the tragedy of this neoliberal enterprise is twofold. Firstly, in destroying an integrated public service responsible for rehabilitation, neoliberal ideology has widened the distance between the community and its offenders on so many levels – philosophical, practical and democratic. Secondly, it has degraded the safety and quality of life for all of us. Wilkinson and Pickett's *The Spirit Level: Why More Equal Societies Almost Always Do Better* (2010) provided telling international evidence for this. Drawn from case studies involving twenty of the richest nations, the evidence, they argued, showed that "In societies with greater inequality, where the social distances between people are greater, where attitudes of them and us are more entrenched and where lack of trust and fear of crime is rife, public and policy makers alike are more willing to imprison people and adopt punitive attitudes towards the criminal elements of society" (2010: 155). They concluded that the greater the disparity between the richest and the poorest, the higher the crime rates and the greater the use of imprisonment. This followed a similar pattern for a range of social, educational and health problems. We can only conclude from this that social mobility and equality of opportunity take society only so far and that greater material equality would actually benefit everyone. As Wilkinson and Pickett conclude, "... greater equality is the material foundation on which better social relations are built" (2010: 265).

Although Michael Sandel's work, referred to earlier in this chapter, has caught the contemporary imagination, it is also worth reminding ourselves that the late Richard Titmuss in his brilliant comparative study of blood-donor systems fifty years ago concluded that commercialised blood systems were wasteful, inefficient, more expensive and much more likely to distribute contaminated blood than public systems. He said of the commercialisation of blood donor relationships, that it

> Repress the expression of altruism, erodes the sense of community, lowers scientific standards, limits both personal and professional freedoms, sanctions the making of profits in hospitals and clinical laboratories, legalizes hostility between doctor and patient, subjects critical areas of medicine to the laws of the marketplace, places immense social cost on those least able to bear them – the poor, the sick and the inept – increases the danger of unethical behaviour in medical science and practice, and results in situations in which proportionately more and more blood is supplied by the poor, the unskilled, the unemployed, Negros (sic) and other low income groups ...
>
> *(1970: 245–246)*

Whilst the rehabilitative endeavour in 2014 and blood donor systems of the 1960s are separated by half a century and are not directly comparable, what Titmuss alerted us to is not only the material outcomes of private delivery mechanisms, but, unintended or otherwise, their corrosive impact on relationships. Since the publication of Titmuss's *The Gift Relationship,* the onward march of neoliberalism has been relentless at the global level, across the economies of nation states and within their social institutions, but its all-pervasive ideology (or rather *common sense as ideology*) creates individuals in its own likeness as sometimes customers, sometimes providers, in a world of competition where value is roundly expressed in monetary terms. What we hope our work has demonstrated, nevertheless, is that academics and practitioners have joined forces over the past decade or more to reimagine rehabilitation as a process that benefits those who offend and those who do not. It now requires our political leaders to do likewise and reimagine a world where social and economic equality brings us all closer together.

A final word about the quote from Alan Bennett's diary entry of November 2013 that began this book. We wanted to begin with it because it captures, as only he can, the mundane, the important and complex with effortless ease and economy. It not only reflects the situation the Probation Service currently finds itself in, but having now completed the book, we realise that it captures the essence of our entire project.

References

Allen, R. (2013) Paying for justice: Prison and probation in an age of austerity, *British Journal of Community Justice,* 11(1): 5–18.

BBC (2014) File on 4 Programme on Repeat Offenders broadcast on 23 February, http://www.bbc.co.uk/programmes/b03vf0f7 (Accessed on 2 April 2014).

Beetham, D. (2013) How widely should we define 'corruption'? *Criminal Justice Matters*, 94(1): 4–5.

Bell, E. (2011) *Criminal Justice and Neoliberalism*, Palgrave Macmillan: London.

Berry, N. and Winterburn, L. (2014) Stop bulk buying public services and save £16bn. *The Guardian*, http://www.theguardian.com/public-leaders-network/2014/mar/13/bulk-buying-public-services-16bn-contracts (Accessed 10 April 2014).

Box, S. (1987) *Recession, Crime and Punishment*, London: MacMillan.

Burke, L. and Collett, S. (2008) Doing with or doing to: What now for the probation service? *Criminal Justice Matters*, 72: 9–11.

Canton, R. (2013) The point of probation: On effectiveness, human right and the virtues of obliquity, *Criminology & Criminal Justice*, 13(5): 577–593.

Collett, S. (1993) Beyond reason and understanding: the everyday understanding of crime, *Probation Journal*, 40(4): 184–187.

Corston, J. (2007) *The Corston Report: A report by Baroness Jean Corston of the review of women with particular vulnerabilities in the criminal justice system*, London: Home Office.

Dorling, D., Gordon, D., Hillyard, P., Pantazis, C., Pemberton, S. and Tombs, S. (2005) *Criminal obsessions: Why harm matters more than crime*, (Second Edition), London: Centre For Crime And Justice Studies.

Dudman, J. (2014) Chiefs of privatised public services have hit the jackpot. Government has not. *The Guardian*, 3 April 2014, http://www.theguardian.com/public-leaders-network/2014/apr/03/privatised-public-services-chief-executives-pay (Accessed 10 April 2014).

Garland, D. (2011) *The Culture of Control*, Oxford: Oxford University Press.

Gavrielides, T. (2012) *Calling for evidence-based user-led sentencing policy: IARS writes to the Justice Minister*, www.iars.org.uk (Accessed 10 July 2012).

Gould, I. (2013) Dear Mr Grayling, *British Journal of Community Justice*, 11(2/3): 207–211.

Hedderman, C. (2013) Payment by Results: hopes, fears and evidence, *British Journal of Community Justice*, 11(2/3) Winter 2013: 43–59.

Keegan, W. (2011) Planned penury is leading us to ruin, *The Guardian*, http://www.theguardian.com/business/2011/jul/10/this-isnt-an-age-of-austerity-this-looks-like-a-lost-decade (Accessed 10 April 2014).

Klein, N. (2007) *The Shock Doctrine*, London: Penguin.

Mair, G. and Burke, L. (2011) *Redemption, Rehabilitation and Risk Management: A History of Probation*, London: Routledge.

Marples, R. (2013) Transforming rehabilitation: The risks for the voluntary, community and social enterprise sector in engaging in commercial contracts with tier 1 provider, *British Journal of Community Justice*, 11(2/3) Winter 2013: 21–33.

Mawby, R. and Worrall, A. (2013) Working with offenders: Someone has to do it ... but not just anyone can, *British Journal of Community Justice*, 11(2/3) Winter: 115–119.

Ministry of Justice (2013) *Strategic objectives for female offenders*, London: Ministry of Justice.

Ministry of Justice (2014) *Update on delivery of the Government's strategic objectives for female offenders*, London: Ministry of Justice.

McNeill, F. (2011) Probation, credibility and justice, *Probation Journal*, 58(1): 9–22.

McNeill, F. (2012) Counterblast: A Copernican correction for community sentences? *The Howard Journal of Criminal Justice*, 51(1): 94–9.

McWilliams, W. (1987) Probation, pragmatism and policy, *The Howard Journal of Criminal Justice*, 26(2): 97–121.

Parker, H., Bakx, K. and Newcombe, R. (1988) *Living With Heroin*, Milton Keynes: Open University Press.

Prison Reform Trust (2012) *Prison Reform Trust Response to the Ministry of Justice Consultation, Punishment and Reform: Effective Community Sentences*, www.prisonreformtrust.org.uk (Accessed 10 July 2012).

Riots, Communities and Victims Panel (2012) *After the Riots: The Final Report of the Riots, victims Panel*, London: Riots, Communities and Victims Panel.

Sandel, M. (2012) *What Money Can't Buy – The Moral Limits of Markets*, London: Allen Lane.

Social Exclusion Unit (2002) *Reducing re-offending by ex-prisoners*, London: Office of the Deputy Prime Minister.

Titmuss, R. (1970) *The Gift Relationship: From Human Blood to Social Policy*, London: George Allen & Unwin.

Underdown, A. (1998) *Strategies for Effective Offender Supervision, Report of the HMIP What Works Project*, London: Home Office.

Wacquant, L. (2004) *Punishing the Poor: The Neoliberal Government of Social Insecurity*, London: Duke University Press.

Wilkinson, R. and Pickett, K. (2010) *The Spirit Level: Why More Equal Societies Almost Always Do Better*, London: Allen Lane.

INDEX